LONG LIVE MEN!

LONG LIVE MEN!

The Moonshot Mission to Heal Men, Close the Lifespan Gap, and Offer Hope for Humanity

JED DIAMOND, PhD

Waterside Productions

First Printing, 2022

ISBN-13: 978-1-958848-36-4 print edition
ISBN-13: 978-1-958848-37-1 e-book edition

Waterside Productions
2055 Oxford Ave
Cardiff, CA 92007
www.waterside.com

CONTENTS

INTRODUCTION

MY SEVENTY-FOUR-YEAR JOURNEY HEALING MEN

I was five years old when my uncle drove me to the mental hospital. I was confused and afraid.

"Why do I have to go?" I asked Uncle Harry.

He looked at me with his round face and kind eyes. "Your father needs you."

"What's the matter with him?" I was beginning to cry, and I clamped my throat tight to stop the tears.

He turned away and looked back at the road. In our family, we didn't talk about difficult issues. I knew that my father was in a hospital and that it was my duty to visit him. It never occurred to me to ask why my mother didn't come to visit. She told me I was being her "brave little man," and I felt proud to be the one to help my father.

I shivered thinking about father's angry outbursts and cold silences and wondered how he would be when I saw him in the hospital. Entering Camarillo State Mental Hospital fifty miles north of our home in the San Fernando Valley was like entering an Alice-in-Wonderland world.

"But I don't want to go among mad people," Alice remarked.

"Oh you can't help that," said the Cat. "We're all mad here. I'm mad. You're mad."

"How do you know I'm mad?" said Alice.

"You must be," said the Cat, "or you wouldn't have come here."

I later learned that the movie *The Snake Pit* starring Olivia de Havilland was filmed at Camarillo. The hospital is also rumored to be the Eagles' inspiration for the classic rock song "Hotel California."

After going with my uncle to visit my father every Sunday for a year and later learning that my father escaped, the last lines of the song still chill me:

Last thing I remember, I was
Running for the door
I had to find the passage back
To the place I was before.
"Relax," said the night man
"We are programmed to receive."
"You can check out any time you like"
"But you can never leave!"
Welcome to the Hotel California
Such a lovely place (such a lovely place).

During the twelve months I visited my father, I watched him deteriorate. Shortly after he was admitted, my uncle took him out of the hospital to be treated for stomach ulcers that nearly killed him, but my father was forced to return because he was still under a court-ordered commitment as being "mentally ill" and therefore in need of "long-term treatment."

As a six-year-old, I imagined I could save my father. But he kept getting worse, and I couldn't do anything to help him. My own mental health was draining away, though I didn't realize it at the time. Finally, my mother agreed that I should stop the visits. She seemed to have moved on with her life, and I tried to follow her example.

As I advanced in school, other kids asked about my father. I was ashamed that he was "in a nut house," and it became easier to say that "my father died." Instead of the teasing and ridicule I had received when I told them he was in a mental hospital, I got some care and sympathy. Yet, I was driven to understand more about men's mental health and what I could do to improve it.

It would be years before my father was able to get on with his own life. When he was committed to Camarillo, treatment for those in despair was primitive at best. If you were getting worse, the doctors gave you more drugs, more electroshock treatments, convinced that more of the same would eventually save you. My father had a different plan, though it took him a long time to implement it. After seven years being "treated" for his mental illness, he escaped, changed his name, was never caught, and created a new life for himself. I wrote about his journey in my memoir, *My Distant Dad: Healing the Family Father Wound.*

I grew up wondering what happened to my father, whether it would happen to me, and how I could prevent it from happening to other men and their families. I went on to college and later graduate school, getting a master's degree in social welfare and later a PhD in international health. My doctoral research study, not surprisingly, involved male depression, and my dissertation was published as a book: *Male vs. Female Depression: Why Men Act Out and Women Act In.*

It was shortly after my first son, Jemal, was born on November 21, 1969, that my mother found some old journals in the attic that my father had written before he was hospitalized. They gave me a glimpse into the tortured months leading up to his overdose and commitment to the mental hospital.

They still bring me to tears when I realize what was lost and how much suffering he went through before he finally got the help he needed. Here is a note from my father's first journal, written when he was his old self:

"I feel full of confidence in my writing ability. I know for certain that someone will buy one of my radio shows. I know for certain that I will get a good part in a play. Last night I dreamt about candy. There was more candy than I could eat. Does it mean I'll be rewarded for all my efforts? Has it anything to do with sex?"

I also feel the deep sadness as I watch him slipping closer to the edge of hopelessness and his hospitalization in Camarillo. In the last journal, I found these entries. My father wanted so much for me, but like so many fathers who found it difficult to give what he had never received, he struggled.

July 3, 1948: "Oh, Christ, if I could only give my son a decent education—a college decree with a love for books, a love for people, good, solid knowledge. No guidance was given to me. I slogged and slobbered and blundered through two-thirds of my life."

So many men feel trapped in the *Man Box*, surrounded by walls that they beat themselves bloody trying to get through.

August 8, 1948: "Sunday morning, my humanness has fled, my sense of comedy has gone down the drain. I'm tired, hopelessly tired, surrounded by an immense brick wall, a blood-spattered brick world, splattered with my blood, with the blood of my head where I senselessly banged to find an opening, to find one loose brick, so I could feel the cool breeze and could stick out my hand and pluck a handful of wheat, but this brick wall is impregnable, not an ounce of mortar loosens, not a brick gives."

Men often blame themselves when they are out of work. The breadwinner role is deeply embedded in us, and when we can't fulfill that role, too many of us feel helpless and worthless.

September 14, 1948: "How much can Edie stand? When in this world will I ever have a piece of bread that isn't encrusted with fear and doubt, with all those moldy devils turning my blood to water and my stomach to mush. I feel like a gutless zero."

We look around and it seems that so many people seem to be doing better than we are. We compare ourselves to others and conclude that we are failing ourselves and those we care about the most.

December 8, 1948: "Your flesh crawls, your scalp wrinkles when you look around and see good writers, established writers, writers with credits a block long, unable to sell, unable to find work. Yes, it's enough to make anyone, blanch, turn pale and sicken."

Amazing to see my father writing about *The Snake Pit* when a year later he would find himself as a court-committed inmate. Our subconscious minds are always at work, sometimes giving us glimpses into our future and the challenges we will face.

January 29, 1949: "Seeing the movie *The Snake Pit*, starring Olivia de Havilland, was some experience. It was the first time the door was unlocked on the chaos of mental illness, the first time that light was shown into the darkness. De Havilland gave a touching, beautiful, striking, performance. Here was a girl hurt, bruised, terrified, plunged into a pit by the guilt complexes of a lifetime; and woven into this guilt pattern were her own weaknesses. The one encouraging ray of light was the fact that no matter how mentally ill a person is, they can get better. There's hope, but that hope wears thin under the bludgeoning and battering of the life she is struggling with."

More and more men today are having trouble keeping up with a world that is increasingly accelerating like a runaway truck going downhill. Our one goal is simply to support our families, but that goal is increasingly out of reach for so many.

February 24, 1949: "Faster, faster, faster, I walk. I plug away looking for work, anything to support my family. I try, try, try, try, try. I always try and never stop."

Every man reaches a breaking point at some time. We know that the suicide rate for middle-aged men begins to increase dramatically and continues to rise as men age. In his book *Dying to Be Men*, Dr. Will Courtenay cites CDC statistics that show the suicide rate for males forty-five to fifty-four is three times higher than it is for females of the same age and increases to more than six times higher for males sixty-five to seventy-four.

June 18, 1949: "A hundred failures, an endless number of failures, until now, my confidence, my hope, my belief in myself, has run completely out. Middle aged, I stand and gaze ahead, numb, confused, and desperately worried. All around me I see the young in spirit, the young in heart, with ten times my confidence, twice my youth, ten times my fervor, twice my education. I see them all, a whole army of them, battering at the same doors I'm battering, trying in the same field I'm trying. Yes, on a Sunday morning in June, my hope and my life stream are both running desperately low, so low, so stagnant, that I hold my breath in fear, believing that the dark, blank curtain is about to descend."

Shortly after this June entry, my father took an overdose of sleeping pills, was diagnosed, given a psychiatric label, and court-committed to the hospital.

I experience tears of grief and joy reading my father's journals. Grief at feeling his deepening pain and rising fear as he suffers because he can't support his family financially. I also feel joy to hear and feel the intimate words of my father as he reaches out through the years to tell me what was in his heart and soul and how hard he worked to be there for me and my mother.

I have gone on to help thousands of men and their families live healthier, more engaged, and loving lives. I've written more than a thousand articles and sixteen books. At this stage of my career, spanning more than fifty years, I want to use the time I still have to make the most positive impact I can so that I can continue to help men and their families.

There are millions of men, like my father, who hunger to be fully alive and well. My colleagues Randolph Nesse, MD, and Daniel Kruger, PhD, examined premature deaths among men in twenty countries. They found that in every country, men died sooner and lived sicker than women, and their shortened health and lifespan harmed the men and their families.

Among their conclusions were these two statements:

- **"Being male is now the single largest demographic factor for early death."**
- **"Over 375,000 lives would be saved in a single year in the U.S. alone if men's risk of dying was as low as women's."**

The primary reason men die sooner and live sicker than women is due to mental health problems such as male depression and aggression. Mentally healthy men don't kill themselves and others. They don't express their pain through road rage and domestic violence. They aren't involved with mass shootings.

Google's [X] is known as their "Moonshot Factory." Those who work there aim to improve the lives of millions, even billions, of people. Their goal is a 10x impact on the world's most intractable problems, not just a 10 percent improvement. We need a moonshot mission to revitalize men's mental health.

This book is a call to action to create our own moonshot for *mankind* and humanity. We hope all individual men and women and organizations who care about healing men will join us. You can learn more here: https://menalive.com/about/my-moonshot-mission/

Thank you for being part of this journey. Let's continue as we explore the nature of the problem we face.

PART I
THE PROBLEM

In every country studied, males, as a group, live sicker and die sooner than females. In part 1, I detail the reasons why this is so and the data that support these findings. I show the impact of male violence—both self-directed resulting in increased suicides and other-directed resulting in increased domestic violence—community violence, and worldwide conflicts. I look at the impact of the stresses going on in the world and whether they are leading to collapse or transformation. Finally, I show that all these problems lead to poor mental health for men and to increasing depression and aggression, which, I believe, are key causes of the problems we face in the world. These problems impact not only men, but also women, children, communities, and the environmental health and balance that is needed for humanity to survive and thrive.

CHAPTER 1

WHY MEN LIVE SICKER AND DIE SOONER THAN WOMEN

I was accepted at UC Santa Barbara in September 1961. I wanted to get away from my home in Los Angeles, but not too far away. Also, it was rumored that there were three girls for every guy at the school. When my buddy and I visited the campus the summer before enrollment, a car full of girls honked and waved at us. I knew I was in the right place at the right time.

As a nerdy, shy, withdrawn kid, I thought I had died and gone to heaven. I had never dated in high school and was too afraid to ask anyone to the senior prom, but I imagined I would start a new life and meet the woman of my dreams. I had pretty much forgotten about my father. When he escaped from Camarillo, my mother was notified and she had me stay with neighbors for a week, afraid he might come and harm me or steal me away. I was afraid but secretly hopeful that he might care enough to come back for me. I imagined him fully healthy, wealthy, and wise. He'd drive up in a new car and my broken life would magically be put back together. But he never came back.

Although I had consciously put him out of my mind, he lived in some part of my repressed psyche. I had gotten good grades in high school and took pre-med classes at UCSB. If you had asked me why, I would have said because I wanted to get a good job in a challenging field. Subconsciously, I might have said, "I want to go on to medical school, become a psychiatrist, so I can save other men like my father and make my father proud of me. Maybe then, he'll come home and become the father I always longed to have."

I didn't find my father in college, but I did find a father figure. Although I took classes like biology, chemistry, and psychology, I also took a philosophy course from one of the world's leading figures in the field, Paul Tillich. He was a visiting professor and shared views that inspired many of us. His words of wisdom have stuck with me through the years.

"Every serious thinker must ask and answer three fundamental questions: (1) What is wrong with us? With men? Women? Society? What is the nature of our alienation? Our dis-ease? (2) What would we be like if we were whole? Healed? Actualized? If our potentiality was fulfilled? And (3) how do we move from our condition of brokenness to wholeness? What are the means of healing?"

I was most interested in the question, "What's wrong with men?" I wanted to understand why my father, and other men I knew growing up, became stressed and depressed. My own mother, and other women I knew growing up, seemed to be doing better than the men. Why was that? I recognized the women had their challenges, and neither men nor women had a corner on the market for physical and emotional pain.

I learned that men and women have different experiences of pain and must address different underlying causes. Sigmund Freud said, "Love and work are the cornerstones of our humanness." For men like my father, and for many men, work holds a special place in their lives. We often judge our value as men and human beings on how successful we are at work. Being unemployed can be devastating.

After achieving some success in New York as an actor, my father came to California to write for the movies and the emerging television industry. However, these were times when the country was in the grips of "the red scare," and Senator Joe McCarthy and the House Un-American Activities Committee (HUAC) were hunting for communists.

Their investigations often focused on Hollywood actors and screenwriters. Although my father was not as well known as others who were *blacklisted*—such as screenwriter Dalton Trumbo, singer Pete Seeger, actor Orson Welles, or author Dashiell Hammett—like them, he was soon unable to find work.

My father never blamed others when he couldn't find a job. He took it personally and it ate away at him every day. Here is an entry from his journal during this period:

"I need a full day's work and accomplishment. But jobs are few and far between. I know that to live you must work. To stop working means to die. Not all at once, but from that minute that you stop using hand and brain to bring in bread for the family you begin to die. Hope, initiative, spirit, understanding, beauty—all begin to experience the first tremors of death rattles."

Before my father had his "nervous breakdown" as my mother and her women friends referred to it, I overheard a conversation they were having in the kitchen that forever changed my life and is a key to understanding why men live sicker and die sooner than women. I must have been four years old at the time, and my father was out of work.

"I wish Muni could find a job," my mother told her friends. My father's name was Morris, but from the time he was young, everyone called him Muni. "He can't find work and he's either depressed or angry all the time. I know it's not his fault. Lots of men are out of work these days. He mopes around or blows up at me if I try and comfort him. It's like having another child at home."

Each of the other women also had complaints about their husbands. Their words seared into my four-year-old brain. I hated the women for dumping on men I knew and cared about, and I was ashamed of my father and the other men for being so deeply disrespected. Worse than the words were the feelings that went with the words. There was a mixture of contempt, pity, and disdain.

I'll die before I ever let a woman talk about me like that, I vowed. In my four years of life experience, I didn't know how I'd do it, but I made three promises to myself:

I'll never be out of work.

- I'll never show weakness.
- I'll never let anyone disrespect me.

These three promises were like poison seeds that began to grow inside me. As an adult, they become the core of the fears that drive me:

My feelings will destroy me if I let them.

1. I'll go crazy like my father.
2. I will be a failure at work and lose my family's respect.
3. There is something dangerous and violent in me waiting to destroy the people I love the most.
4. Women will say they love me, but underneath the surface they'll feel contempt and pity.
5. I will kill if I must in order to keep from being disrespected.

I buried the fears, but they seethed inside to become the Ten Commandments that I must live by.

1. Thou shalt not be weak, nor have weak gods before thee.
2. Thou shalt not fail thyself, nor fail as thy father before thee.
3. Thou shalt not keep holy any day that denies thy work.
4. Thou shalt not express strong emotions, neither high nor low.
5. Thou shalt not cry, complain, nor ask for help.
6. Thou shalt not show thy feelings.
7. Thou shalt not be uncertain or ambivalent.
8. Thou shalt not be dependent on others.
9. Thou shalt not acknowledge thy death nor thy limitations.
10. Thou *shalt* do unto other men before they do unto you.

Before going on, take a little time to reflect on the fears and commandments that show up in your own life. Which ones resonate for you? Which ones did you grow up with? Which ones still influence you now? Which ones influenced the lives of important men in your life?

You may want to keep a journal to write down your experiences, thoughts, feelings, and insights that come up for you as you read this book.

I have found our beliefs, more than anything else, determine whether we live fully healthy lives or live sicker and die sooner. Delving more deeply into the material and seeing what fits in your own life can go a long way in helping you create the life you are meant to live.

There are some physical realities about being male that we need to accept about ourselves before we can change the patterns that keep us locked in a destructive Man Box of our own making.

The Facts of Life and Death for Men

David Gremillion, MD, is a retired Air Force colonel and retired professor of medicine, University of North Carolina School of Medicine. He serves on the board of directors of the Men's Health Network. "There is a silent health crisis in America," says Dr. Gremillion. "It's a fact that, on average, American men live sicker and die younger than American women." The facts of men's health or lack of it begin early and life and last until the end. Here are some other facts detailed by the Men's Health Network:

Although 115 males are conceived for every 100 females, the male fetus is at greater risk of miscarriage and stillbirth.

- 25 percent more newborn males die than females.
- 60 percent of sudden infant death (SIDS) victims are boys.
- Men suffer hearing loss at twice the rate of women.
- Men die at higher rates than women from nine of the top ten causes of death and are the victims of over 92 percent of workplace deaths.

When Drs. Nesse and Kruger examined the overall male-to-female mortality ratio for eleven specific leading causes of death across age groups in the US over the course of the lifespan and in twenty different countries, they found that in every country studied, males lived sicker and died sooner than females.

They not only concluded that over 375,000 lives would be saved in a single year in the US alone if men's risk of dying was as low as women's, they also concluded that reducing the risk would do more good in the world than curing cancer. By helping hundreds of thousands of men to live longer and healthier lives, we not only help fathers, sons, brothers, grandsons, husbands, and partners; we also help mothers, daughters, sisters, granddaughters, wives, and partners.

It may not be possible for male mortality to be as low as that of females, but we can go a long way to achieving healthy equality. There is a genetic component to why males are at higher risk for earlier death than females.

All females have two X chromosomes (XX), while all males have only one (XY). Sharon Moalem, MD, PhD, is a researcher who has been interested in gender medicine and men's health for most of his professional life. In his book *The Better Half: On the Genetic Superiority of Women*, he begins by saying, "Here are some basic facts: Women live longer than men. Women have stronger immune systems. Women are less likely to suffer from a developmental disability, are more likely to see the world in a wider variety of colors, and overall are better at fighting cancer. Women are simply stronger than men at every stage of life. But why?"

Dr. Moalem concludes, "Having the use of two X chromosomes makes females more genetically diverse. And the ability to rely on that diverse genetic knowledge is why females always come out on top. Whether it's an infant girl's survival in the Neonatal Intensive Care Unit, a woman's ability to fight infections, or a genetic female's decreased risk of having an X-linked intellectual disability, it all boils down to the simple fact that females have a degree of genetic flexibility that males lack."

Some take these facts to mean that men are doomed to live sicker and die sooner than females. But here's another fact that should give us pause. The Centers for Disease Control and Prevention (CDC) reports that in 1920, women lived, on average, one year longer than men. Now, men, on average, die almost five years earlier than women. Men's and women's genes haven't changed in the last hundred years, but our behaviors have.

Further, the science of epigenetics demonstrates conclusively that genes are not destiny. As Drs. Kenneth R. Pelletier and Andrew Weil say in the book *Change Your Genes, Change Your Life: Creating Optimal Health with the New Science of Epigenetics*, "Biology is no longer destiny. Our DNA doesn't rigidly determine our health and disease prospects. Our genetic profile may signal an inherited vulnerability to a disease, but those genes cannot predict your future. Instead, our daily choices and lifestyle behaviors determine whether these vulnerable genes will be switched on or switched off. And that means our actions have a direct and powerful effect on our genes."

The Real Reasons Men Live Sicker and Die Sooner than Women

Some men engage in more healthy practices than some women. But on the whole, our health practices leave a lot to be desired. Here is a summary of the underlying reasons men live sicker and die sooner than women. I've drawn these from my own work over the years and from colleagues including Will Courtenay, author of *Dying to Be Men: Psychosocial, Environmental, and Biobehavioral Directions in Promoting the Health of Men and Boys*, and Marianne J. Legato, author of *Why Men Die First: How to Lengthen Your Lifespan*.

Males Have Less Healthy Lifestyles

Men and boys, in general, have lifestyles that are less healthy than women and girls. They engage in fewer health-promoting behaviors like eating more fruits and vegetable and less meat. Men as a group are more overweight than women and are much less likely to get help to lose weight.

For years I tried to lose weight on my own, figuring it just took willpower and commitment. When I continued to be overweight,

I asked myself what I would recommend to my clients. I would tell them to get some support. Losing weight isn't easy. Join a program. I finally went to a WeightWatchers meeting, which helped me lose more than 10 percent of my body weight. But there were very few men there, and though the information was helpful, the way the meetings were conducted were not always conducive to men.

Likewise, men eat more meat, fat, and salt and less fiber, fruits, and vegetables than women. There's a joke I heard in a bar. An Irish coffee is one of the healthiest drinks you can get because it contains your four basic food groups: alcohol, sugar, caffeine, and fat.

Men use fewer medications, vitamins, and dietary supplements. My wife, Carlin, has taken much better care of herself than I have. It's taken me a long time to begin to adopt her healthier practices. One of the things I've admired about her is how she exercises. Every morning she walks on her treadmill. In the evening she stretches, meditates, easily falls asleep, and generally sleeps through the night. I continue to struggle with sleep.

Males Engage in More Risk-Taking Behavior

Men and adolescent males engage in more reckless and illegal driving, and they drive drunk more frequently than women and adolescent females. They also have more sexual partners than women. I wrote a book, *Looking for Love in All the Wrong Places: Overcoming Romantic and Sexual Addictions*, in which I talk about my own period of sexual obsession and how common it is in men. Guys also engage in significantly more high-risk physical activities—such as dangerous sports and leisure-time activities—and physical fights. They are also more likely than women to carry guns or other weapons, and they engage in more criminal activity.

Males More Often Have Problems with Drugs and Alcohol

Compared to women, men use more alcohol and other drugs. More men than women use tobacco products, and they have more dangerous patterns of tobacco use. Although not everyone who uses drugs or alcohol becomes addicted, men are more likely to continue using even when they experience negative consequences. As one man told me in counseling, "My drug of choice is *more*." For him, like many men who become addicted, too much is never enough. I believe addiction is the disease of lost self-hood. Addicts are looking for pleasure and escape from pain in all the wrong places. Like confused homing pigeons, they seek the safety and security of family and friends, but they fly 180 degrees in the wrong direction.

Males Misperceive Their Susceptibility to Risk

Men are consistently less likely than women to perceive themselves as being at risk for illness, injury, and a variety of health problems. Despite being at greater risk from drug and alcohol use, for example, males of all ages perceive significantly less risk than females associated with the use of cigarettes, alcohol, and other drugs. With rare exceptions, people who think they are invulnerable take fewer precautions with their health—and thus have greater health risks—than people who recognize their vulnerability.

Males Are Less Likely to Change Unhealthy Behaviors

Men believe less strongly than women that they have control over their future health or that personal actions contribute to good health. Further, women are more likely than men to contemplate changing unhealthy habits or to maintain healthy habits. Men, however, are more likely than women not to consider changing unhealthy behaviors and deny that these behaviors are problematic.

Males Have Traditional Views of Masculinity that Often Conflict with Health

There is a high level of agreement among people in the United States regarding typical feminine and masculine characteristics. Men and boys, in particular, experience a great deal of social pressure to conform to these stereotypical characteristics. These dominant norms of masculinity dictate, for example, that men should be self-reliant, strong, robust, and tough; that men should welcome danger; and that men should never reveal vulnerability, back down, or do anything "feminine." These idealized norms of masculinity create a conflict with actions that we could do to take care of ourselves or to be taken care of by those who love us.

In his book *The Hazards of Being Male*, psychologist Herb Goldberg says, "The male has paid a heavy price for his masculine 'privilege' and power. He is out of touch with his emotions and his body. He is playing by the rules of the male game plan and with lemming-like purpose he is destroying himself—emotionally, psychologically and physically."

Males Don't Express Their Emotions or Acknowledge Distress

In general, women are more emotionally expressive than men—except when it comes to expressing anger. Men also report less fear or emotional distress than women do, and they are less likely than women to cry. Men's inexpressiveness can have both direct and indirect effects on their health and well-being. Self-disclosure, for example, is associated with improvements in immune functioning and physical health. Men are also more likely than women to exhibit emotionally inexpressive type A behavior and to experience or express hostility, both of which are strongly linked with increased health risks—particularly for cardiovascular disease. Men are also disinclined to discuss experiences of pain or physical distress.

Males Have a Harder Time Dealing with Unemployment

With our economic system going through major transformations, more people are unemployed. Unemployment is consistently linked with a variety of negative health effects, and there is evidence that these negative effects are greater for men than for women. Unemployed men are more likely to commit suicide than unemployed women. One study among youth found that unemployment is also a risk factor for increased alcohol consumption, increased tobacco use, illicit drug use, suicide, and unintentional injuries, particularly for males.

This was certainly true for my father and me. I remember getting laid off from work for the first time in my life. I was the clinical director of an agency where I had worked for nearly ten years and was respected by staff and clients alike. Even though I had grown tired of the job and was looking for another, I was devastated when I was told I was being let go.

Even though I had planned to leave and the reasons they were letting me go were clear and had nothing to do with anything I had done wrong, I still felt that I had somehow failed. I knew I was being cut for purely economic reasons. Yet, I still felt that I had done something wrong and was being punished. I knew my wife understood and we both were confident I would soon find another job. But I couldn't get it out of my head that she secretly was talking to her friends and they were commiserating with her about having a loser for a husband.

I knew it was foolish, but I couldn't seem to stop castigating myself. I quickly slipped into a deep depression, and it took months of therapy to help me get back to a semblance of normal.

Boadie Dunlop, MD, from Emory University School of Medicine says, "Compared to women, many men attach a great importance to their roles as providers and protectors of their families. Failure to fulfill the role of breadwinner is associated with greater depression and marital conflict."

Even though my logical brain knew the truth, deep down inside I couldn't shake the feeling of failure that kept running through my waking thoughts and intruding into my sleepless nights. The old values that a man must be a good provider, or die trying, is deeply engrained in many men. It takes considerable reprogramming to dislodge these old beliefs and create new, healthier ones.

Males Have Fewer Social Supports

Males have much smaller social networks than women do. Men and boys also have fewer, less intimate friendships, and they are less likely to have a close confidant, particularly someone other than a spouse. Men's restricted social networks limit their levels of social support. In times of stress, for example, men mobilize less varied social networks than women. There is consistent evidence that the lack of social support is a risk factor for premature death—especially for men. Men with the lowest levels of social support are two to three times more likely to die than men with the highest levels of social support. Men's social isolation significantly decreases their chance of survival of heart disease, cancer, and stroke.

Males Are Lonelier and More Isolated

"Many of my male friends are also struggling with loneliness—and I have struggled with it at many points in my life. But it's not something we often talk about," says Vivek H. Murthy, MD, who served as the nineteenth Surgeon General of the United States. In his book *Together: The Healing Power of Human Connection in a Sometimes Lonely World*, Dr. Murthy says, "Quite simply, human relationship is as essential to our well-bring as food and water. Just as hunger and thirst are our body's ways of telling us we need to eat and drink, loneliness is the natural signal that reminds us when we need to connect with other people."

We know that heart disease is still the biggest killer of males, but disconnection and isolation may be the underlying causes. "All the usual risk factors for heart disease—smoking, obesity, a sedentary lifestyle, and a high-fat diet—account for only half of all cases of heart disease," says heart expert Dr. Dean Ornish. "Every so-called lifestyle risk factor laid at the door of cardiovascular illness by the medical community has less to do with someone having a heart attack than does simple isolation—from other people, from our own feelings and from a higher power."

Yet, millions of men are lonely and isolated, and many aren't even aware of it. Through most of my career, I've been very successful and very busy. When I was at the height of my successful career, if someone would have asked if I was lonely, I would have laughed at them. I was too busy to be lonely. I learned that many of the most successful people feel emotionally alone but often don't slow down enough to let their feelings catch up with them.

In his book *Lonely at the Top: The High Cost of Men's Success*, Thomas Joiner says, "Men's main problem is not self-loathing, stupidity, greed, or any of the legions of other things they're accused of. The problem, instead, is loneliness; as they age, they gradually lose contacts with friends and family, and here's the important part, they don't replenish them."

As the suicide statistics verify, men often feel increasingly alone as they get older, even when they are surrounded by those who care about them. "A postmortem report on a suicide decedent," says Joiner, "a man in his sixties read, 'He did not have friends.... He did not feel comfortable with other men ... he did not trust doctors and would not seek help even though he was aware that he needed help.'" Does this sound familiar? When I first read these words, I felt like tiny bombs had exploded in my brain. Each one was very true for my father before he took the overdose of pills. They also felt true for me earlier in my life and helped motivate me to join a men's group, which I will describe later in the book.

Before moving on, I suggest you review the ten factors listed above. Which ones resonate with you? It is easy to become accustomed to long-standing feelings and behaviors so that we don't even notice them. It may be helpful to ask a loved one to give you their honest feedback on which of these factors may be operating in your life. Write down what you learn, and let it motivate you to move ahead to learn ways of addressing the ones that may be harming your relationship health.

What's Wrong with Men May Be the Wrong Question. What Happened to Us Offers New Opportunities for Healing

Even as a five-year-old child visiting my father in the mental hospital, I wondered what happened to him, not what was wrong with him. I thought if I could figure out what happened to him, I could understand why he changed. I still remember little snapshots of our early times together:

Me riding on his shoulders, holding on to his ears, both of us laughing as I rode him around the little park in Encino, near our home in the San Fernando Valley.

- Being introduced to his friends. "Here's my little fella…" I beamed with pride and pleasure.
- Feeling excitement and joy going with him to the TV studio where I was going to be on a kid's show he had written.

The show was called "The Squeaky Mulligan Show." Squeaky was a cat puppet, and I was one of the children who sat in front listening to the stories the little star of the show delivered, much to the delight of all the kids.

But then something changed. I didn't know when or why, but something must have happened. He didn't play with me as much. When he did, he seemed preoccupied. He became more irritable and short-tempered. I overheard my mother trying to talk with him in their bedroom. She seemed concerned, but he said little and there were a lot of silences. On my visits with my uncle to the mental hospital to see my father, I asked him what had happened to him. All he would say was that he was "sick" but would be getting well soon. Well, soon never came.

When I was in graduate school, I learned about mental health and mental illness. We were required to read the Diagnostic and Statistical Manual of the American Psychiatric Association. It is used by health care professionals in the United States and much of the world as the authoritative guide to the diagnosis of mental disorders. There were hundreds of diagnostic labels that were applied at the time to people like my father, including major depressive disorder, manic-depressive disorder (now called bipolar disorder), and psychotic depression.

Clearly, something serious was wrong with my father. This is true for millions of other men who become irritable, angry, stressed, and depressed. I know because I am one of those men. Growing up, I was generally a nice, well-behaved child. But periodically I would have fits of anger and rage. I still remember becoming enraged at my dog, Spotty, when he accidentally knocked me down when I was eight or nine years old. I grabbed him by the throat and began choking him. I only held him for an instant and immediately let him go. I didn't know what came over me, and I immediately felt ashamed and reached out for my dog and hugged him gently.

Dogs are much more forgiving than wives. In my first marriage, I was also a nice, well-behaved husband, but periodically would flare up and yell at my wife, usually triggered by some small slight where I felt disrespected and discounted, or when I felt jealous. My anger was one of the factors that led to our divorce. A similar pattern occurred in my second marriage.

Discovering I Had 4 ACEs Changed My Life

It never occurred to me that my lifelong anger and depression, and later my two broken marriages, had anything to do with my past. All that changed in 1998 when I reached out to a colleague, Dr. Charles Whitfield, because I couldn't seem to heal my depression despite the fact that I was receiving good therapy and was taking medications. He told me that the missing piece in my healing might be addressing childhood trauma.

Dr. Whitfield introduced me to the Adverse Childhood Experiences (ACEs) studies developed by Vincent Felitti, MD, the head of Kaiser Permanente's Department of Preventive Medicine in San Diego, and Dr. Robert Anda, a medical epidemiologist at the CDC. "The information the studies have provided us is not just helpful," said Whitfield, "it is astounding."

He went on to describe the original studies and what they learned. "Felitti and Anda and their colleagues looked at 9,508 middle-class, middle-aged people in Southern California. All were members of Kaiser's health maintenance organization, who were medically evaluated, and then each completed a sixty-eight-question survey about seven categories of childhood trauma and subsequent illness. The researchers also had the medical records of each patient with which to verify the findings."

They found that a large percentage of this general medical clinic population reported the following traumatic experiences from their childhoods.

- Physical abuse
- Sexual abuse
- Emotional abuse
- Physical neglect
- Emotional neglect
- Exposure to domestic violence
- Household substance abuse
- Household mental illness
- Parental separation or divorce
- Incarcerated household member

Their findings rocked the world of health care. It offered a whole different approach for understanding, treating, and preventing disease—everything from cancer and heart disease to obesity and depression. All these problems, and more, had roots in our childhood experiences of trauma. Childhood wounds provided a psychosocial basis for a whole range of problems that impact brain function, even those that were assumed to be purely physical.

They found the following to be true:

- More than half of respondents reported at least one ACE.
- If you have one ACE, you are highly likely to have two or more ACEs.
- The more ACEs you have as a child, the more likely you are to have a whole range of physical and emotional problems as an adult.

I was surprised to learn that mental, emotional, and relationship problems can be caused by the experiences we may have had as children. I was even more surprised to find that even physical problems such as asthma, diabetes, heart disease, and cancer were also connected to ACEs.

I was anxious to see how I would score and answered the following questions developed by the ACE researchers for the general public:

Prior to your eighteenth birthday:

1. Did a parent or other adult in the household often or very often ... Swear at you, insult you, put you down, or humiliate you? Or act in a way that made you afraid that you might be physically hurt? No___. If Yes, enter 1 ___.

2. Did a parent or other adult in the household often or very often ... Push, grab, slap, or throw something at you? Or ever hit you so hard that you had marks or were injured? No___. If Yes, enter 1 ___.

3. Did an adult or person at least five years older than you ever ... Touch or fondle you or have you touch their body in a sexual way? Or attempt or actually have oral, anal, or vaginal intercourse with you? No___. If Yes, enter 1 ___.

4. Did you often or very often feel that ... No one in your family loved you or thought you were important or special? Or your family didn't look out for each other, feel close to each other, or support each other? No___. If Yes, enter 1 ___.

5. Did you often or very often feel that ... You didn't have enough to eat, had to wear dirty clothes, and had no one to protect you? Or your parents were too drunk or high to take care of you or take you to the doctor if you needed it? No___. If Yes, enter 1 ___.

6. Were your parents ever separated or divorced? No___. If Yes, enter 1 ___.

7. Was your mother or stepmother: Often or very often pushed, grabbed, slapped, or had something thrown at her? Or sometimes, often, or very often kicked, bitten, hit with a fist, or hit

with something hard? Or ever repeatedly hit over at least a few minutes or threatened with a gun or knife? No___. If Yes, enter 1 ___.

8. Did you live with anyone who was a problem drinker or alcoholic, or who used street drugs? No___. If Yes, enter 1 ___.
9. Was a household member depressed or mentally ill, or did a household member attempt suicide? No___. If Yes, enter 1 ___.
10. Did a household member go to prison? No___. If Yes, enter 1 ___.

Now add up your "Yes" answers: ____. This is your ACE score.

I found I had four ACEs, which is great if you're playing poker. However, in the game of life, four ACEs are very risky. The study found the following increased risk factors for those who had four or more ACEs compared to those who had none:

- A four- to twelve-fold increase of health risks for alcoholism, drug abuse, depression, and suicide attempt.
- A two- to four-fold increase in smoking, poor self-rated health, having more than fifty sexual intercourse partners, and sexually transmitted disease.
- A 1.4- to 1.6-fold increase in physical inactivity and severe obesity.

New Understandings from the ACE Studies

Since the first ACE studies were reported in 1998, there have been hundreds of further studies that have validated the basic findings: Adverse Childhood Experiences (ACEs) can cause later physical and emotional problems in adulthood. The latest information about current research on ACEs is available on two websites developed by journalist Jane Ellen Stevens: www.AcesTooHigh.com and www.AcesConnection.com. Stevens has been a newspaper and magazine journalist focusing on health, science, and technology for more than thirty years and has been reporting on ACE study and related research since 2005.

Subsequent to the original ACE study, other ACE surveys have expanded the types of ACEs, so if you have had any of the following experiences, add another number to your ACE score.

1. Did you experience racism?
   No___. If Yes, enter 1 ___.
2. Did you experience gender discrimination?
   No___. If Yes, enter 1 ___.
3. Did you witness a sibling being abused?
   No___. If Yes, enter 1 ___.
4. Did you witness violence outside the home?
   No___. If Yes, enter 1 ___.
5. Did you witness a father being abused by a mother?
   No___. If Yes, enter 1 ___.
6. Were you bullied by a peer or adult?
   No___. If Yes, enter 1 ___.
7. Were you hospitalized, in foster care, or forced to live away from your family?
   No___. If Yes, enter 1 ___.
8. Did you grow up and live in a war zone?
   No___. If Yes, enter 1 ___.
9. Did you grow up in an unsafe neighborhood?
   No___. If Yes, enter 1 ___.
10. Was a family member deported or did you live in fear of deportation?
    No___. If Yes, enter 1 ___.

Take a break now and reflect on your own ACEs. How many do you have? What adult problems might connect to early experiences growing up?

How ACEs Early in Life Can Lead
to Problems Later in Life

It took me many years to really understand how events in childhood, even relatively common ones such as having parents who divorced or had mental health problems, could lead to an increased risk for adult depression or broken marriages.

The doctors who designed the initial research had some tentative ideas. Now these ideas have been tested and accepted. They are posted on the Centers for Disease Control and Prevention website. The mechanism for our childhood traumas leading to later problems as adults goes like this:

Adverse Childhood Experiences (ACEs) lead to faulty neurodevelopment, which leads to social, emotional, and cognitive impairment, which leads to adoption of risky health behaviors, which leads to disease, disability, and social problems, which lead to a shortened life and early death.

This has helped me understand how ACEs had contributed to the problems I experienced as a child and also later in life. As noted earlier, I experienced **4 ACEs** growing up. I came to understand that the effect of these early traumatic experiences had caused a disruption in how my brain functioned. As a child, I felt different. With my father locked up in a mental hospital and my mother terrified that I would end up like my father, I went on with my life, but I always felt afraid. I worried constantly about whether I would end up like my father. Would I be locked up? Would I feel so depressed I would want to die?

I learned that ACEs can not only undermine our physical and emotional health and well-being but can undermine our relationships. Understanding ACEs can go a long way toward helping us understand why men live sicker and die sooner than women.

Male Attachment Disorders: How ACEs
Can Undermine a Man's Relationships

Not only are relationships an important part of our lives, but a good relationship can make our lives worthwhile and keep us healthy. In their book *Loneliness: Human Nature and the Need for Social*

Connections, social scientists John Cacioppo and William Patrick report that "When people are asked what pleasures contribute most to happiness, the overwhelming majority rate love, intimacy, and social affiliation above wealth, or fame, even above physical health."

One of the great tragedies of having unhealed ACEs is that they undermine our ability to have healthy, joyful, relationships. Looking back, it's clear that my unrecognized ACEs contributed to my two divorces and that healing my ACEs has contributed to the fact that Carlin and I have been happily married for forty-two years now.

Too many men suffer from what I call *Male Attachment Disorder,* or MAD for short. Our childhood wounds keep us irritable, angry, stressed, and depressed and undermine our ability to be truly intimate in our love lives. Here are eight aspects of MAD.

1. Agitation and anger.

    Our Adverse Childhood Experiences undermine our ability to trust others and have a healthy sex and love life as an adult. For men, the pain often expresses itself as irritability and anger. I was always agitated like a cat on a hot tin roof and easily triggered. Men's anger causes them to become increasingly cut off from others, which increases our loneliness and makes us even angrier.

2. Male-type depression.

    Depressed women often turn their sadness inward. Depressed men become more irritable and angrier. Male-type depression usually goes unrecognized, and irritable and angry men usually cause others to withdraw from them, which increases their pain and suffering. Feeling misunderstood and cut off from others, they tend to deny their own contribution to the problem and often blame their wives or partners.

3. Impulsiveness and risk-taking.

    MAD men are impulsive and take more risks. I was successful in my work, wrote books, and spoke all over the world. Risk-taking could be an asset at work, but at home it kept everything on edge. You never knew what I might do next. Men, in general, take more risks than women, but men who suffer from ACEs take greater risks than most. One client of mine continued to have unprotected sex with strangers despite knowing that he was putting himself at risk of getting AIDS.

4. Need for control.

When men grow up with unrecognized and unhealed ACEs, their lives become increasingly out of control. Inside they feel confused and frightened. Yet, they are often unwilling to address their internal fears, and so they do everything they can to control others. One of my clients tried to control every aspect of his wife's social life. He wanted her to dress in clothes that he approved of for her, and if she was a minute late getting ready for an outing, he would go into a rage.

5. Resistance to love and support.

Men are hungry for and love and support, but we often resist it at every turn. Even caring offers of support or suggestions about taking better care of ourselves or going to the doctor for a checkup may be met with angry resistance. Carlin often tried to tell me that I needed help, but I refused vehemently. Since I couldn't trust my caregivers growing up, I had a horrific time trusting those who loved me later. It took me years to let myself be guided and be open to getting help.

6. Denial and blame.

Men often deny that they are responsible for any of the problems in their lives. They blame the government, the people at work, and most often the people closest to them. They have fights with their children and often become enraged. They may blame their wives or partners. For years I refused to recognize and accept that I had a problem. I blamed it on everything else—stress, work, politics, my kids, my wife—anything but my life and what was really causing the problem. When I talk to male clients, I often have to get them to see that it isn't their *wife* that is the problem, but it is their *life*. I help them to stop trying to get others to change and begin getting them to change their own lives.

7. Addictive personality and behavior.

One of the most common ways men attempt to deal with the pain and discomfort of unhealed ACEs is the increased use of alcohol and other drugs. Often, use begins with a natural desire to relax from the stresses of life, but it becomes habitual as the unhealed wounds from the past make relationships increasingly stressful. Many then drink, use drugs, or find other means of relief, and a vicious cycle begins.

8. Confusion and helplessness.

Since men don't often recognize the underlying cause of their problems, their relationships become increasingly frustrating and dysfunctional, and they feel increasingly confused and helpless. The men often withdraw even more, may have an affair in an attempt to find the love they so desperately need, but as the title of one of my most popular books says, they are *Looking for Love in all the Wrong Places*.

Fortunately, addressing our ACEs and childhood trauma can help men heal from male attachment disorders. For now, reflect on the eight aspects of MAD. Which ones do you notice in your own life?

Trauma: It's Not What You Think

When most of us think of trauma, we think of extreme situations—soldiers facing extreme stress in battle, children being sexually abused, or an adult being raped. We don't think of trauma as the more subtle and common events that occur in most of our lives as we are growing up. The ACE studies have shown conclusively that events don't need to be extreme in order to have serious, negative consequences later in our lives.

In their book *Code to Joy: The Four-Step Solution to Unlocking Your Natural State of Happiness*, George Pratt, PhD, and Peter Lambrou,

PhD, illustrate the way in which we underestimate the effect of common ACEs. They ask you to imagine you are standing just outside your home, surrounded by a dense fog so thick you can't see the other side of the street in front of you. You look to the left, to the right, but can't see more than fifty feet in any direction. You are surrounded. You feel cut off from everything, and you feel frightened and alone.

They ask, how much water does it take to create the blanket of fog that has completely isolated you from your world? The surprising answer is *a few ounces*. The total volume of water in a blanket of fog one acre around and one meter deep would not quite fill an ordinary drinking glass. The fog actually contains four hundred billion tiny droplets suspended in the air creating an impenetrable cloak that shuts out light and makes you shiver.

This is what happens when we have painful experiences that we just can't shake. Pratt and Lambrou call it "the fog of distress," and it is this fog that occurs when we experience one or more ACEs. The underlying cause may be as common as a few ounces of water, but the impact can change our lives.

"Typically, this vague sense of unease parks itself in the background," say Pratt and Lambrou, "like the annoying hum of a refrigerator or air conditioner we have learned to block out from our conscious awareness." We get on with our lives and forget the ACEs we grew up with. However, as the studies show, they affect our lives nonetheless. "Whether we are aware of it or not, it pervades our existence like an insistent headache, interfering with our ability to have healthy relationships, to perform to our potential at work, or to have lives that are anywhere near as fulfilling as they could be."

Their conclusion is similar to what the researchers found with the ACE studies. **"Over the years, that background hum can sabotage our careers, friendships, marriages."** It's not surprising that since the wounds occur in our most intimate relationships in our families, their impact is felt in our most intimate adult relationships.

Bessel van der Kolk, MD, is one of the world's leading experts on trauma. In his book, *The Body Keeps the Score: Brain, Mind, and Body in the Healing of Trauma,* he says, "Trauma affects not only those who are directly exposed to it, but also those around them. The wives of men who suffer from PTSD tend to become depressed, and the children of depressed mothers are at risk of growing up insecure and anxious. ... Long after a traumatic experience is over, it may be reactivated at the slightest hint of danger and mobilize disturbed brain circuits and secrete massive amounts of stress hormones."

According to Lynne McTaggart, award-winning journalist and author of the best-selling books *The Field* and *The Bond,* "An enormous body of research reveals that the root of stress and ultimately illness is a sense of isolation, and most toxic of all appears to be our current tendency to pit ourselves against each other." I will address these issues in the next chapter as we explore the problem of violence in our lives and in the world.

CHAPTER 2

MALE VIOLENCE IS INCREASING— FROM SCHOOL SHOOTINGS, TO DOMESTIC VIOLENCE AND INSURRECTION AT THE US CAPITOL, FROM IRRITABILITY AND ANGER TO DEPRESSION AND SUICIDE

Most men don't consider themselves to be violent, but many men recognize that we have a "short fuse" and can sometimes "fly off the handle" when provoked. It slowly began to dawn on me that I might have an anger problem when my first wife said she was frightened of me. I heard what she said, but I didn't believe her. "How can you say that?" I wanted to know, my voice becoming louder with every word. "I've never laid a hand on you."

Learning about my Adverse Childhood Experiences (ACEs) helped me understand that you don't have to become physically violent to cause harm to others. I still remember my father's irritability and anger, his cold and threatening silences, and his occasional outburst. He never hit me or my mother, but I always felt his rage was barely under control.

My irritability and anger weren't the only cause of our divorce after being married ten years, but they were certainly contributing factors. I still saw myself as a nice guy who was not violent and only got seriously angry when he was provoked. I married again, this time to a woman who slept with a gun under her pillow. That should have been a tipoff that anger and violence might be a problem in my life, but again, I didn't recognize it the time.

Like many angry men who are beginning to recognize their problem but don't understand it, I thought the solution was to keep my anger under control, to be nicer, kinder, more understanding. Not everyone with an anger problem chooses a woman with an anger problem, but our subconscious works in mysterious ways.

My second wife and I were together for just two years, and it was a roller coaster of highs and lows. She would get angry at something I did. I would try to be nice and understanding, and her anger would escalate until I would finally blow up, and we'd be in a fight. She became physically abusive, though I never called it that at the time. She would punch me, pinch me, throw things at me, break things that were important to me. But I had been in fights as an adolescent so I could easily defend myself. I figured if she didn't physically injure me, then she wasn't being abusive.

Our marriage ended shortly after our last confrontation. We had agreed that when our fights escalated, we would disengage and go in separate rooms until we cooled down. It didn't stop our fights, but it kept them from becoming physical. I was getting tired of being hit and having to restrain myself.

On this occasion we had been arguing for an hour, and as it escalated, I screamed, "That's enough. We have to separate." She yelled one final obscenity as I left. I went into my room, and she went into hers. I tried to calm my breathing and felt the rage subsiding. Suddenly she burst into my room. She wouldn't leave when I screamed for her to get out but came at me and continued her diatribe about what a worthless piece of shit I was.

Then she began to pound my chest with her finger, making her point with each word she spat in my face. At that point, I completely lost it. All rational control flew out of me and all I could see was red rage and an animal that was trying to kill me. I pulled my fist back and knew I was going to hit her and knew I would kill her if I did.

At the last second, I turned and smashed my fist into the wall. I pictured my fist going through the wall and coming out the other side outside the house. That didn't happen. I hit a stud and I screamed in pain as I heard the bones break.

My wife drove me to the emergency room. The ER doctor X-rayed my hand. "My God," he said. "What did you do? Are you a boxer? The last time I saw a hand this broken was with a fighter who came in following a bloody confrontation in the ring." I sheepishly told him I was a counselor not a boxer. I just got angry and punched the wall. He said I would need immediate surgery, admitted me to the hospital, and called the best hand surgeon in town.

I had multiple steel pins put in the bones of multiple fingers, and it took months for me to regain the use of my right hand and many more months of physical therapy to regain full function. But I was lucky—very lucky. I didn't kill anyone, though I came close, I knew. I did get out of the relationship, though it wasn't easy.

I came to understand why women don't leave abusive relationships. Over the years, our self-esteem slowly drips away, one day, one minute, at a time. We say to ourselves we don't believe the mean things they say to us or that we somehow deserve what we're getting, but over time we lose our will to escape. We cling to the abuse we know rather than risk the unknown that we fear may be worse. It took me a full year following my broken-hand surgery before I found the strength to leave for good.

Reflection: Take a moment to reflect on your own experiences of violence. Did you grow up in a home where a father or mother raged or was physically or emotionally violent? Were you ever bullied or observe violence on the streets in your neighborhood?

Violence comes in many forms and is a problem throughout the world. Nelson Mandela said, "Many who live with violence day in and day out assume that it is an intrinsic part of the human condition. But this is not so. Violence can be prevented. Violent cultures can be turned around. In my own country and around the world, we have shining examples of how violence has been countered. Governments, communities, and individuals can make a difference."

Violence Is a Worldwide Problem with Many Related Aspects

The World Health Organization (WHO) produced an in-depth analysis of violence and published the information under the title, "The World Report on Violence and Health." The report is the result of three years of work, during which WHO drew on the knowledge of more than 160 experts from more than seventy countries.

In order to treat and prevent violence, we must understand what it is and its underlying causes. This report examines what is known about the epidemiology and prevention of violence from research and programs throughout the world. It addresses several types of violence, including:

- Child abuse and neglect by caregivers.
- Youth violence, including violence by adolescents and young adults.
- Intimate partner violence.
- Sexual violence.
- Elder abuse.
- Self-inflicted violence, including suicide.
- Collective violence, including the use of violence by one group against another to achieve political, social, or economic objectives; for example, war or terrorism.

Although things like school shootings, terrorism, and war grab the headlines, most violence involves self-harm. The report noted the following:

- War-related violence accounted for 18.6 percent of the total.
- Homicide accounted for 31.3 percent.

- Suicide accounted for a whopping 49.1 percent of the total violence in the world.

We often think of males as being the perpetrators of violence, but males are also the primary victims. In the US as in other countries, violence touches some groups more than others. The Men's Health Network cites the following differences:

- The chances of being a homicide victim are 1 in 30 for black males versus 1 in 179 for white males.
- The chances of being a homicide victim are 1 in 132 for black females versus 1 in 495 for white females.

What We Can Learn from The Violence Project

Mass shootings in America are becoming part of our daily lives. We are frightened and horrified when another incident occurs, but often a real understanding of the facts and the underlying cause is missing.

Frustrated by reactionary policy conversations that never seemed to convert into meaningful action, special investigator and psychologist Jill Peterson and sociologist James Densley created "The Violence Project," the first comprehensive database of mass shooters. Their goal was to establish the root causes of mass shootings and figure out how to stop them by examining hundreds of data points in the life histories of more than 170 mass shooters—from their childhood and adolescence to their mental health and motives. They've also interviewed the living perpetrators of mass shootings and people who knew them, shooting survivors, victims' families, first responders, and leading experts to gain a comprehensive firsthand understanding of the real stories behind them, rather than the sensationalized media narratives that too often prevail.

Key Findings include:

- Psychosis played no role for nearly 70% of mass shooters. Clearly the idea that all mass shooters must be crazy isn't accurate.

- Many mass shooters experienced feelings of **suicidality** either before or during their attack. According to the findings, 31% felt suicidal prior to the attack, 40% during the attack, and 59% died at the scene. Suicide and murder are often linked.

- Mass shootings occur where people live and work and where they feel uncared for. For example, 31.5% occur the workplace, 16.7% in retail establishments, 13.7% in restaurants, 8.3% outdoors, 7.7% in residences, 6.5% in houses of worship, 6.5% in K-12 schools, 5.4% in colleges and universities, 3.4% in government buildings.

- Motivations of mass shooters have varied over time. Most recently, 30% have domestic or relationship issues, 23% employment issues, 20% interpersonal conflict, 19% hate, 19% psychosis, 13% legal issues, 7% fame-seeking.

- Hate-motivated mass shootings and fame-seeking perpetrators have rapidly increased since 2015.

- Eighty percent of mass shooters were in noticeable crisis prior to their shooting. The idea that shootings are unpredictable and a person just "snaps" are myths.

- Some signs of a crisis were more common than others, with more than two-thirds of shooters experiencing increased agitation before their shooting. Among these, 23.8% experienced paranoia, 24.4% inability to complete daily tasks, 27.3% mood swings, 29.7% depressed moods, 33.1% loss of reality, 39.5% increasing isolation, 41.9% abusive behavior, 66.9% increased agitation.

Feminist activist Caitlin Roper, writing in a *Huffington Post* blog, says, "Male violence is the worst problem in the world." She goes on to say, "While many of us have been directly harmed by male violence, the threat alone is enough to keep women as a class in a state of fear, controlled, pliable. Yet when reporting on male violence, mainstream media neglects to call it what it is, with headlines often stating the sex of the victim while downplaying the sex of the perpetrator, if even mentioning him at all."

Violence often starts at home with stresses in our interpersonal relationships. Irritability, anger, abusive behavior, depression, mood swings, and agitation are important signs. Clearly mass shootings are rare events, but the more common acts of aggression and violence are ones we need to better understand.

The Irritable Male Syndrome: The Roots of Violence Begin at Home

Once I got out of my own abusive relationship, I began to write. Writing is the way I make sense of my life and express my pain so I can understand the causes and cures. The result was two books. The first was *The Irritable Male Syndrome: Understanding and Managing the 4 Key Causes of Depression and Aggression* and *Mr. Mean: Saving Your Relationship from the Irritable Male Syndrome.*

> Q: What do you call a man who is always tired, miserable, and irritable?
> A: Normal.
> Q: How can you tell if a man has Irritable Male Syndrome?
> A: You ask him to pass the salt and he yells: "Take, take, take—that's all you ever do!"

These little zingers, which appeared in the *London Daily Mirror,* illustrate some important aspects of what many men, and those who must live with them, are experiencing these days. First, it seems that stress has become a normal part of modern life, and more and more men are taking our frustrations out on those closest to us. Second, men's irritability, blame, and anger seem excessive and more explosive. You ask an innocent question, and he jumps down your throat. What's going on here?

For some, this kind of irritability has come on slowly over a period of months and years. For others, it seems like someone has flipped a switch and Mr. Nice has turned into Mr. Mean. "God, it's like he's hormonal," one woman said. When I told her she wasn't too far from the truth, she snapped back, "I knew it." Since I began my study of this subject, I have received thousands of letters from men and women describing their experiences.

What follows are typical of what women and men have been telling me.

A Woman's View

This letter I received is typical of what women experience with men suffering from the Irritable Male Syndrome:

For about a year now (it could be even longer, it's hard to know exactly), I have gradually felt my husband of twenty-two years pulling away from me and our family. He has gradually become more sullen, angry, and moody. His general life energy is down, and his sex drive has really dropped off.

Recently he has begun venting to anyone who will listen about how horrible we all are. He is particularly hard on our nineteen-year-old son, Mark. It's so surprising because our son has always been super industrious and competent. My husband has always shared my view that Mark is one of the hardest working kids we know. But all of a sudden that has all changed. Mark still works from 6:30 a.m. until 4:30 p.m. every day, but now his dad accuses him of being unmotivated, lazy, and anything else he can think to say that is negative.

If the kids aren't living up to his standards, it is my fault. When they're good, it is because he has been such a positive influence in their lives. If there's a problem, it must be because of the way I've raised them. I know that sounds bizarre, but that's how he is thinking.

He blames me for everything these days. If his socks or underwear are missing, I must have put them somewhere or done something with them to piss him off. I'm not kidding, that's what he tells me. The thing that bothers me the most is how unaffectionate he has become. I don't even get the hugs and affection like I did in the past, and when he does touch me, I feel grabbed rather than caressed. My husband used to be the most positive, upbeat, funny person I knew. Now it's like living with an angry brick!

Women often feel baffled by men's irritability and anger. I know this was true for my wife. Like many women, she felt that just about anything would set me off. She didn't know what to do and would often close down and withdraw to protect herself. This would usually cause me to become afraid and would trigger more anger.

A Man's View

Although men are generally not as aware of their problem or willing to admit that they are suffering from the Irritable Male Syndrome, this man was unusually expressive. He had filled out the IMS questionnaire on my website and responded to my request for more in-depth feedback about his experience of the Irritable Male Syndrome. Rick is a fifty-two-year-old married man with children ages twenty-two and twenty-six. His responses are typical of many men who have spoken out:

> I think my irritability is related to the time of life I am in and to the stresses that seem to be mounting both at work and at home. I'm an electrical engineer and work for a large company in the Midwest. There has been a great deal of "consolidation" over the last few years and many people have been let go or forced into early retirement. Even though I have been here a long time and don't think I am vulnerable to losing my job, I still worry.
>
> There is always so much to do and there never seems to be enough time to do it all. I have trouble staying on top of it all. I don't have much physical or mental energy these days. All of this is affecting my sleep. My wife keeps asking me what's wrong. I don't know what to tell her. I usually answer that nothing is wrong. When she persists I often snap at her.
>
> Although I love my wife, I feel we have grown apart over the years. We used to be very close, but now we often seem like opposites and that creates its own kind of stress. I often feel unappreciated, unheard, uncared about. She says the same. Neither of us are getting what we need, but we don't seem to be able to do anything about it. It's very discouraging and depressing.
>
> For me, depression and irritability are closely linked. I don't really lash out that often. I mostly hold the feelings in. I don't want

to fight, but sometimes things erupt and I blow up at her. I can tell she's hurt. I feel guilty and that makes me angrier. It seems to be a vicious cycle. She says I am often sarcastic and cutting. I don't think I am, but maybe she's right.

Another thing she complains about is how I drive. You might say that I have a good deal of "road rage." When people cut me off or drive in a manner dangerous to others around them, I get furious. I'll yell, pound the steering wheel, and once I even chased someone off the freeway to teach them a lesson. I was clearly out of control. My wife and I generally carpool to work and she hears all my cussing and sees all my gesturing. I know it makes her uncomfortable and she's admitted that it makes me look more than a little crazy.

When we're out having fun, I can go from being happy-go-lucky to being crabby in the blink of an eye. Something small will happen. I take it personally and become irrationally angry. For instance, I'll be at a bar with some friends and if the waitress is slow in getting to the table, it infuriates me. Sometimes I'll say something hurtful, like "it's about time you got around to doing your job." Other times I'll just leave and go home, fuming all the way.

I know I lack a sense of general well-being much of the time. I have come to doubt my ability to be a reliable, dependable, likeable person. My confidence in myself is low. When I feel hateful or annoyed with everyone I just want to isolate myself. That way I don't have to deal with them and I won't do things I'll regret later. As a result, I have become estranged from my wife and children. Even at work, which used to be a place I felt comfortable and where I had a lot of friends, I feel cut off and isolated.

This depression/irritability "syndrome" affects EVERYTHING in my life. I feel that I have achieved very little of what, as a young man, I had hoped to achieve. I long to be much more confident and competent, much more relaxed, much more self-sufficient and much more successful.

Men are often not aware of the extent of their anger or how destructive it is to their relationship with their wife or partner. When they are aware of the anger, they feel justified and tell themselves some-one else is responsible for causing them to be angry. I still remember screaming at my wife, "I'm not angry, goddamn it!" She just looked at me, with the unspoken words, *Do you hear yourself? Give me a break, of course you're angry.* I then followed with an angry, "What the hell do you expect when you ... " And on it would go.

Irritable Male Syndrome: Up Close and Personal

One of the reasons I wrote *The Irritable Male Syndrome* was to help the many men and women who are suffering through a problem they don't understand. As a therapist, it makes me sad to see so many couples splitting up at the very time of life that they could be enjoying each other the most. I'm often frustrated seeing the tension that builds between young men and their families, tensions that can tear a family apart and can lead to alcohol or drug abuse, aggression, violence. It makes me angry to see so many of our young men—good, caring guys—who end up involved with the criminal justice system.

The other reason is a lot more personal and closer to home. After many years of being in a wonderful marriage, something seemed to be eating at the very roots of our joy and commitment. Carlin and I had both been married before and had merged our families when we got together. She had three sons, and I had a son and a daugh-ter. We raised her youngest son and my daughter together. There were difficulties, stresses, and strains, but we worked through them pretty well. We each felt we had found the love of our life, the per-son we would spend the rest of our days with. We felt we had learned a lot about ourselves, healed a good deal of our past wounds, and knew how to create a healthy marriage and family.

The change was nearly imperceptible at first. Looking back, it seems to have begun close to the time our last child left home. We were together without the day-to-day responsibilities of parent-ing. My psychotherapy practice was growing, and we had the extra money to enjoy a few more luxuries and some trips together. Carlin seemed to blossom. After coming back from a personal retreat, she started a school—The Diamond Wise School for Sacred Living and Joyful Action.

Her school quickly drew the kind of students she was looking for—adults who wanted to explore new aspects of their lives and create a balance between the spiritual and the practical, the inner and the outer world. I joined the school as well and liked putting my professional role aside to become a student again. It was a new experience, but one that felt right, to have Carlin teaching me the things that she knew best.

Though the changes all seemed to be positive, they created major shifts in our lives. I was glad Carlin was becoming increasingly successful in her work, but I began to feel slightly uneasy. The thoughts rarely broke through the surface, but just underneath I wondered whether she would surpass me in success. (She had just written her first book and everyone, including me, thought it was exceptional.) My conscious mind was delighted at her success, but my less-conscious self was feeling threatened and competitive.

I'd often dreamed of a time when she would move out in the world more directly, take on more of the financial responsibility for our family. I saw myself as taking more time to rest, relax, and have more time for non-work-related activities. I thought I might like to learn to play the guitar, sing, or dance. I'd always wanted to learn metal sculpture. But somehow it wasn't happening. Rather than cutting back on work, I was doing even more. I told myself it was so we'd have more money to do the things we both wanted to do. The truth was, I had spent so much of my life on the run, winning races, reaching for success, I didn't know how to slow down or shift gears.

Although I talked about it a lot, we didn't take more time for ourselves. I was frustrated with myself and uneasy about my future, but I couldn't see that. Instead, my gaze turned outward. Something wasn't right, and through my distorted lenses, it looked like the problem was Carlin. I started to become more critical, impatient, and dissatisfied. At the beginning, I kept the feelings bottled up inside. Things were mostly good, I told myself. If there were some problems, I was sure they would clear up and go away.

I did find myself withdrawing a bit, holding back my thoughts, not saying how I felt about things. The truth was I didn't really know how I felt about things. I rationalized my withdrawal by telling myself I didn't want to appear negative and ruin the times we did have together. Something was changing, but I knew whatever the change, "it was no big deal." Things would return to normal, I was sure.

I am an excellent counselor and therapist. I have been helping people lead healthy, productive, lives for over thirty-eight years now. Unfortunately, being a good therapist doesn't mean we are immune to problems that most people have to deal with. Sometimes it allows us to blind ourselves to our situation. We tell ourselves that we are professionals. If we were having problems, we would see them and correct them. Too many of us in the health care professions break down and even die because we are blind to our own difficulties until they create a major crisis in our lives.

If I had seen someone like this Jed character in my practice, I would have told him he was heading for a fall. I can usually tell when someone is under a great deal of stress, and I can often predict that if they don't take action to reduce the stress, there is going to be some kind of breakdown in their body, their mind, or both. But this Jed Diamond guy was not a client, and I couldn't be an objective, concerned therapist. I was too close to see clearly.

I had gotten to a point where my mind was spinning out of control, though I was still telling myself I wasn't in trouble. I just had so many interesting things to think about, I had to keep them all going. I was like a juggler who had six balls in the air, feeling the adrenaline rush of living at the edge of his abilities, and who couldn't resist putting a seventh ball in the mix.

The crash came one day when I lost my job. It was a job I had grown tired of and I was looking for something else, but I was told I was being terminated because of budget considerations. I felt ashamed. I knew there was nothing wrong with my performance, but I felt like a failure. Without knowing it, I was falling into the feelings of hopelessness that almost killed my father.

Two women helped stop my downward spiral. The first was Kay Redfield Jamison, an expert on depression who wrote *An Unquiet Mind: A Memoir of Moods and Madness*. These words totally nailed what I was feeling in a way that forced me to see reality. **"You're irritable and paranoid and humorless and lifeless and critical and demanding and no reassurance is ever enough. You're frightened, and you're frightening, and 'you're not at all like yourself but will be soon,' but you know you won't."**

The other woman was my wife, Carlin, who was kind but insistent. "I know you're depressed, and you need help. Your anger is killing us." With her help and support, I was finally willing and able to reach out for help and began long-term therapy with a woman psychiatrist, Dr. Betty Lacy, who helped save my marriage and my life.

The Origin of the Irritable Male Syndrome (IMS)

The term Irritable Male Syndrome has an interesting history. In early 2002, a colleague sent me a copy of an article by Dr. Gerald A. Lincoln, a researcher in Edinburgh, Scotland. Dr. Lincoln had recently published the results of his studies on animals in the journal *Reproduction, Fertility, and Development*. He titled the paper "The Irritable Male Syndrome" and described what he observed in the animals following the withdrawal of testosterone.

In the introduction to his paper, he said that the "irritability-anxiety-depression syndromes associated with withdrawal of sex steroid hormones are well recognized in the female." They are, he noted, connected with changes associated with the ovarian cycle and include premenstrual syndrome, postnatal depression, and menopause.

He went on to write, "The occurrence of a potentially similar behavioral syndrome in males following withdrawal of testosterone (T) has received less attention. A clear behavioral response to T withdrawal is predicted, however, because T has well-defined psychotropic effects in relation to sexuality, aggression, performance, cognition and emotion."

After reading about Dr. Lincoln's work, I decided I needed to visit him in Edinburgh, Scotland. I wondered what kind of man would find an interest in studying irritable males. The opportunity presented itself when I was invited to present my research at the World Congress on Men's Health in Vienna, Austria. I asked Dr. Lincoln if my wife and I might stop by for a visit on our way to the conference. He readily agreed and said he would pick us up at the airport on our arrival. When I asked how we'd recognize him, he told me "I'm tall, gray, and balding, and I'll be carrying a sign."

On first appearance, Dr. Lincoln seems the opposite of the irritable male. He is tall, thin, and greeted us with a wonderfully friendly smile. He was relaxed and immediately put us at ease. We gathered our things and bundled into his small car for the twenty-five-mile drive to Fife, a country village where he and his family have a wonderful old cottage. We settled in and had dinner with him, his wife, and their teenage daughter. The next day we walked around the property, saw the hundreds of trees he had planted, the pond he had dug, the treehouse he had built, the metal sculpture of a Soay ram, and the sheep he breeds for his experiments. He seems to be a man who enjoys life, has a passion for his work, and cares deeply about people.

Dr. Lincoln told us that originally he had been doing experiments in an attempt to create a male birth control pill. In his experiments with Soay sheep and other animals, he tried lowering testosterone levels in the hope that he could find a level that prevented conception but still allowed for regular hormonal function.

He failed at developing a male contraceptive but succeeded in creating a lot irritable and angry rams. He also coined a new term, Irritable Male Syndrome, and defined it this way. "IMS is a behavioral state of nervousness, irritability, lethargy, and depression that occurs in adult male mammals following withdrawal of testosterone."

He told me he assumed this was true of *all* male mammals but had never studied humans. I told him the studies I had conducted for my books *Male Menopause* and *Surviving Male Menopause* supported his findings, though I felt that human IMS was not only caused by low testosterone, but other factors as well. I told him I planned to write a book about this, and he gave me his support for titling the book *The Irritable Male Syndrome.*

Irritable Male Syndrome in Adult Male Human Mammals

I first recognized the symptoms of IMS when I did research on Male Menopause, the time of life where men's testosterone levels begin to drop. Later it became clear that IMS could occur at any age and was not only caused by low testosterone. Here is the definition of Irritable Male Syndrome that I developed and use.

Irritable Male Syndrome (IMS): **A state of hypersensitivity, anxiety, frustration, and anger that occurs in men and is associated with biochemical changes, hormonal fluctuations, stress, and loss of male identity.**

Let me share with you what went into this particular definition. Working with males (and those who live with them) who are experiencing IMS, I have found there are four core symptoms that underlie many others.

The first core emotion is hypersensitivity.

The women who live with these men say things like the following:

- I feel like I have to walk on eggshells when I'm around him.
- I never know when I'm going to say something that will set him off.
- He's like time bomb ready to explode, but I never know when.
- Nothing I do pleases him.
- When I try and do nice things, he pushes me away.
- He'll change in an eyeblink. One minute he's warm and friendly, the next he's cold and mean.

The men don't often recognize their own hypersensitivity. Rather their perception is that they are fine but everyone else is going out of their way to irritate them. The guys say things like:

- Quit bothering me.
- Leave me alone.
- No, nothing's wrong. I'm fine. Quit asking me questions.
- Why don't you ever ... fill in the blank. ... want sex, do what I want to do, do something with your life, think before you open your mouth, do things the right way.
- You damn ... fill in the blank. ... fool, bitch, etc. As IMS progresses, the words get harsher and more hurtful.
- They don't say anything. They increasingly withdraw into a numbing silence.

One concept I have found helpful is the notion that many of us are "emotionally sunburned," but others don't know it. We might think of a man who is extremely sunburned and gets a loving hug from his wife. He cries out in anger and pain. He assumes she knows he's sunburned, so if she "grabs" him, she must be trying to hurt him. She has no idea he is sunburned and can't understand why he reacts angrily to her loving touch. You can see how this can lead a couple down a road of escalating confusion.

The second core emotion is anxiety.
Anxiety is a state of apprehension, uncertainty, and fear resulting from the anticipation of a realistic or fantasized threatening event or situation. As you will see as you delve more deeply, IMS men live in constant worry and fear. There are many real threats that they are dealing with in their lives—sexual changes, job insecurities, relationship problems, threats of disease, political unrest, environment crises such as climate change. There are also many uncertainties that led men to ruminate and fantasize about future problems.

These kinds of worries usually take the form of "what ifs." What if I lose my job? What if I can't find a job? What if she leaves me? What if I can't find someone to love me? What if I have to go to war? What if something happens to my wife or children? What if my parents die? What if I get sick and can't take care of things? The list goes on and on.

The third core emotion is frustration.
The dictionary offers two relevant definitions that can help us understand this aspect of IMS.

1: the feeling that accompanies an experience of being thwarted in attaining your goals. Synonym is defeat.

2: a feeling of annoyance at being hindered or criticized.

The dictionary offers an enlightening example to illustrate the use of the word: "Her constant complaints were the main source of his frustration."

IMS men feel blocked in attaining what they want and need in life. They often don't even know what they need. When they do know, they often feel there's no way they can get it. They often feel defeated in the things they try to do to improve their lives. The men feel frustrated in their relationships with family, friends, and on the job. The world is changing, and they don't know where, how, or if they fit in.

Author Susan Faludi captured this frustration in her book *Stiffed: The Betrayal of the American Man.* The frustration is expressed in the question that is at the center of her study of American males. "If, as men are so often told, they are the dominant sex, why do so many of them feel dominated, done in by the world?" The frustration, that is often hidden and unrecognized, is a key element of IMS.

The fourth core emotion is anger.
Anger can be simply defined as a strong feeling of displeasure or hostility. Yet anger is a complex emotion. Outwardly expressed it can lead to aggression and violence. When it is turned inward it can lead to depression and suicide. Anger can be direct and obvious or it can be subtle and covert. Anger can be loud or quiet. It can be expressed as hateful words, hurtful actions, or in stony silence.

For many men, anger is the only emotion they have learned to express. Growing up male we are taught to avoid anything that is seen as the least bit feminine. We are taught that men "do" while women "feel." As a result men are taught to keep all emotions under wrap. We cannot show we are hurt, afraid, worried, or panicked. The only feeling that is sometimes allowed many men is anger. When men begin going through IMS, it is often anger that is the primary emotion.

Whereas feelings like anger, anxiety, and frustration can occur quickly and end quickly, irritability can develop into a mood state that can last over a long period of time and can trigger these feelings over and over again. It can have a major impact on our whole lives. "When we're in a mood it biases and restricts how we think," says Paul Ekman, who is professor of psychology and director of the Human Interaction Laboratory at the University of California Medical School in San Francisco. Dr. Ekman is one of the world's experts on emotional expression.

In describing these kinds of negative moods, Ekman continues and describes what happens to us and offers a clear and compelling understanding of how IMS can cause harm:

"It makes us vulnerable in ways that we are normally not. So the negative moods create a lot of problems for us, because they change how we think. If I wake up in an irritable mood, I'm looking for a chance to be angry. Things that ordinarily would not frustrate me, do. The danger of a mood is not only that it biases thinking but that it increases emotions. When I'm in an irritable mood, my anger comes stronger and faster, lasts longer, and is harder to control than usual. It's a terrible state… one I would be glad never to have."

As we explore IMS in more depth, be aware that we are talking about a problem that isn't easily categorized or circumscribed. It is slippery and elusive. It can wreak havoc in the lives of men and those who love them and remain hidden from scrutiny.

Like everything else in life, causes are complex. When I did the original research on Irritable Male Syndrome, I said there were four key causes. I now believe there are five.

The First Key Cause of IMS Is Decreasing Testosterone

In order to understand the way in which hormonal fluctuations cause IMS in men, we need to know something about testosterone. Theresa L. Crenshaw, MD, author of *The Alchemy of Love and Lust*, describes testosterone this way: "Testosterone is the young Marlon Brando—sexual, sensual, alluring, dark, with a dangerous undertone." She goes on to say that "it is also our 'warmone,' triggering aggression, competitiveness, and even violence. Testy is a fitting term." We know that men with testosterone levels that are too high can become angry and aggressive. But recent research shows that most hormonal problems in men are caused by testosterone levels that are too low.

Dr. Gerald Lincoln, who coined the term "Irritable Male Syndrome," found that lowering levels of testosterone in his research animals caused them to become more irritable, biting their cages as well as the researchers who were testing them. Larrian Gillespie, MD, an expert on male and female hormones, says, "Low testosterone is associated with symptoms of Irritable Male Syndrome."

I first recognized the importance of testosterone and what happens when levels begin to go down when I did my original research that led to the publication of my book *Male Menopause* which was published in 1997. At the time there was little real research and the book was soon translated into fourteen foreign languages in addition to English.

The primary symptoms that received all the headlines were that older men began to lose sexual desire and potency. I was one of the first researchers to report on a new experimental drug, later called Viagra, that helped older men to improve their erections. Yet, there was another symptom I found that was not being reported, and that was male irritability and anger. Testosterone levels decline naturally as we age, and if they get too low, we can become irritable and angry.

The Second Key Cause of IMS Is Low Serotonin

Most people have heard of the brain neurotransmitter serotonin. When we have enough flowing through our brains, we feel good. When there isn't enough, we feel bad. Siegfried Meryn, MD, author of *Men's Health and the Hormone Revolution*, calls serotonin "the male hormone of bliss." Women have the same hormone in their brains, and it has an equally positive effect on them. "The more serotonin the body produces," says Dr. Meryn, "the happier, more positive and more euphoric we are. Low serotonin can contribute to a man's irritability and aggression."

One of the most common causes of low serotonin levels are our eating and drinking habits. For instance, research has shown that protein, if consumed in excessive quantity, suppresses central nervous system serotonin levels. Many men were taught to believe that eating lots of meat would make them manly. Not only are there hormones injected in meat to make the animals fatter, but the protein contained in the meat can be harmful as well.

Judith Wurtman, PhD, and her colleagues at the Massachusetts Institute of Technology found that a high protein, low carbohydrate diet can cause increased irritability in men. They found that men often mistake their cravings for healthy carbohydrates, such as those found in vegetables like potatoes, rice, corn, squash, and so on, with cravings for protein found in meat. "Eating protein when we need carbohydrates," says Wurtman, "will make us grumpy, irritable, or restless."

Wurtman's team also found that alcohol consumption increases serotonin levels initially. However, chronic use dramatically lowers serotonin, resulting in depression, carbohydrate cravings, sleep disturbances, and proneness to argumentativeness and irritability. It may be that the male propensity to eat too much meat and drink too much alcohol is contributing to lower serotonin levels in brain chemistry, which leads to symptoms of IMS.

The Third Key Cause of IMS Is Increasing Stress

We all know the feeling. We've had another one of those days at work. One deadline after another, and there isn't enough time to breathe. Someone is always making more demands, and no matter how hard we try to stay on top of things, we seem to be getting further and further behind. Many of us have lost our jobs. If we have a job, we're often working more hours for less money. The economy is in turmoil. Our savings are dwindling, and our hopes for retirement seem to be fading away. The weather is crazy and heat waves and fires can no longer be ignored.

We all recognize the feeling of being stressed out. But what exactly is stress and why is stress-reduction so important? In my experience as a psychotherapist, I have found that too much stress underlies most of the psychological, social, and medical problems that people face in contemporary society, including IMS. For most of us, stress is synonymous with worry. If it is something that makes us worry, then it is stressful.

We can't avoid stress, nor would we want to. Life is change and change is life. The problem arises when there is too much change in too short a time. We might think of the problem that leads to the Irritable Male Syndrome as "dis-stress" or "overstress." Stress is unavoidable, necessary, invigorating, and life-enhancing. Distress and overstress can cause untold difficulties if not understood and prevented.

The Fourth Key Cause of IMS Is Loss of Male Identity and Purpose

For most of human history, the male role was clear. Our main job was to "bring home the bacon." We hunted for our food and shared what we killed with family and tribe. Everyone had a role to play. Some were good at tracking animals. Others excelled at making bows and arrows or spears. Some men were strong and could shoot an arrow with enough force to kill a buffalo. Others were skilled at singing songs and doing dances that invoked the spirit of the animal and made the hunt more effective.

But now many of us work at jobs that we hate, producing goods or services that have no real value to the community. We've gotten further and further away from the basics of bringing home food we've hunted or grown by ourselves. The money we receive is small compensation for doing work that is meaningless. And the men with some kind of job, no matter how bad, are the lucky ones. More and more men are losing their jobs and can't easily find new ones.

In her book *Stiffed: The Betrayal of the American Man,* author Susan Faludi concludes that male stress, shame, depression, and violence are not just a problem of individual men, but a product of the social betrayal that men feel as a result of the changing economic situation we all face. One of the men Faludi talked to at length, Don Motta, could be speaking for millions of men in this country who have been laid off, been downsized, or part of a company that has gone under.

"There is no way you can feel like a man," says Motta. "You can't. It's the fact that I'm not capable of supporting my family. When you've been very successful in buying a house, a car, and could pay for your daughter to go to college, though she didn't want to, you have a sense of success and people see it. I haven't been able to support my daughter. I haven't been able to support my wife. I'll be very frank with you," he said slowly, placing every word down as if each were an increasingly heavy weight. "I. Feel. I've. Been. Castrated."

This was certainly how my father felt when he couldn't find work. As Faludi interviewed men all across the country, she uncovered a fact that most men and women know all too well. Men put a lot of their identity and sense of self-worth into their jobs. If we aren't working or can't support our family, we feel that we're not really men. Motta's feeling of being castrated speaks volumes. Even men who choose to retire often feel lost and inadequate. We need to help men know that there is more to who they are than a paycheck. But we also have to develop societies that create meaningful work that can provide a decent living.

The Fifth Key Cause of IMS Is the Existential Terror that We Are Killing Ourselves

There is an increasing recognition among more and more people that humans are seriously out of balance with nature, and we seem unable to solve our problems. The headlines reporting a 2021 study on the climate crisis were startling: MORE THAN HALF OF YOUNG PEOPLE FEEL HUMANITY IS DOOMED.

The lead author, Caroline Hickman from Bath University, said, "The young feel abandoned and betrayed by governments." The researchers said they were moved by the scale of distress. One young man said, "I don't want to die, but I don't want to live in a world that doesn't care for children and animals."

We all are impacted by climate change, but there is a particular kind of pain men feel when they know we are leaving a world for our children and grandchildren that is quite literally burning up. Men who have been taught that it is our job to "protect and serve" feel ashamed, stressed, and depressed with what we are doing to our children.

In the next chapter, we will address the state of the world and how it impacts men and their families, and more importantly, how we can change things for the better.

CHAPTER 3

THE STATE OF THE WORLD— CHAOS, COLLAPSE, OR TRANSFORMATION

This is a difficult chapter to write because I must face the reality that my children and grandchildren and the other children of the world are in despair. The reason I wrote this book is because I believe we need to engage a Moonshot Mission for Mankind and humanity. My website MenAlive speaks to the need for healthy male leadership by men who are fully alive to themselves, each other, and their families.

The recent worldwide study "Young People's Voices on Climate Anxiety, Government Betrayal and Moral Injury: A Global Phenomenon" reported 75 percent of young men and women feel the future is frightening, and 56 percent think humanity is doomed. According to what its authors say is the world's largest ever study into young people's fears about the climate crisis, 45 percent of sixteen- to twenty-five-year-olds said climate-related anxiety and distress is affecting their daily lives and ability to function normally.

Almost 60 percent of the ten thousand young people surveyed across ten countries attributed this to their national governments, who they said were "betraying" them and future generations through their inaction. The study, published in *Lancet Planetary*

Health in September 2021 and led by academics and professionals at the University of Bath, Stanford Medicine Center for Innovation in Global Health, Oxford Health NHS Foundation Trust, and others, found that people from countries more directly and immediately impacted by climate change tended to be more worried about the future. Ninety-two percent of young people in the Philippines said they felt like the future was frightening, compared to just 56 percent in Finland.

"This study paints a horrific picture of widespread climate anxiety in our children and young people," said Caroline Hickman, a coauthor and a researcher at the University of Bath in the United Kingdom, in a statement. The results lend credence to lawsuits in which young people have taken their governments to court over climate change, arguing that political leaders have failed to protect their futures and their right to a healthy environment.

The study uses "climate anxiety" as a catch-all to describe the many emotions that people feel when confronted with the facts about climate change: worry, fear, anger, grief, despair, guilt, even hope. These feelings, the authors write, are a rational response. But they are often disregarded by others: among the 81 percent of respondents who said they talked to people about their concerns, nearly half said they were ignored or dismissed.

"I grew up being afraid of drowning in my own bedroom," said Mitzi Tan, a twenty-three-year-old from the Philippines, in a statement accompanying the study. "Society tells me that this anxiety is an irrational fear that needs to be overcome—one that meditation and healthy coping mechanisms will 'fix.' At its root, our climate anxiety comes from this deep-set feeling of betrayal because of government inaction. To truly address our growing climate anxiety, we need justice."

The children of the world need our support as never before. But before we can truly protect and serve, we must face our own fears and feelings of hopelessness. If I believed humanity was doomed, I would join others who were escaping into a make-believe world and pretend that everything is working out well. But escape is not an option. Facing the reality of the world we are living in requires that we do some serious soul searching.

We can begin by addressing the questions the young people answered in the survey. Please read the following statements and indicate if they apply to you. (You may want to circle or write down your own responses.):

1. To what degree are you worried that climate change threatens people and the planet?
    - Not worried
    - A little worried
    - Moderately worried
    - Very worried
    - Extremely worried

2. Does climate change make you feel any of the following?
    - Sad
    - Helpless
    - Anxious
    - Afraid
    - Optimistic
    - Angry
    - Guilty
    - Ashamed
    - Hurt
    - Depressed
    - Despair
    - Grief
    - Powerless
    - Indifferent

3. Do your feelings about climate change negatively affect any of the following aspects of your daily life?
    - Eating
    - Concentrating
    - Work
    - School
    - Sleeping
    - Spending time in nature
    - Playing
    - Having fun
    - Relationships

4. Does climate change make you think any of the following?
    - I'm hesitant to have children.
    - Humanity is doomed.
    - The future is frightening.
    - My family's security will be threatened (e.g., economic, social, physical security).

- I won't have access to the same opportunities that my parents had.
- The things I most value will be destroyed.
- People have failed to take care of the planet.

5. Yes or no: When I try to talk about climate change, have other people ignored or dismissed me?

6. I am reassured by governments' action on climate change.
   - Not at all
   - A little
   - Moderately
   - Very
   - Completely reassured

7. Yes or no: In relation to climate change, I believe that my government is/other governments are …
   - Taking my concerns seriously enough.
   - Doing enough to avoid a climate catastrophe.
   - Dismissing people's distress.
   - Acting in line with climate science.
   - Protecting me, the planet and/or future generations.
   - Can be trusted.
   - Lying about the effectiveness of the actions they're taking.
   - Failing young people across the world.
   - Betraying me and/or future generations.

8. When I think about how my government is / other governments are responding to climate change, I feel very or extremely:
   - Anguished
   - abandoned
   - afraid
   - hopeful
   - angry
   - valued
   - ashamed
   - belittled
   - protected

There are certainly other challenges the world faces other than climate change. But I believe that the change that occurred six to ten thousand years ago, when human societies shifted from being in partnership with nature to trying to dominate nature, was the original trauma that has led to many of the other problems we face in the world today.

The way we tried to dominate the earth and all the creatures of the earth began a cascade of trauma. What men did to the earth we did to ourselves, then to women and children. The healing that must occur, which I'll describe starting with chapter 4, begins by healing our relationship to ourselves, then to other men, women, and children, and finally healing our relationship to the earth.

Religious historian Thomas Berry spoke eloquently to our need to be honest about our present situation. "We never knew enough. Nor were we sufficiently intimate with all our cousins in the great family of the earth. Nor could we listen to the various creatures of the earth, each telling its own story. The time has now come, however, when we will listen or we will die."

Another truth-teller is Sam Keen, who in his words, was "overeducated at Harvard and Princeton" and was a professor of philosophy and religion at "various legitimate institutions" and a contributing editor of *Psychology Today* for twenty years before becoming a freelance thinker, lecturer, seminar leader, and consultant. He is the author of a baker's dozen books, including *Faces of the Enemy: Reflections of the Hostile Imagination, Fire in the Belly: On Being a Man,* and *Prodigal Father, Wayward Son: A Roadmap to Reconciliation* written with his son, Gifford Keen.

He says, "My work as a writer, lecturer and workshop leader has focused on exploring these questions":

- How can I find a meaning, purpose, vocation for my life?
- What can I know?
- What ought I to do?
- For what may I hope?
- Is there life beyond death?

- Whom do I love? Who loves me?
- What curtails my freedom?
- How can I escape from the constricting social, political, sexual, and economic myths that were imposed on me by my family and culture?
- To what cause, ideal, faith may I surrender without destroying the integrity of my self?
- What does it mean to experience the sacred?
- How can I live a spirited life in a world dominated by a secular-technological-economic vision of reality?
- How can we create a more just and peaceful world?

Which questions most intrigue you? Which ones are you wrestling with now?

I've known Sam for many years. He offered this quote for my 1994 book *The Warrior's Journey Home: Healing Men, Healing the Planet*: "Down to earth advice about the path that leads away from the kingdom of the hollow men."

In the book I quote Sam, who offers a simple challenge to all.

The radical vision of the future rests on the belief that the logic that determines either our survival or our destruction is simple:

1. The new human vocation is to heal the earth.

2. We can only heal what we love.

3. We can only love what we know.

4. We can only know what we touch.

Clearly the healing he describes really must begin with our own healing. We each might say that our personal human vocation begins with healing ourselves. We can only heal by loving ourselves. We can only love by getting to know ourselves. We can only know by getting in touch with ourselves.

One of the Things We Need to Know About Ourselves Is That We Are Driven by Dopamine

My colleague Daniel Z. Lieberman, MD, along with physicist Michael E. Long, has written a compelling book about the things that drive us, from falling in love to going to war, from our addiction to drugs to our dependence on fossil fuels. It's called *The Molecule of More: How a Single Chemical in Your Brain Drives Love, Sex, and Creativity—and Will Determine the Fate of the Human Race.*

The authors offer a scene that is familiar to most of us:

> Shawn knew he was in love. His insecurities melted away. Every day made him feel on the brink of a golden future. As he spent more time with Samantha, his excitement about her grew, and his sense of anticipation became constant. Every thought of her suggested limitless possibilities. As for sex, his libido was stronger and ever, but only for her. Other women ceased to exist. Even better, when he tried to confess all this happiness to Samantha, she interrupted him to say, she felt exactly the same.
>
> Shawn wanted to be sure they would be together forever, so one day he proposed to her. She said yes.

Many of us have experienced the joys of falling in love, and many of us have been disappointed when the relationship began to change.

I've been a marriage and family counselor for more than fifty years. I've had a lifelong interest in understanding how we come to fall in love and why so many relationships start off like Shawn and Samantha's and then end in heartbreak and disappointment. My interest has been personal as well as professional since I went through two marriages and divorces before I learned the secret of why our attractions are so powerful and our hopes so high and why so many end in disaster.

Understanding the underlying causes of why we fall in love and why relationships don't always last can help us understand a lot about the state of the world and why so many things start off as a gift and end up as a disaster.

In *The Molecule of More,* Drs. Lieberman and Long offer this thought experiment:

Look down. What do you see? Your hands, your desk, the floor, maybe a cup of coffee, or a laptop computer or a newspaper. What you see when you look down are things within your reach, things you can control right now, things you can move and manipulate with no planning, effort, or thought. They are things in your possession.

Now look up. What do you see? The ceiling, perhaps pictures on the wall, or things out the window: trees, houses, building, clouds in the sky—whatever is in the distance. To reach them, you have to plan, think, calculate. Unlike what we see when we look down, the realm of up shows us things that we have to think about and work for in order to get.

They tell us that the brain is structured to address these two basic realms. There are a number of *down* chemicals—neurotransmitters—the brain uses to let you experience satisfaction and enjoy whatever you have in front of you. Lieberman and Long call them the *Here & Nows*. When you turn your attention to the world of *up*, your brain relies on a different chemical, a single molecule called dopamine.

"Mammals, reptiles, birds, and fish all have this chemical inside their brains," say Lieberman and Long, "but no creature has more of it than a human being. It is a blessing and a curse, a motivation and a reward. Carbon, hydrogen, oxygen, plus a single nitrogen atom—it is simple in form and complex in result. This is dopamine, and it narrates no less than the story of human behavior."

Dopamine was discovered in the brain in 1957 by Kathleen Montagu, a researcher in London. Only 0.0005 percent of brain cells produce dopamine—one in two million—yet these cells exert an outsized influence on behavior. In fact, under the right circumstances, pursuit of *feel-good* dopamine activation can become impossible to resist.

Initially some scientists christened dopamine *the pleasure molecule* and the brain pathway, the *reward circuit*. Early experiments with drug addicts showed that the more activity in the dopamine reward pathways, the greater the high. But further experiments expanded their understanding.

"It seemed more likely that the evolutionary processes that harnessed dopamine were driven by the need to motivate survival and reproductive activity," said Lieberman and Long. "Dopamine, they discovered, isn't about pleasure at all. Dopamine delivers a feeling much more influential."

Understanding dopamine, Lieberman and Long concluded, was key to explaining a great deal about human behavior, but if dopamine is not about pleasure, what is it about? After reading the book and learning the science of dopamine, I felt like I knew this important molecule. I imagined it talking to us all and revealing its secrets:

I'm all about the **pursuit**, not about attaining pleasure. I love to live in the **fantasy** world of **"what if."** What if I could get that sexy creature in bed with me? What if we could fly like the birds? Once I have what I seek, or I've invented a new way to travel, my job is done, I want to look for the next rush of excitement. I live in the future, not in the here and now.

No matter how attractive the person is, once we spend time together and get to know each other, the novelty wears off and I want to try something or someone new. I crave the **unexpected, the strange, the exotic**. That's why pornography is so attractive, particularly to men.

A drug addict completely understood me when he acknowledged, "My drug of choice is more." Too much is never enough for me. I drive every economy in the world, and I'll never stop. There may, in fact, be human limits, but for me, I'll keep making more and more whether its babies, bombs, or the carbon dioxide and methane that are heating the planet to dangerous levels.

From my point of view, **having is uninteresting**. It's only **getting** that matters.

The reality of **what is** becomes boring to me. I want to dream about what **could be. Glamour** is me personified. It creates **desires that can never be fulfilled** because they crave what can only exist in our imaginations.

I'm **never satisfied**. Mick Jagger told his biographer in 2013 he had been with about **four thousand women**—a different sex partner every ten days of his adult life. It is no wonder the Rolling Stones' hit song was "(I Can't Get No) Satisfaction." It is all about **anticipation**, never about *having what we seek. I'm all about **falling in love or lust**, never about the here and now, actually loving someone and having a satisfying sex life.*

*There are a number of **here and now chemicals** (H&Ns) such as **serotonin, oxytocin, endorphins** (your brain's version of morphine), and **endocannabinoids** (your brain's version of cannabis). **When I'm turned up, these H&Ns are turned down.***

Although women are driven by me too, men have a special affinity for me. That's why so many of the captains of industry are men as well as the dictators that are never satisfied with what they have. They always want more. Men don't have more of me than women, but testosterone, which is so much higher in males, forces the release of dopamine.

Dopamine is a wonderful gift to life. It drives our desires, creativity, and search for a partner. However, like most things, we need to balance the desire for *more* with the joy of *what is*. Through most of human history we had a better balance between the search for more and the joy of what is, between finding a loving partner and creating the joy of an ongoing relationship.

Throughout 99 percent of our human history, where partnership practices were the rule rather than the exception, we were more intimately involved with nature and with each other. There was a greater balance between getting more of the things that we needed like food, friends, and mating partners. But as we moved to a time of domination, these here and now needs were replaced by a desire for more.

One of the main reasons humans become addicted to substances like cocaine or heroin is that it artificially releases dopamine, which creates an endless hunger for more. And since dopamine can never satisfy our here and now pleasures, we become like confusing homing pigeons flying ever faster toward a home that gets farther and farther away.

The key element of the domination system is that it is built on fear. Dopamine makes us believe that what we have and who we are is not enough. We must always strive for more. Of course, the molecule of more is the perfect chemical for a dominator system that is driven by profits. We measure success by how much stuff we create and consume, not how satisfied or happy our people are.

In the final chapter of *The Molecule of More*, called "Harmony: Putting it All Together, in Which Dopamine and the Here and Now, H&Ns, Find Balance," the authors say, "Living our lives in the abstract, unreal, dopaminergic world of future possibilities comes at a cost, and that cost is happiness." They conclude saying, "We have to overcome the seduction of endless dopaminergic stimulation and turn our backs on our never-ending hunger for more. If we are able to intermingle dopamine with H&N, we can achieve that harmony." To do that, we may have to change the way we live.

The Men's Movement Meets the Sinking Ship of Civilization

I had been doing men's work since 1969 when my son, Jemal, was born. During that time I attended a number of men's conferences, but the 1993 Men's Leaders' Conference in Indianapolis, Indiana, sponsored by *Wingspan Magazine* changed my life forever. I saw what humanity was up against and the two choices that would determine our future. It started off like many other conferences I had attended. We shared stories, read poetry, talked about our children, our wives, lovers, friends, and neighbors. We caught up with old friends and heard about what was going on with men and their relationships in other parts of the country.

But this gathering had something new to offer: a sweat lodge ceremony. I'd attended a few in the past, led by Native American elders. I've had asthma since I was a kid and worried about being in a hot, enclosed space, but I joined others who wanted to experience this ancient healing ceremony.

The sweat lodge is a small structure made of a frame of saplings and covered with animal skins and blankets. A depression is dug in the center into which hot rocks are positioned. Water is thrown on the rocks to create steam, and a small flap opening is used to regulate the temperature.

As we touched the earth and made a prayer for "all our relations," we crawled naked through the doorway and took our positions around the stone pit. We were told there would be three "rounds" where we would chant and pray. In between rounds, the flap would be opened to allow us to cool down. With each round, more stones were added, the lodge became hotter, and the experience became more intense.

As it turned out, I was at the back of the lodge where it was the hottest. In the third round, it became so hot that many of the men crawled out. I was one of the few men left inside, but I didn't feel the heat. I felt transported to another time and another place, where I experienced a vision of the future. In the vision I "saw" the ending of our present civilization so strongly influenced by values of domination, conflict, and disconnection and the choice of a new way of life based on partnership, cooperation, and connection:

We are all on a huge ocean liner. Everything we know and have ever known is on the ship. People are born and die. Goods and services are created, wars are fought, and elections are held and disputed. Species come into being and face extinction. The ship steams on and on, and there is no doubt that it will continue on its present course forever.

There are many decks on the ship, starting way down in the boiler room where the poorest and grimiest toil to keep the ship going. As you ascend the decks, things get lighter and easier. The people who run the ship have suites on the very top deck. Their job, as they see it, is to keep the ship going and keep those on the lower decks in their proper places. Since they are at the top, they are sure they deserve to acquire more and more of the resources of the earth.

Everyone on the lower decks aspires to get up to the next deck and hungers to get to the very top. That's the way it is. That's the way it has always been. That's the way it will always be. However, there are a few people who realize that something very strange is happening. What they come to know is that the ship is sinking. At first, like everyone else, they can't believe it. The ship has been afloat since time before time. It is the best of the best. That it could sink is unthinkable. Nonetheless, they are sure the ship is sinking.

They try to warn the people, but no one believes them. The ship cannot be sinking, and anyone who thinks so must be mentally ill. When they persist in trying to warn the people of what they are facing, those in charge of the ship silence them and lock them up. The ship's media keeps grinding out news stories describing how wonderful the future will be. Any problems that are occurring will surely be solved with the wonders of our civilized, technological lifestyle.

The leaders of the ship smile, wave, and promise prosperity for all. But water is beginning to seep in from below. The higher the water rises, the more frightened the people become and the more frantically they scramble to get to the upper decks. Some believe it is the end and actually welcome the prospect of the destruction of life as we know it. They believe it is the fulfillment of religious prophesy. Others become more and more irritable, angry, and depressed. Like caged rats they bite their own tails and those of their cage mates who appear to be a threat.

But as the water rises, those who have been issuing the warnings can no longer be silenced. More and more escape confinement and lead the people toward the lifeboats. Though there are boats enough for all, many people are reluctant to leave the ship. Many questions are asked. "The old stories tell us that we've been on this ship for more than six thousand years, isn't it safer to stay aboard? Could things really be so bad that we have to leave? Where will we go? Who will lead us? What if this is all there is? What if we all die?"

Nevertheless, the ship is sinking. Many people go over the side and are lowered down to the boats. As they descend, they are puzzled to see lettering on the side of the ship: T-I-T-A-N-I-C. When they reach the lifeboats, many are frightened and look for someone who looks like they know what to do. They'd like to ride with those people. However, they find that each person must get into their own boat and row away from the ship in their own direction. If they don't get away from the ship as soon as possible, they will be pulled down with it. When everyone who wants to leave, each in their own boats, rowing in their own direction, reaches a certain spot, a new web of life will be formed. It will be the basis for a new way of life that will replace the life that was lived on the old ship of civilization.

I slowly came back to the present and found myself alone at the back of the sweat lodge. I wasn't quite sure what had happened, but the vision was clear in my head and has remained so. Since that fateful day in 1993, I have been trying to understand what I had been given in the vision and how to best share it with others. Here's what I have learned thus far:

1. **Working to achieve success in a "business-as-usual world" is like getting a better deck chair on the *Titanic*.**

    When the ship sinks, it doesn't matter which deck you've managed to reach. "The world we have created is not sustainable," says Ervin Laszlo, the editor of the international periodical *World Futures* and two-time nominee for the Nobel Peace Prize. "Whether we realize it or not, we have entered a state of global emergency."

2. **The ship of civilization is a six-thousand-year-old way of life that has been based on extracting more and more resources from the earth.**

    In the last 150 years, fossil fuels have been critical. But this way of life is coming to an end. In his prescient 2003 book *The Party's Over: Oil, War and the Fate of Industrial Societies*, Richard Heinberg says, "The world is changing before our eyes—dramatically, inevitably, and irreversibly. The change we are seeing is affecting more people, and more profoundly, than any that human beings have ever witnessed. I am not referring to war or terrorist incident, a stock market crash, or global warming, but to a more fundamental reality that is driving terrorism, war, economic swings, climate change, and more: the discovery and exhaustion of fossil energy resources."

3. **We have reached the end of growth, and everything is changing.**

    Our whole way of life has been based on the idea of continued growth. Once we accept that in many areas of our lives growth is coming to an end, the way we look at the world will change dramatically. "Economic growth as we have known it is over and done with," asserts Heinberg in his book *The End of Growth: Adapting to Our New Economic Reality*.

He defines growth as being the expansion of the overall size of the economy, with more people being served and more money changing hands, with increasing quantities of energy and material goods flowing through it. Endless growth can no longer continue.

4. **Indicators of a failing system are increasingly evident and hard to ignore.**

A report by The Commission for the Human Future headed by cardiologist and physician Arnagretta Hunter says, "Human activity and numbers are transforming our world. Wildfires, floods, droughts, melting ice caps, large-scale extinctions of plants and animals, shortages of water, loss of soil, forests and sea life combined with rising food insecurity, universal pollution, pandemic diseases, collapsing states, wars and refugee crises are a wakeup call that our very way of life is at risk."

5. **Signs of collapse have been with us for some time.**

Rebecca D. Costa, author of *The Watchman's Rattle: A Radical New Theory of Collapse*, helps us understand why civilizations such as the Mayans, the Romans, and others grew ever larger and more complex and eventually collapsed.

Reflecting on our present situation, she quotes her mentor, world-renowned biologist E. O. Wilson, who has been called "the Darwin of the twenty-first century." According to Wilson, "The real problem of humanity is that we have paleolithic emotions; medieval institutions; and god-like technology."

The danger we face, concludes Costa, is this: "From an evolutionary perspective, social progress moves fast, but our brains—the apparatus that must process all this new information—evolve over millions of years. So while the world is changing in picoseconds, my brain is struggling to keep up."

She goes on to say there are two signs of impending collapse:

- The first is *gridlock*, which occurs when civilizations become unable to comprehend or resolve large, complex problems, despite acknowledging beforehand that these issues may lead to their demise. More parts of the system break down and effective problem-solving grinds to a halt.

- *Beliefs become a substitute for facts.* Since we can't seem to get our heads around complex problems, we simplify the issues, reduce our emphasis on scientific understanding, and cling to our beliefs. ("I don't care what the scientists say. I believe global warming is a myth.")

6. **Men are the "canaries in the coal mine" alerting us for the need to change.**

Canaries were once used in coal mining as an early warning system. Toxic gases such as carbon monoxide and methane in the mine would kill the bird before affecting the miners. Male mental illness and breakdown are the world's early warning signs of impending catastrophe. Things like Irritable Male Syndrome, male depression and aggression, and high suicide rates are alerting us to the toxic nature of our current lifestyles.

7. **Personal healing and social justice must go together.**

In the vision, each person had to get into their own boat and get off the sinking ship. We each have to do our own personal healing if we are going to succeed during these times of change. But personal healing isn't enough. We have to band together with other like-minded people to bring about the social change that is necessary for us to survive and thrive. Those who have gotten the most economic benefit from the old ship of state will try to take possession of as many planetary resources as possible. We must link together to stop them and protect ourselves, our communities, and our planet.

All enlightened activists know social justice must accompany personal healing. As environmental activist Chico Mendez said before he was murdered in Brazil, "At first I thought I was fighting to save rubber trees. Then I thought I was fighting to save the Amazon rain forest. Now I realize I am fighting for humanity."

8. Collapse need not be the end. It can be a new beginning.

In the sweat lodge vision, there were two main characters. The first was the huge sinking ship of the dominator civilization. The second was the individual lifeboats each with a courageous captain leaving the old ship and connecting with others to create a new way of life.

There are also two sets of feelings involved. When we focus on the sinking ship, we feel fear. But when we focus on the adventure of striking out for a new world and connecting with others, we feel love. Both feelings are with us, and we can choose where we want to focus our attention.

Our human ancestors have been on the planet for two million years. We have never been perfect partners with the community of life, but our partnership roots are deep. Although city-state civilization has been around for six thousand years, that is a relatively short time in the whole of our human story. Further, it has only been in the last 150 years that we have become reliant on fossil fuels to drive our civilization and have been heating the planet and destroying our life-support system.

We have a choice to make about whether we want to continue the delusion that humans are somehow separate from and superior to the rest of the players in the symphony of life on this unique planet known as *Gaia* or jump ship and join others who are committing ourselves to creating a new, more loving world. As Charles Eisenstein puts it, we have the opportunity to "create the more beautiful world our hearts know is possible."

How Domination and Partnership Have Shaped Our Lives and Will Determine Our Future

I first met Riane Eisler in 1987 shortly after the publication of her book *The Chalice & the Blade: Our History, Our Future.* I remember discussing our views on the future of humanity and the healing that needed to occur between men and women. My first book,

Inside Out: Becoming My Own Man, had been published in 1983, in which I described my own healing journey. At a time when many female writers were blaming men for the problems in the world, I appreciated that Riane understood that the problem was not men, but the system of domination that harmed both women and men.

When I first read these words in *The Chalice & the Blade*, I was moved by their simplicity, vision, and truth:

> Underlying the great surface diversity of human culture are two basic models of society. The first, which I call the *dominator* model, is what is popularly termed either patriarchy or matriarchy—the *ranking* of one-half of humanity over the other. The second, in which social relations are primarily based on the principle of *linking* rather than ranking, may best be described as the *partnership* model. In this model— beginning with the most fundamental difference in our species, between male and female—diversity is not equated with either inferiority or superiority.

In her book *Nurturing Our Humanity: How Domination and Partnership Shape Our Brains, Lives, and Future*, written with anthropologist Douglas P. Fry, Riane describes her early influences and insights. When Riane was six, the German and Austrian Nazis took over her native Vienna. Riane's father was dragged off by the Gestapo. Her mother miraculously obtained his release, and the family fled to Cuba.

They were on one of the last ships before the *MS St. Louis*, carrying 930 Jewish refugees from Europe, was turned back by Cuban authorities. Because neither Cuba nor the United States nor any other country in the Western hemisphere let the *St. Louis* dock, it was forced to return to Europe, where many on board eventually died in Nazi death camps.

Riane remembers standing at the Havana waterfront watching how, after long days of waiting and hoping they would be permitted to disembark, the doomed families on the *St. Louis* disappeared over the horizon.

With her move to the United States in 1946 came further formative experiences. As she and her parents arrived at last to the promised land of American liberty and equality, they found in Miami, their port of entry, yet another disempowered out-group, or "other." In the rigidly segregated South of that time, they discovered one more variation of the all-too-familiar use of cultural narratives to justify the persecution and subordination of "inferior" beings.

The accumulation of these kinds of experiences brought recurrent questions. Are patterns of prejudice, cruelty, and violence inevitable? Are they human nature? Or is something else at work? When Riane studied sociology at the University of California, these questions were at the back of her mind. They were there as she became involved first in the civil rights movement and then in the feminist movement.

Riane says that we have seen the domination system historically in the rule by terror of Genghis Khan and the autocratic family patriarch of earlier times. Nowadays, we see it in the despotic rulers, such as the religious heads of ISIS or secular Kim Jong-un, and at the familial level in abusive parental behavior. Whether within a family or more generally within a society, social systems that orient closely to the domination side of the continuum are ultimately held together by fear and force, as illustrated by customs of child and wife beating, persecution of minorities, threats or displays of torture and death, and wars of conquest.

In contrast, the partnership configuration is more peaceful, egalitarian, gender-balanced, and environmentally sustainable. As in the strivings of countless families, businesses, and communities today, the partnership system consists of beliefs and structures that support relations based on mutual benefit, respect, and accountability. Fear and force are not woven into the cultural tapestry of the partnership system because they are not needed to maintain rigid top-down rankings, whether it is man over man, man over woman, race over race, religion over religion, or nation over nation.

Riane believes that the domination and partnership of these two systems exist on a continuum, and we can influence which direction things move. On her website, Partnerism.org, she contrasts the two systems:

Domination	Partnership
• In groups and out groups	• Everyone matters
• Hierarchies of domination	• Hierarchies of actualization
• Power maintained by force and fear	• Increase in liberty and expression
• Inequality	• Equality: gender, race, etc.
• Ignores economic value of caring	• Care is valued economically
• Violence and abuse	• Human flourishing and creativity

Whether we are looking at the US or the entire world, we see evidence of these two contrasting systems, domination and partnership, competing for our attention. Our future hangs in the balance.

In *Nurturing Our Humanity*, Eisler and Fry conclude, "There is strong evidence that over the millennia of human biocultural evolution, most societies were constructed along partnership lines. Yet domination systems—with their inherent exploitation of people and nature, social and economic inequalities, and direct and structural violence—came to predominate on the global stage."

Is the US and the World Facing Collapse?

I first met Rebecca Costa in 2010 following the publication of her book *The Watchman's Rattle*. She invited me to be a guest on her syndicated radio program *The Costa Report*, where we discussed the state of the world and the challenges we are facing.

In addition to the early warnings of gridlock and substituting beliefs for facts, Costa describes a number of what she calls *supermemes*, which most of us have seen but haven't fully comprehended.

"A supermeme," says Costa, is **"any belief, thought, or behavior that becomes so pervasive, so stubbornly embedded, that it contaminates or suppresses all other beliefs and behaviors in a society."**

Costa says, "It's important to remember that supermemes are often a response to accelerating complexity." She identifies the following five supermemes:

1. Irrational Opposition

   Costa says, "Irrational opposition occurs when the act of rejecting, criticizing, suppressing, ignoring, misrepresenting, marginalizing, and resisting rational solutions becomes the accepted norm." We see this supermeme operating in our initial response to the coronavirus and our continued difficulty coming together as a country to agree on a rational response.

2. The Personalization of Blame

   Costa says, "Throughout history civilizations have had a clear pattern of *foisting the responsibility for complex problems onto the shoulders of individuals whenever complex problems persist.*" We see this supermeme operating in many aspects of our lives. "Sometimes we blame religious leaders. Sometimes our boss, ex-wife or husband, lawyer, neighbors, doctor, parents, or broker are responsible for our troubles. And sometimes we turn the blame inward toward *ourselves* in harsh and unforgiving ways."

3. Counterfeit Correlation

   "Counterfeit correlation occurs," says Costa, "as a result of three convenient practices:
   - Accepting correlation as a substitute for causation.
   - Using reverse-engineering to manipulate evidence, and
   - Relying on consensus to determine facts."

   Costa goes on to say, "The reason counterfeit correlation has become so popular is easy to understand: Casually observing a relationship—any relationship—between two events is magnitudes easier than the grueling effort required to prove one thing actually *causes* another to occur."

4. Silo Thinking

"Silo thinking," says Costa, "is the compartmentalized thinking and behavior that prohibits the collaboration needed to address complex problems." She goes on to say, "Instead of encouraging cooperation between individuals and groups that share a common objective, silo thinking causes undermining, competition, and divisiveness. As silos prevent sharing and coordination across organizational boundaries, information that is already difficult to acquire becomes even more inaccessible."

In his book *The Premonition: A Pandemic Story*, Michael Lewis described the silo thinking that limited the government's ability to develop a national strategy to address the COVID-19 pandemic. In chapter 4, "Stopping the Unstoppable," Lewis says, "One day some historian will look back and say how remarkable it was that these strange folk who called themselves 'Americans' ever governed themselves at all, given how they went about it. Inside the United States government were all these little boxes. The boxes had been created to address specific problems as they arose. . . . Each box became its own small, frozen world, with little ability to adapt and little interest in whatever might be going on inside the other boxes."

5. Extreme Economics

"Every person I know," says Costa, "has a strange relationship with money. They want more of it. They spend too much of it. They invest, inherit, protect, and live in fear they'll run out of it. Some people never talk about money. And some can't quit talking about it. Marriages break up over it and children are spoiled by it. But mostly we wear money on our shirtsleeves where we once wore our hearts."

Costa goes on to say, "The economics supermeme occurs when *simple principles in business, such as risk/reward and profit/ loss, become the litmus test for determining the value of people and priorities, initiatives and institutions.*"

She concludes, "Unlike the first four supermemes, *irrational opposition, the personalization of blame, counterfeit correlation,* and *silo thinking,* which are easy to see as harmful, *extreme economics* feels more like a relative who came to visit and stayed too long. We have mixed feelings."

Costa goes on to examine the collapse of past civilizations including the Mayan, Khymer, and Roman empires. She found that the underlying cause of collapse had not been fully understood or addressed. What she discovered was that a society's inability to deal with complexity was the root cause of collapse.

As Costa's mentor, the world-renowned sociobiologist Edward O. Wilson said in the book's foreword, "The clash of religions, and civilizations, Costa argues, is not the cause of our difficulties but a consequence of them. The same is true of the global water shortage, climate change, the decline of carbon-based energy, our cheerful destruction of the remaining natural environment, and all the other calamities close to or upon us. **The primary cause of all threatening trends is the complexity of civilization itself, which cannot be understood and managed by the cognitive tools we have thus far chosen to use.**"

We certainly see these indicators of collapse in the United States and throughout the world. It is a fearful thought that our country is not working well for many people, but one that more and more people are recognizing. It is even more frightening to think our present civilization itself is sinking, and the whole world may be heading for collapse.

A New Paradigm for Understanding the State of Our World: From Collapse to Transformation

Humans are storytelling animals. The stories we tell about the world and our lives can either make us sick or restore our health. Clearly the reality of our situation at this time in human history is dire. Many people see the facts as an indication that we are experiencing collapse.

For me, the world "collapse" is frightening. It brings up images of the World Trade Center collapsing after being hit by a plane on 9/11 with each floor collapsing onto the next with a devastating loss of life.

Telling the story as one of collapse makes many people want to deny the reality or see our situation as hopeless. I have a different image of our situation that is one of transformation. An old, dominator system is ending, and we are going "back to the future" and reclaiming our partnership roots that have been present for more than 99 percent of human history.

As Czech statesman, author, poet, and playwright Václav Havel said during times of a major change in his world, "I think there are good reasons for suggesting that the modern age has ended. Today, many things indicate that we are going through a transitional period, when it seems that something is on the way out and something else is painfully being born. It is as if something were crumbling, decaying, and exhausting itself, while something else, still indistinct, were arising from the rubble."

This way of looking at things brings to mind the story of the insignificant and often ugly caterpillar who will wrap himself in his silk bud or cocoon and emerge a glorious winged creature. The image is more comforting but leaves out the death and destruction that is the reality that many in the world are experiencing.

Kirstin Vanlierde calls herself "a walker between worlds, a writer, artist, and weaver of magic." In a beautiful article "Chrysalis—or why the caterpillar must die: A little story on death and resurrection," she offers a more realistic and hopeful story. Here is an excerpt from her article:

> I had always taken the butterfly—and the transformation it stood for—for granted; the image had long turned into a cliché, like all clichés losing its taste and its sting in the process. We use the symbol, but we no longer know what it means.
>
> Fortunately years ago, reading Bill Plotkin's *Soulcraft*, a book on how personal transformation is attained not only by reaching higher for your better self but also by descending

into the darkness of your subconscious, I changed my mind about the butterfly completely.

If you were to open the chrysalis halfway through its nympha stage, Plotkin asserts, emerging from the capsule would not be some hybrid creature, half caterpillar half butterfly, but a puddle of liquid.

In order to be able to become a butterfly, the caterpillar has to fall apart completely, decompose down to its very essence, devoid of any shape or consciousness. It literally dies. There is nothing left of it.

And from this liquid essence, the butterfly starts to put itself together, from scratch.

Ever since I first came across this image almost ten years ago, I have stood in awe for its depth and force.

I believe we are going through a major transformation in human history. The outcome is not preordained, and change, like birth itself, will be painful and bloody. It will call on courage and bring out the best and the worst in many of us.

One of the guides I draw upon for wisdom and strength during these challenging times is Margaret Wheatley. Since 1966, Margaret (Meg) Wheatley has worked globally in many different roles: a speaker, teacher, community worker, consultant, adviser, formal leader. In her book *Who Do We Choose to Be? Facing Reality, Claiming Leadership, Restoring Sanity*, Meg challenges us to become "Warriors of the Human Spirit."

Says Wheatley, "A Warrior of the Human Spirit is a decent human being who aspires to be of service in an indecent, inhumane time. Throughout time, warriors arise when the people need protection."

When I wrote the book *The Warrior's Journey Home: Healing Men, Healing the Planet*, I quoted meditation master Chögyam Trungpa who says that we must separate the life of the warrior from the destruction of war. "Warriorship here does not refer to making war on others. Aggression is the source of our problems, not the solution. Here the word 'warrior' is taken from the Tibetan *pawo* which literally means 'one who is brave.' Warriorship in this context is the tradition of human bravery, or the tradition of fearlessness. Warriorship is not being afraid of who you are."

When I've said I've been on seventy-four-year journey healing males, what started out as a five-year-old's fantasy to heal his father's mental illness has turned into a seventy-nine-year-old's hope to find my own warrior spirit and encourage others to join together on a Moonshot Mission for Mankind in support of humanity.

In the next section we will turn our attention to the healing practices and understandings that are needed to address the big problems humanity faces and how effectively addressing men's mental health issues offers the greatest hope not only for men, but for women and children.

Part 2
Revitalizing Men's Mental Health: Our Moonshot Mission for Mankind and Humanity

When I enrolled in medical school in 1965, my hope was to become a psychiatrist. I wanted to learn everything I could about why men became angry, stressed, and depressed. I wanted to do for other families what I could not do for my own. I couldn't save my father or prevent my mother from her debilitating anxiety and fear of loss. But I soon learned that medical school offered a very restricted and narrow view of health and well-being.

I dropped out of medical school and transferred to the School of Social Welfare at UC Berkeley. It was a good move for me, and I did expand my understanding of men's mental health and well-being, but I wanted more. I eventually went back to school and earned a PhD in international health. My work to expand and deepen our understanding of gender-specific healing and men's health continues.

In the next seven chapters, I will delve even more deeply into how we can improve men's health and well-being. This is a moonshot mission that will require a large number of men and women who know that improving men's mental health is the hope for humanity.

Chapter 4

Embracing The Masculine Soul.
The Truth About Being Male

Boys and girls really are different, and so are the men and women they become. It is not, for me, a cliché or a pleasantry to say that I think we are very fortunate as a species to be able to acknowledge that.

—Melvin Konner, MD

To improve men's mental health, we have to fully embrace everything that goes into being male. That journey begins even before we are born. I learned early that my father wasn't the typical male and my mother wasn't the typical female. My father exemplified more of the traditional feminine qualities. He was emotional to the point of melodrama. His poetry was of sunsets and beauty and odes to his mother. He was more interested in quoting Shakespeare than making money—much to my mother's frustration and concern. My mother, on the other hand, spent her life making money and focusing on job security. She was a social activist who was still marching at age seventy-five—this time for the rights of senior citizens. She had a framed saying on her wall with a call to action: "Seniors: On your feet and off your rockers."

My father was gentle and tender. My mother was dry and logical. He was very physical and enjoyed playing games with me, picking me up and riding on his shoulders. My mother always seemed cold and distant. She was always present, but she never seemed to be comfortable getting close. If I read poetry and wept, was I being manly? It was all very confusing.

I've been interested in maleness for as long as I can remember. My parents wanted a child, but after ten years of trying to conceive, they had nearly given up. They learned about an experimental procedure of injecting my father's sperm into my mother's womb. They were overjoyed when they learned my mother was finally pregnant. "I walked down 5th Avenue in New York," my mother used to tell me. "I was overjoyed knowing we were finally going to have a baby. I walked gingerly trying to be sure I didn't lose you."

They were sure I was going to be a girl and had only considered girl's names. But when I came into the world with my little penis proudly displayed, they were surprised. "It's a healthy baby boy," the doctor announced, and my parents had to rethink what to name me. My father decided I should be named Elliott Diamond. Following Jewish tradition, he had picked the name of his nephew who had recently died.

He hoped that in receiving the name Elliott I would carry some of the virtues of his sister's first child. Elliott was beloved in the family, and before his untimely death at age nineteen, he had demonstrated his father's musical talents and had begun composing popular songs. But my mother didn't like the name and recalled, "I cried for three days in the hospital until your father agreed to pick another name for you." They settled on John Elliott Diamond. John was my mother's father's name, and he had died at age thirty when my mother was five years old.

So, early on in my life, I was also confronted with issues of male and female, mother's preference versus father's preference in names. It wasn't until I went to college that I decided to change my name to Jed. I thought it sounded manlier than Johnny, which is what I had been called my whole life up until then. J. E. D. captured in my initials both my mother's and father's heritage but was my own name, which I've carried ever since.

I grew up with a fierce interest in understanding the mysteries of male and female. When I went to college at UC Santa Barbara, I wanted to be a doctor, ostensibly to make my mother proud and make a good living. Deep down, I wanted to become a psychiatrist so that I could protect myself from *going crazy* like my father and help men like my dad so that I would finally be able to do what I couldn't do as a child—save my father and other men like him.

In college I took classes in biology, zoology, psychology, and some of the first courses offered in ecology and evolution. Later in graduate school and throughout my life since, I've been learning what it means to be male.

When I was in graduate school in the 1960s, there was a great debate about what was more important in understanding human beings, our biological heritage as controlled by our genes or what we learned from our environment. Were we controlled by our genes or by our life experiences?

Within the scientific community, that debate has ended. We now know we are products of both. Our genes provide the blueprint of who we can be, but the environment determines how that blueprint is read. There is a new field of science called epigenetics, which demonstrates that we can actually change the way our genes operate, and hence change our lives. In his book *Change Your Genes, Change Your Life: Creating Optimal Health with the New Science of Epigenetics*, Dr. Kenneth Pelletier says, "Epigenetics is the study of the chemical tags that park themselves on the genome that literally control the activities of our genes. In a sense, these markers appear 'above' the genes—and is thus signified by the Greek prefix 'epi,' which means 'above' or 'upon.'"

Similarly, there has been debate about what constitutes male and female. Are there essential differences between the sexes, or are male and female traits determined by our culture? Again, the answer is both. Yet, questions of male and female stir strong feelings in most people.

The strong feelings are understandable. For a long time, whenever differences between males and females was postulated, the differences were used to suggest that one sex, usually the female, was inferior, or too weak to engage in certain activities. Differences were often based on politics, not science, and were used to keep women and men in our places, separate but not equal.

Yet, science shows there are differences, and denying them harms women and men. It is better to change the system of domination that harms both males and females than to try and deny the realities of male and female.

The Biological Realities of Maleness

Let me be clear. **What I will share about males and females are *generalizations.*** A generalization, by definition, applies to the majority within a population, allowing plenty of room for individual exceptions. If I told you that *men are taller than women,* you would recognize that this is not true of all men. As a five-foot, five-inch-tall guy, I'm very aware that this is a generalization—though I still wish I could magically become an *undersized* six-foot-five basketball forward.

Yet, the generalizations can tell us a lot about who we are and why we evolved the thoughts, feelings, and behaviors that make us who we are. Because men tend to be a certain way does not mean that men are better than women or that these qualities are fixed and can't change. They just offer the findings on the biological nature of males and females.

We might think about the things that distinguish boys and girls, that is, genitals (penis/vagina or chromosomes [XY/XX]). Biologists have a very simple and useful definition of what is male and what is female, whether we are fish, ferns, or human beings. An individual can either make many small gametes (sex cells) or fewer but larger gametes. The individuals who produce smaller gametes are called "males," and the ones who produce larger gametes are called "females."

The female strategy produces gametes that are large and have a high rate of survival and fertilization. The male strategy is to produce as many as possible to increase the chances of finding a large one. About four hundred eggs are ovulated in a woman's lifetime.

A healthy male produces five hundred million sperm per day. Many men believe that size matters. Yet, most of us are not aware of the difference in size between a sperm and an egg. A human egg is one hundred thousand times larger than a sperm.

Dr. Stephen Emlen is professor of behavioral ecology at Cornell University and a world authority on the social behavior of animals. He says, "Because of all the resources a female will put into each egg, it makes sense, in most cases, for her to be choosy about whose genes she allows to combine with it, and to continue to invest in its growth and survival after fertilization. For the male, it usually pays best to compete with other males for access to as many eggs as possible. This tends to give rise to the more traditional male/female sex roles."

An individual must either invest in a few large eggs or in millions of sperm. Thus, there will always be many times more sperm than there are eggs. Consequently, sperm must compete for access to those rare eggs. The egg is not passive in the process but gives off a chemical substance that allows one sperm to enter and rejects the rest. Although these basic facts of life may be obvious, the importance and implications may not be.

In fact, this difference in the size of our sex cells makes a huge difference in how we act as males. As we will see, it helps explain why males compete with other males, take more risks than females, fight more, and die sooner. "The cellular imbalance is at the center of maleness," says geneticist Dr. Steve Jones. "It confers on males a simpler sex life than their partners, together with a host of incidental idiosyncrasies, from more suicide, cancer and billionaires to rather less hair on the top of the head."

Generally, it is easier to move the smaller sperm to the larger egg than vice versa, and so it is the male who seeks out the female and the female who makes the selection from those males who come courting. Dr. Jones concludes, "From the greenest of algae to the most blue-blooded of aristocrats their restless state hints at an endless race in which males pursue but females escape."

Of course, if females escaped completely, there wouldn't be babies, and that would be the end of that species. Yet, it does help us to recognize the different challenges males and females face in the mating process.

Jungian therapist Eugene Monick concludes that these biological realities of sperm competition can tell us a lot about male insecurity and fear of failure. "What the sperm experiences in its life struggle toward the ovum is the ground or archetypal pattern for a man's daily struggle for virility. Body awareness that but one sperm will succeed, two million will die, is the raw material of masculine psyche, the fuel for a male's terror of fate."

In recent years, more attention has been paid to sexual variation beyond XX and XY. Marianne J. Legato, MD, is an internationally recognized academic, physician, author, and founder of The Partnership for Gender-Specific Medicine. She is the author of numerous books, including *Plasticity of Sex: The Molecular Biology and Clinical Features of Genomic Sex, Gender Identity and Sexual Behavior*, which collects all the evidence-based research on issues of gender identity and transition to provide a comprehensive view on the development and variations of human sexuality.

"We now understand more about the molecular biology of people who transition," explains Dr. Legato. "It isn't just a whim or a fashionable decision. It comes from a profound variation in molecular biology in which people are classified as one gender, but in fact, in their mind and in their awareness of who they are, are another gender."

Nevertheless, the basic differences between male and female are important to understand and can help us become the best versions of ourselves. The evolution of male and female is a long one. In his book *The Hidden Spirituality of Men: Ten Metaphors to Awaken the Sacred Masculine*, Matthew Fox says, "The universe invented sex and sexuality about one billion years ago."

There Are Ten Trillion Cells in Your Body and Every One is Sex Specific

David C. Page, MD, is professor of biology at the Massachusetts Institute of Technology (MIT) and director of the Whitehead Institute. He is one of the world's leading experts on the fundamental differences between males and females. "At the Institute," says Dr. Page, "we focus on understanding the biology and evolution of sex chromosomes (X and Y), the role that the X and Y chromosomes play in fundamental sex differences beyond the reproductive tract, and the origins and development of germ cells—the precursors of eggs and sperm."

Dr. Page and his colleagues have been studying the Y chromosome since the early 1990s, and their findings can help us all better understand what it means to be male. "There are ten trillion cells in the human body and every one of them is sex specific," says Dr. Page. "So, all your cells know on a molecular level whether they are XX or XY."

"It has been said that our genomes are 99.9% identical from one person to the next," says Dr. Page. "It turns out that this assertion is correct, as long as the two individuals being compared are both men. It's also correct if the two individuals being compared are both women. However, if you compare the genome of a man with the genome of a woman, you'll find that they are only 98.5% identical. In other words, the genetic difference between a man and a woman are 15 times greater than the genetic difference between two men or between two women."

Males Differ Genetically from Females and the Differences Are Significant

If you think a 1.5 percent difference in genetic makeup isn't a lot, consider that the human genome and the chimpanzee genome differ by 1.5 percent. It helps explain a lot to me when I recognize that I am as different genetically from my wife as I am from a male chimpanzee.

Dr. Larry Cahill, a neuroscientist at the University of California, Irvine, admits that like many fellow scientists, he used to think men and women were fundamentally the same outside the obvious areas of reproduction and sex hormones. However, following research on the different ways males and females react to certain medications, he changed his mind. He says Ambien (known generically as zolpidem) is a case in point. "We now know that women metabolize Ambien differently than men," says Dr. Cahill. "Women reach maximum blood levels *45 percent higher* than those of men.

"That is a textbook example of what is wrong," says Cahill. "How did it happen that for 20 some years, women, millions of them, were essentially overdosing on Ambien?" This may be true for many other drugs, but we don't know it. And the reverse may also be true. While women are getting too much of a medication, men may not be getting enough.

This focus on important gender differences is not just going on in laboratories headed by men. In 1992, cardiologist Marianne J. Legato, MD, published *The Female Heart: The Truth about Women and Coronary Artery Disease* and revealed that women presenting symptoms of heart disease are taken less seriously than men, and when women undergo cardiac surgery, they are less likely than men to survive.

Dr. Legato says, "Everywhere we look, the two sexes are startlingly and unexpectedly different not only in their internal function but in the way they experience illness." Rather than pretending there are no differences or trying to minimize the differences, we would do well to celebrate them. Sex and gender differences are central to our lives.

On the Genetic Superiority of Females

Throughout the ages many believed that males were superior in every way. But recent science shows that in many ways females are superior to males. This is true at the very core of who we are, at the level of our genes, according to Sharon Moalem, MD, PhD.

Dr. Moalem is an award-winning scientist and physician. He is the author of the *New York Times* bestseller *Survival of the Sickest* as well as other books. His most recent book, *The Better Half: On the Genetic Superiority of Women*, offers sobering but important truths about what it means to be male and its impact on the genetic roots that cause males, as a group, to live sicker and die sooner than females.

"Here are some facts," says Dr. Moalem. "Women live longer than men. They have stronger immune systems. They're better at fighting cancer and surviving famine, and even see the world in a wider variety of colors. They are simply stronger than men at every stage of life." Doctor Moalem wondered why that was. It turned out the facts of life have to do with a simple yet profound reality: a genetic female has two X chromosomes, one from her mother and one from her father. A genetic male has only one X chromosome from his mother and one Y chromosome from his father.

For a long time, biologists have understood that XX chromosomes give females an advantage in some arenas. For instance, having the use of a spare X in case the other is somehow defective is why females are less susceptible to disorders like color blindness.

"But we're only just now beginning to understand the full advantage that this extra X chromosome confers," says Dr. Moalem. "It's not just that women have a spare X chromosome to swap in. Rather, the more than 2,000 genes that, combined, make up two X chromosomes, are used by cells that actually *interact* and *cooperate* within a woman's body. Each cell predominantly uses one X chromosome over the other—so if one X chromosome has genes that are better at recognizing invading viruses, for instance, immune cells using that X can focus on that task, while immune cells using the other X chromosome focus on, say, killing the invading cells." This is one of the reasons Dr. Moalem believes that women, as a group, were able to ward off COVID-19 better than males and males had higher death rates than females.

"Typical males, by contrast, are forced to get by in life with just the one X chromosome," says Moalem. "What if a male's particular genes aren't able to competently recognize or kill off cells infected with a coronavirus? In that case, his ability to fight the infection will be limited; his solitary X is the only one he's got."

The bottom line is when it comes to dealing with the trauma and stressors of life—whether it's avoiding a serious congenital malformation, a developmental disability, or fighting off an infection—females have genetic options. And genetic males don't.

"My wife doesn't win only when it comes to overall longevity," says Dr. Moalem. "Her risk for developing cancers in organs we both have, for example, is lower than mine. And if she does develop cancer, she has better odds of surviving, as research shows that women respond better than men to treatments. And our sex chromosomes by and large determine our sex hormones—which also give her an advantage: Higher levels of testosterone appear to suppress the immune system; conversely, estrogens have been found to stimulate a more vigorous immunological response."

I've learned that one of the most important things we can do to live long and well is to accept our weaknesses. Always having to prove how strong we are is a burden we need to release. As we'll see, there are other important differences that impact males and females.

Like Every Other Part of Us, the Male Brain is Significantly Different from the Female Brain

Louann Brizendine, MD, is a professor of clinical psychiatry at the University of California, San Francisco and codirector of the UCSF Program in Sexual Medicine. Dr. Brizendine graduated from UC Berkeley in neurobiology, Yale University in medicine, and Harvard Medical School in psychiatry.

She says, "The brains of females and males are not the same. Male brains are larger by about nine percent, even after correcting for body size. Women and men, however, have the same number of brain cells. The cells are just packed densely in women—cinched corset like into a smaller skull." In her book *The Male Brain*, she says, "Simplifying the entire male brain to just the 'brain below the belt' is a good setup for jokes, but it hardly represents the totality of a man's brain."

Here are some of the significant differences in the brain structure and function Dr. Brizendine describes:

- The anterior cingulate cortex weighs options and makes decisions.

It's the worrywart center, and it's larger in women and smaller in men.

- The medial preoptic area is the area for sexual pursuit.
It's two-and-a-half times larger in the male.
- The temporal parietal junction is the solution seeker.
It's more active in the male brain, comes online more quickly, and races toward a "fix-it-fast" solution.
- The hippocampus is the center for emotional memory.
"It's the elephant that never forgets a fight, a romantic encounter, or a tender moment—and won't let you forget it either," says Dr. Brizendine. She notes that it's larger and more active in women and one of the main reasons that, as Dr. Legato suggests in the title of one of her books, *Why Men Never Remember and Women Never Forget*.

Testosterone: The Holy Grail of Manhood

Larrian Gillespie, MD, calls it the "Holy Grail of Manhood." Testosterone is an androgen that is produced both in the adrenals and testes of men. Women produce this same steroid from their ovaries, but as is true in all aspects of life, quantity is important. "The average male pumps out 260-1000 nanograms of testosterone per deciliter of blood plasma, dwarfing the minuscule 15-70 nanograms a woman gets to play around with in her body," says Dr. Gillespie. She also says men produce estrogens, but in much smaller quantities than do females (at least until women go through menopause and their estrogens drop precipitously).

In her book *The Alchemy of Love and Lust*, Theresa L. Crenshaw, MD, says, "Men have about 20 to 40 times more testosterone than women, which is one reason why our sex drives are so different. This forceful hormone is responsible for the drive associated with sexual appetite and patterns of aggression."

In the interesting article "I Lived Like a Man for a Couple of Weeks. It Helped Me Understand My Husband," writer Ann Mallen describes her experience when her doctor prescribed a "special cream" to boost her testosterone:

I wanted to do them all. Men—young and old, thin and heavy, coiffed and shaggy—walked past my gate in Hartsfield-Jackson as I waited for my connection to visit my sister in Connecticut. Not all rated attractive, but I found the idea of sex with each captivating.

My doctor warned me of "odd symptoms," but she didn't mention this constant sexual distraction. Or the irrational anger. The day before, I dropped a fork in the kitchen and kicked it. It clattered into the base of the cabinet, but that wasn't enough. I picked it up and threw it into the sink with a force intended to harm.

Does this sound familiar? Did you ever think that a man's "excessive" sexual desire, irritability, and anger, was because he was a (fill in the blank of some of the negative things we say and think about men)? It may be more related to his testosterone levels than because he's a son of a bitch.

Mallen shared how her experience helped broaden her view of men. "Living for a few weeks with extra testosterone gave me a new understanding of men. Now, when I notice my husband glancing at an attractive woman, I don't take offense. Testosterone turns your head and makes you look. Sometimes, I whisper, 'Yep, she's beautiful.' He jokes that I'm now one of the guys."

The Essential Difference Between Male-Type Brains and Female-Type Brains

Another research in the field of sex and gender differences is Dr. Simon Baron-Cohen. He is professor of psychology and psychiatry at Cambridge University and has been researching sex differences for over thirty years. In his book *The Essential Difference: The Truth about the Male & Female Brain*, he details the significant differences between male-type brains and female-type brains.

His conclusions are both startling and clear-cut and controversial. "The subject of essential sex differences in the mind is clearly very delicate," he cautions us. But the findings substantiate the fact that males and females are different, in large measure because of the different ways our brains are structured. "The female brain is predominantly hard-wired for empathy," he tells us. "The male brain is predominantly hard-wired for understanding and building systems."

Empathizing, Baron-Cohen tells us, is the drive to identify another person's emotions and thoughts and to respond to these with an appropriate emotion. The empathizer intuitively figures out how people are feeling and how to treat people with care and sensitivity.

Systemizing is the drive to analyze and explore a system, to extract underlying rules that govern the behavior of a system, and the drive to construct systems. "Systems can be as varied as a pond, a vehicle, a computer, a plant, a library catalogue, a musical instrument, a math equation, or even an army unit," says Baron-Cohen. "They all operate on inputs and deliver outputs, using rules." He points out that although most males are better with systematizing and females with empathizing, this isn't true in all cases.

At the end of his book *The Essential Difference*, there are two questionnaires, one to determine your "systemizing quotient (SQ)" and one to determine your "empathy quotient (EQ)." I remember answering the questions for the first time and hoping I would score high on having a male-type brain, though I knew I had great empathy for people.

However, to my dismay, I scored very low on the SQ test. Not only did I score lower on the SQ test than most men, I actually scored lower than most women. But I made up for it on the EQ scale. I scored higher than most men *and* most women. Accepting myself has meant coming to peace with a brain that makes it easier for me to empathize and more difficult for me to systematize.

Dr. Baron-Cohen makes clear that not all males have the typical male-type brain that more easily systematizes and not all females have the typical female-type brain that more easily empathizes. Once again genetics is not destiny. Just as our gene expression can be modified by our life experiences, so too can our brain function be modified. We can all learn to be more empathic and comfortable dealing with large systems. Yet we all have to learn to accept who we are, including our biological limitations.

The Hierarchies of Male and Female: Are Men Really on Top?

Yuval Noah Harari has his finger on the pulse of history. He earned his PhD in history from the University of Oxford and has written three international best-selling books, including *Sapiens: A Brief History of Humankind, Homo Deus: A Brief History of Tomorrow, 21 Lessons for the 21st Century, Sapiens: A Graphic History*, and *Unstoppable Us: How Humans Took Over the World.*

In *Sapiens*, which has thus far sold ten million copies and been translated into fifty languages, he addresses critical issues facing humanity including race, caste, and gender. He says, "All societies are based on imagined hierarchies, but not necessarily on the same hierarchies." He goes on to say that "traditional Indian society classify people according to caste, Ottoman society according to religion, and American society according to race."

"One hierarchy, however, has been of supreme importance in all known human societies," says Harari, "the hierarchy of gender. People everywhere have divided themselves into men and women. And almost everywhere men have got the better deal, at least since the Agricultural Revolution."

Men, in our society—particularly rich, white men—exercise the most power. But the power isn't just over women. It is over men of color, poor men, even men in middle-America who are losing their jobs to automation. Why would we create hierarchies with men of power at the top? There are many theories, but the one that makes most sense to me is based on male competition.

If you think about males throughout history, we competed with other males to rise in the male hierarchy so that we might be chosen by an attractive female who would see us as the best and the brightest. "As men competed against each other for the opportunity to impregnate fertile women," says Harari, "an individual's chances of reproduction depended above all on his ability to outperform and defeat other men. As time went by, the masculine genes that made it to the next generation were those belonging to the most ambitious, aggressive, and competitive men."

However, there is a price to pay for being male. Even white men who have enjoyed a privileged status don't always have it so good. For instance, the high suicide rate for men is particularly high in white males. Psychologist Herb Goldberg, in his book *The Hazards of Being Male*, says, "The male has paid a heavy price for his masculine 'privilege' and power. He is out of touch with his emotions and his body. He is playing by the rules of the male game plan and with lemming-like purpose he is destroying himself—emotionally, psychologically, and physically." We also have to address the reality that a system of domination that is led by a small group of aggressive and often emotionally wounded men is a danger to everyone.

The Dangers of "Strongmen" in a System of Domination

Shortly before he invaded Ethiopia in 1935, Italian dictator Benito Mussolini stated, "I follow my instincts, and I am never wrong." The war he started bankrupted the state, but it made Mussolini popular with Italians as the restorer of the Italian empire. It also further inflated his ego. Ruth Ben-Ghiat is an internationally acclaimed historian and author of *Strongmen: Mussolini to the Present*.

She says, "Ours is an age of authoritarian rulers: self-proclaimed saviors of the nation who evade accountability while robbing their people of truth, treasure, and the protections of democracy. They promise law and order, then legitimize law-breaking by financial, sexual, and other predators." In the book she explores the practices of authoritarian leaders including Jair Bolsonaro in Brazil, Adolph Hitler in Germany, Benito Mussolini in Italy, Vladimir Putin in Russia, Donald Trump in the US, and others.

She says, although women are capable of dictatorial rule, dictators are almost always men. "They use masculinity as a symbol of strength and a political weapon. Taking what you want, and getting away with it, becomes proof of male authority. They use propaganda, corruption, and violence to stay in power."

In *Strongmen*, she points out that these men are not really strong, but often are quite wounded and cover their insecurities and fears by trying to attain and hold on to power. The book came out in 2020. She notes that "the AUTHORITARIAN PLAYBOOK has no chapter on failure." In describing Donald Trump, she says, "Trump's desire to stay in office indefinitely reflected the fear of meeting a bad end, losing immunity from prosecution, or becoming a nobody. 'You've got to put your name on stuff or no one remembers you,' said the former president, who showed familiarity with the anxious irrelevance that spur authoritarians' demands for loyalty and attention, especially at the end stage of rule."

The Most Unappreciated Fact About Men

Here's a thought experiment that will help us get to a key element of maleness. If our species was on the brink of extinction and we were desperate to repopulate the world, would we be better off having a hundred men and one woman or a hundred women and one man? Most of us would pick the latter choice. If we had a hundred men and one woman, the men would likely compete and battle each other. They might end up killing each other and the lone woman would be out of luck, mumbling to herself, "Damn, with survival on the line, all the men can think about is fighting each other, I'm left alone, and the human species dies." With one man, he has plenty of sperm to impregnate all one hundred women. The women would likely talk about the situation, empathize, and decide to share the man among themselves.

Think back to our male ancestors in the animal kingdom competing for access to females. Think about sperm competing to be the first one to the valuable egg. In the scheme of things, females are more valuable and males are more expendable. In his book *Is There Anything Good About Men?*, social scientist Roy F. Baumeister, describes things this way:

"Of all the people who ever reached adulthood, maybe 80% of the women but only 40% of the men reproduced." He goes on to say, "That's a stunning difference. Of all humans ever born, most women became mothers, but most men did not become fathers. You wouldn't realize this by walking through an American suburb today with its tidy couples." But it is an important fact throughout our male history. "I consider it the single most under-appreciated fact about the differences between men and women," says Baumeister.

At the most basic level of life, males are likely to take great risks to be successful. We start new businesses. We risk crossing the ocean to the new world in search of riches. Most of us die young or fail at what nature considers the ultimate game of life, producing more offspring. In this game, females more often and more easily succeed.

Females can also afford to play it safer in life. Their reproductive success is assured. Not only will women become mothers, but all mothers know the baby is hers. Males can never be as sure. Was the baby mine or could she have had a secret tryst with the plumber? Men can never rest easy as far as reproductive success. Hence the saying, "Mother's baby. Father's maybe."

The World of Males Is Bipolar

Guys live in a bipolar world. I don't mean we all suffer from a mental illness, though some of us do. I mean that one of the corollaries of the "most unappreciated fact about men" is that when we look at the highest rungs in our society—the president of the United States, those who represent us in Congress, Supreme Court justices, heads of corporations, and so on, we see mostly males.

Some feminists look at the fact that men occupy these positions of power and assume that the males are trying to keep the females from exercising their full potential. They feel men are the cause of women's inability to break through the glass ceiling. In some cases, this is true.

But there is another reality that some men's activists tune into. They see mostly males at bottom rungs on the societal ladder, too.

Boys drop out of school at higher rates than girls and get more
Ds and Fs. Our prison population is mostly male. More males are
violent and the victims of violence. More males than females are
homeless. Males commit suicide at three to eighteen times the rate
of females of the same age. Males suffer from nine of the top ten
leading causes of death at rates higher than females. Males live
sicker and die sooner than females.

Some feminists look up and see men above them in the social
hierarchy and assume men are keeping them down. Some male
activists look down and see men at the bottom and assume that its
women's fault. They think women now have it good and men are
being kept down. It's a bipolar world of winners and losers, but why?

Why do males go to extremes? Why do we live in a bipolar world
of winners and losers? Remember our earlier thought experiment
about repopulating the world? We only need a few males, but lots
of females. Baumeister concludes, "Nature plays the dice more with
men than women."

One of the great gifts of maleness is that we have the potential to
become wildly successful, but only if we're willing to risk falling on
our face. Males are often the innovators, the creators, the builders of
new systems. We risk becoming losers, but we all strive for greatness.
One of the things I've learned about myself as a man is that we can
learn a lot from our mistakes. Some of the most creative experiences
of my life came when I'd hit bottom, when I wasn't sure I could go
on living. I still remember the depression I went through when I lost
my job at a health clinic. It took me a year to work through my anger,
shame, and grief. I had to reevaluate my life and what I was doing
with it. The downtime led me to make a more serious commitment
to writing and inspired my book *Male vs. Female Depression: Why Men
Act Out and Women Act In* and a series of articles, "Why Healing Male
Depression Will Do More Good than Curing Cancer."

The world is changing. Men don't face the same odds of reproductive failure as we did in the past. We can afford to play it safer,
empathize more, and care about ourselves, the women in our lives,

and our children. The new challenge for many men is taking the risk to learn how to love deeply and well.

Understanding the Power of Your Unconscious Mind

"There's someone living in your head besides you," says Daniel Z. Lieberman, MD, in the introduction to his book *Spellbound: Modern Science, Ancient Magic, and the Hidden Potential of the Unconscious Mind.* "You think you're calling all the shots—that you're in charge of your thoughts, feelings, and choices. You're not. When it comes to how you think and feel your way through life, at best you're the copilot. At worst, you're along for the ride, at the mercy of a part of your brain that's overwhelmingly powerful but entirely unseen, influential but utterly secret from you."

Clinical psychologists George Pratt and Peter Lambrou offer this insightful story in their book *Code to Joy: The Four-Step Solution to Unlocking Your Natural State of Happiness.*

Once upon a time there was a flea who believed that he was king of the world.

One day he decided he wanted to go to the beach for a swim. But the western shore was many miles away, and on this own, the flea could travel only inches at a time. If he was going to reach the shore during his lifetime, he would need transportation.

So he called out to his elephant. "Ho, there Elephant, let's go out!"

The flea's elephant came to his side and kneeled down. The flea hopped up and, pointing to the west, saying, "That way—to the beach!"

But the elephant did not go west. He rather felt like taking a stroll in the forest to the east, and that is what he did. The flea, much to his dismay, could do nothing but go along for the ride, and spent the day being smacked in the face by leaves and branches.

The next day, the flea tried to get the elephant to take him to the store to buy salve for his face. Instead, the elephant took a long romp in the northern mountains, terrifying the poor flea so badly that he could not sleep that night. The flea stayed in his bed for days, beset by nightmares of thundering along mountain roads, certain he would fall to his death, and awoke each morning in a cold sweat.

After a week, finally feeling well enough to rise from his bed, the flea beckoned the elephant to his side, clambered up, and said, "I'm not well. Please, take me to the doctor."

But the elephant merrily trundled off to the western shore, where he spent the day swimming. The flea nearly drowned.

That night, sitting by the fireplace and trying to warm himself, the flea had a thought. He turned to the elephant and said, "About tomorrow... um, what are your plans?"

What's the moral of the story? If you are a flea riding an elephant, before you make any plans, you might want to check out what your elephant has in mind.

"This point is more important to your life than it might seem," say Pratt and Lambrou. "The flea of the story represents your conscious mind which includes your intellect and power of reason, your ambitions and aspirations, your ideas, thoughts, hopes, and plans. In short, everything you think of as you. And the elephant? That's your subconscious mind."

Here the terms subconscious and unconscious are used interchangeably. Some researchers describe the subconscious as the part of consciousness that is not currently in focal awareness while the unconscious consists of the processes in the mind that occur automatically and are not available to introspection.

George Miller, PhD, one of the founding fathers of modern cognitive psychology, says that the conscious mind puts out an average of between twenty and forty neuron firings per second while the unconscious mind puts out between twenty and forty million firings per second. So, when we're talking about the activity of the subconscious mind versus the conscious mind, we're looking at a difference of one million to one, which is roughly the difference in weight between an elephant and a flea.

New research from the field of energy psychology has high-lighted the importance of healing early life trauma, often held in the subconscious energy fields of our bodymind. Only by healing the way these traumatic memories are held in our subconscious mind can we learn to be more joyful and productive in our lives. Pratt and Lambrou offer this thought experiment to help us understand how it works:

> Imagine you are standing just outside your home surrounded by a dense fog so thick you can't see the other side of the street in front of you. You look to the left, to the right, but can't see more than fifty feet in any direction. You are surrounded.

How much water does it take to create the blanket of fog that has completely isolated you from your world?

A few ounces. The total volume of water in a blanket of fog one acre around and one meter deep would not quite fill an ordinary drinking glass. The fog actually contains four hundred billion tiny droplets suspended in the air creating an impenetrable cloak that shuts out light and makes you shiver.

This is what happens when we have painful and traumatic experiences in our lives that we just can't shake. Pratt and Lambrou call it "the fog of distress," and we've all experienced it. What is it made of? "It is partly feelings, partly beliefs, and partly bioelectrical memory traces locked into our bodies," say Pratt and Lambrou. "Most importantly, it operates below the level of our conscious minds.

Humans are adaptable and generally we handle the ups and downs of life without any lasting negative effect. After one of those "bad days," the experience simply vanishes from our minds without a trace, and we end up a little older and wiser as a result. "But not always," say Pratt and Lambrou. "Sometimes, especially when we are very young, we have experiences that we cannot shake. Even if they seem insignificant, no more substantial than a glass of water, when these upsetting experiences evaporate, they then condense into billions of droplets of anger, fear, self-doubt, guilt, and other negative feelings, surrounding us with a suffocating blanket that suffuses every aspect of our lives for years to come."

"Many people are familiar with Freud's model of the unconscious, particularly his descriptions of the instinctual drives of sexual desire and aggression. Carl Jung, who was a student of Freud's, also identified the unconscious as the seat of human instinct, but he believed the instincts found there were more varied and sophisticated."

Compared to human instincts, animal instincts are equally powerful but much simpler. "In fact," says Lieberman, "human instincts are so complex that our conscious minds are incapable of grasping them. Jung called these instincts *archetypes*, and since they form a part of our shared evolutionary heritage, he described them as the collective unconscious."

We will explore some of the powerful archetypes of the male psyche in the next chapter of this book. You'll learn about the billion-year-old archetype of the male spirit as well as more modern archetypes called the King, Warrior, Magician, and Lover.

CHAPTER 5

CELEBRATING THE MALE'S JOURNEY HOME: OUR BILLION-YEAR HISTORY

The natural world is the largest sacred community in which we belong. To be alienated from this community is to become destitute in all that makes us human. To damage this community is to diminish our own existence.

—Thomas Berry

One of the first things I wondered as I began gathering information for my book *12 Rules for Good Men* was when did males begin? In his book *The Hidden Spirituality of Men: Ten Metaphors to Awaken the Sacred Masculine*, Matthew Fox says, "The universe invented sex and sexuality about one billion years ago."

According to mathematical cosmologist Brian Swimme and historian Thomas Berry, in their book *The Universe Story*, life first evolved on earth about four billion years ago. Prior to the evolution of sexual reproduction, cells divided into individual sister cells. Swimme and Berry call this living organism Sappho. But one billion years ago, a momentous change occurred. The first male organism, they call him Tristan, and the first female organism, they call her Iseult, were cast into the ancient oceans. Here's how Swimme and Berry poetically describe this first sexual adventure:

These special cells were then released by Sappho into the currents of the enveloping ocean. They were cast into the marine adventure, with its traumas of starvation and of predation. Able to nourish themselves but no longer capable of dividing into daughter cells, such primal living beings made their way through life until an almost certain death ended their 3-billion-year lineage.

But Tristan and Iseult possessed great fortitude and were willing to face adversity and danger in search of a potential lover, no matter the odds of failure.

A slight, an ever so slight, chance existed that a Tristan cell would come upon a corresponding Iseult cell. They would brush against each other, a contact similar to so many trillions of other encounters in their oceanic adventure. But with this one, something new would awaken. Something unsuspected and powerful and intelligent, as if they had drunk a magical elixir, would enter the flow of electricity through each organism.

Suddenly the very chemistry of their cell membranes would begin to change. Interactions evoked by newly functioning segments of her DNA would restructure the molecular web of Iseult's skin, so that an act she had never experienced or planned for would begin to take place— Tristan entering her cell wholly.

This billion-year-old story takes us back to the emergence of the first sperm, the beginning of maleness, and our first male ancestor. Think about the fortitude and courage it took for the first male to overcome the adversities of life in the primordial ocean to find a female who would allow him entry into her body. This is the first love story and the beginning act to a play that continues to unfold today. But as evolution continued and the first multicellular animals appeared seven hundred million years ago, we started on the long journey to becoming the unique men we are today.

The Return of Father Earth

In 1993, my wife and I were privileged to attend an event focused on healing the masculine and feminine spirits with the mythologist Michael Meade and author Clarissa Pinkola Estes, author of *Women Who Run with the Wolves*. It took place at the Palace of Fine Arts in San Francisco and was appropriately titled "Ovarios y Cojones: Labyrinths of Memory and Danger Within Women and Men."

It was a lively interchange and a powerful collaboration between two powerful storytellers, one male and one female, who alternated in sharing their gifts that took us deeply into the male and female experience. Toward the end of the day, something unexpected occurred when Clarissa offered the following poem, which took everyone by surprise. "It's called Father Earth," she intoned in her quiet voice.

Like most, I had associations with God, the Father, and with Mother Earth. But what she offered in her poem took me to a whole new world and healed wounds that had been part of the human experience for thousands of years. The room grew quiet. I felt the hairs on the back of my neck come alive when she named the title of the poem and began:

Father Earth

There's a two-million-year-old man
No one knows.
They cut into his rivers
They peeled wide pieces of hide
From his legs
They left scorch marks
On his buttocks.
He did not cry out.
No matter what they did to him, he did not cry out.
He held firm.
Now he raises his stabbed hands

---

and whispers that we can heal him yet.
We begin with bandages,
The rolls of gauze,
The gut, the needle, the grafts.
Slowly, carefully, we turn his body face up,
And under him,
His lifelong lover, the old woman,
Is perfect and unmarked.
He has laid upon
His two-million-year-old lover
All this time, protecting her
With his old back, with his old, scarred back.
And the soil beneath her
Is fertile and black with her tears.

By the end of her poem, I had tears in my eyes. *Finally, finally a woman understands*, I thought to myself. I've recited the poem at many gatherings of men and women. Everyone is moved. For me, it speaks to a number of personal and archetypal truths:

- Father Earth is real and emerging in the consciousness of women and men today.
- Just as women felt empowered when images of the deity were changed to include the feminine, so too are men changed with the imagery of Father Earth.
- The reality goes back to the beginning of the human story two million years ago and likely even earlier.
- Until recently the reality of "Mother Earth" has been accepted, but an ancient "Earth father" has been hidden from awareness.
- Our disconnection from the earth, from ourselves, from our fathers, from the women and children in our lives has caused a deep wounding in the masculine soul.
- The wounding and pain that men have felt for thousands of years have been suppressed but escape in distorted whispers and violent actions.

- Yet despite all the trauma, pain, and violence the male soul and spirit has experienced, there has been a deeper female soul and spirit that loves us and weeps for us and with us.
- The tenacity of the masculine and the courage and grief of the feminine activate the nourishing waters that can unite and heal us all.

Matthew Fox is another person who recognized the importance of healing the masculine soul through a new understanding of the sacred. In his book *The Hidden Spirituality of Men: Ten Metaphors to Awaken the Sacred Masculine*, he says, "Our culture has latched onto images of God as Male and then defined for us what male means. Male means winning (being number one in sports, business, politics, academia), going to war ('kill or be killed'), being rational, not emotional ('boys don't cry'), and embracing homophobia (fear of male affection). Male means domination, lording over others—whether nature, one's own body, women, or others."

Clearly a new understanding of maleness and masculinity is emerging and demanding our attention and engagement. "It is time for us to take our manhood back," says Fox. "And we must do this before it is too late—before excessive yang energy (which is fire) literally burns the earth up."

This is a calling that can unite mankind and womankind, humanity, and the community of life on planet earth.

Accepting Our Place in the Community of Life

The brain of *Homo sapiens* shows our heritage from reptiles, mammals, and primates. Further, for more than 90 percent of our human history, we were hunter-gatherers, and we still carry those proclivities, skills, and sensibilities. Remembering our roots in the community of life is a powerful help in accepting ourselves as men.

Let's take a look at our reptilian heritage. Reptiles evolved 313 million years ago, according to Swimme and Berry. "The beings who created eggs were the first reptiles. They crowded out the amphibians to become the predominant terrestrial vertebrate."

Modern-day reptiles include crocodiles, snakes, lizards, turtles, and tortoises.

According to Petset.com, the three most popular reptile names for male reptiles are Apollo, Earl, and Bruce. I like Earl as a male representative of our reptilian ancestors. There are three things that are most important to Earl. We can think of them as the three *s*'s: safety, sustenance, and sex.

Men often get a bad rap when we focus so much attention on eating barbeque ribs, fighting, or trying to get attractive women to have sex with us. But that's Earl for you. I'm not saying that we have no control over our desires. If that were true, we'd be constantly feeding our faces when we weren't fighting or f-cking or trying all three at the same time. I'm just saying Earl is part of our maleness, and his desires have to be considered if we're going to understand ourselves and make good decisions about our lives and the lives of others.

Our reptilian brain isn't very social—no one tries to cuddle up with a snake, lizard, or crocodile. Though I think turtles are great, I wouldn't want to get in bed with one. Earl wants what he wants when he wants it, and he isn't much concerned about other's needs. Earl's mantra is "me, me, me, more, more, more."

We may not always embrace Earl's behavior, but he lives within all of us, and reptiles did pretty well for themselves. They're still going strong after 313 million years. Swimme and Berry say that our human lineage came on the scene a mere 2.6 million years ago. I hope humans will be around as long as the reptiles.

Mammals Are Us

When the earth was hit by a giant meteor and possibly a series of massive volcanoes, the dinosaurs and a great deal of other life was extinguished sixty-five million years ago. This opened the world to an explosion of mammalian life including lemurs, tarsiers, monkeys, rodents, bats, whales, horses, and many more.

In their book *The Archaeology of Mind: Neuroevolutionary Origins of Human Emotions*, Jaak Panksepp and Lucy Biven offer the following thoughts in their first chapter, "Ancestral Passion": "This book takes us on an archaeological dig deep into the recesses of the mammalian brain, to the ancestral sources of our emotional minds."

Based on Jaak Panksepp's lifelong study of the neuroscience of emotion, he describes seven primary-process emotional systems that are part of our mammalian heritage. A stickler for language, he capitalized the systems so they wouldn't be confused with how we think about these words in common language: SEEKING, LUST, CARE, RAGE, FEAR, PANIC, and PLAY. Let's look more deeply at each.

In many ways we can think of these systems as part of our collective unconscious, archetypes that can guide us into the deepest recesses of our bodymind.

1. SEEKING

    The SEEKING system gets a mammal moving. It encourages foraging, exploring, investigating, curiosity, and expectancy. "Paradoxically," says Panksepp, "it operates independent of what it might actually find, 'a goad without a fixed goal.' It's like radar that never turns off, or a party guest who keeps scanning the room while holding a conversation, or a web surfer who finds a right-priced pair of Air Jordan 11 Retro shoes on Amazon, but keeps looking."

    Panksepp concludes, "When fully aroused, SEEKING fills the mind with interest and motivates organisms to effortlessly search for the things they need, crave, and desire. In humans, this system generates and sustains curiosity from the mundane to our highest intellectual pursuits."

    As I pointed out in chapter 3, dopamine is the neurotransmitter that is most associated with the SEEKING system. It is always looking to the future to see what is *out there* that can benefit us.

2. RAGE

    When the SEEKING system is thwarted, RAGE is aroused. Anger is provoked by curtailing an animal's freedom of action. We have come to see rage in negative terms and associate it with male violence, but it's a natural part of every mammal's behavior and has the positive purpose of keeping the animal alive and able to seek and find what he needs. It also helps animals defend themselves by arousing fear in their opponents.

"RAGE helps us defend our lives and our resources," says Panksepp. "RAGE is not only activated when we are attacked and need to defend ourselves, but also in situations of frustration, when access to expected reward is thwarted, including territorial conflicts." Certainly, our rage and anger need to be channeled so we can live well with others, but anger and rage are part of our mammalian heritage. Denying our anger and rage denies of huge part of who we are.

3. LUST

Lust is driven by the desire for sexual satisfaction. This system energizes us to want to "get it on." The evolutionary basis for LUST is based on our need to reproduce, a need shared among all living things. Through reproduction, organisms pass on their genes and thus contribute to the perpetuation of their species. Both males and females lust for sex (otherwise we wouldn't be here), but different experiences, different hormones, and different brain neurochemistry create different patterns in males and females.

The hypothalamus of the brain plays an important role in the LUST system, stimulating the production of the sex hormones testosterone and estrogen from the testes and ovaries. While these chemicals are often stereotyped as being "male" and "female" respectively, both play a role in men and women. As it turns out, testosterone increases libido in just about everyone, but since males have a lot more testosterone than females, male lust is more demanding and less discriminating.

4. CARE

The CARE or nurturance system ensures that babies are cared for. CARE is the basis for what later becomes love in human beings. Brain evolution has provided safeguards to ensure that parents, usually the mother, take care of offspring. Some of the chemistries of sexuality, for instance oxytocin, have been evolutionarily redeployed to mediate maternal care, nurturance, and social bonding, suggesting there is an intimate evolutionary relationship between female sexual rewards and maternal motivations. Male mammals can nurture their children, but the drive isn't as strong as it is in females.

5. PANIC

Mammals need parental care in order to survive. When a mammal loses connection with the nurturing parent, they are in danger of losing their lives. The PANIC system energizes the mammal to do everything it can to reconnect with the parent. "Young socially dependent animals have powerful emotional systems to solicit nurturance," says Panksepp. "They exhibit intense crying when lost, alerting caretakers to attend to their offspring."

In humans, panic attacks can be triggered by any threat of losing a needed loved one. Even as adults we feel dependent on our mates for nurturing and support. In males, the jealousy and rage we often see is related to the panic a man feels at the possibility of losing his source of nurture and care.

6. FEAR

When we think of our human feelings, we often associate panic and fear. But in Panksepp's research on the mammalian brain, he has demonstrated that FEAR is a separate system. "The evolved FEAR circuit helps to unconditionally protect animals from pain and destruction," says Panksepp. "FEAR leads animals to flee, whereas much weaker stimulation elicits a freezing response. Humans stimulated in these same brain regions report being engulfed by an intense free-floating anxiety that appears to have no environmental cause."

7. PLAY

The PLAY system is present in all mammals. This is one of the key aspects of Panksepp's research. He worked with rats and not only showed that they play, but found that it is consistently accompanied by positive, intense social joy, signaled in the rats by making abundant high-frequency chirping sounds resembling laughter.

When animals are deprived of play, they look normal and they eat normally, they're just not as socially sophisticated. "Animals deprived of play are more liable to get into a serious fight," says Panksepp. "Play teaches them what they can do to other animals and still remain within the zone of positive relationships." For males, rough and tumble play is part of our heritage. Male mammals love to run, chase, pounce, wrestle, and play fight. Human males are no exception. Boys who grow up without a father often have difficulty with play and are more likely to respond with anger and rage in social situations.

These seven systems work together to form the basis of our emotional lives that gear all mammals to survive and thrive. When I think of these seven systems, I'm reminded of Carl Sandburg's poem "Wilderness," which begins: "There is a wolf in me ... fangs pointed for tearing gashes ... a red tongue for raw meat ... and the hot lapping of blood—I keep this wolf because the wilderness gave it to me and the wilderness will not let it go."

We often try to suppress these basic emotions. Men are often taught not to express fear, panic, or care. We are taught to put a lid on our lust and suppress our anger and rage. Even play is something that we are told we need to outgrow. Sandburg reminds us that we all carry the heritage of our mammalian ancestors.

Take a moment to reflect on the seven mammalian systems that make up our lives. Which systems do you engage most comfortably? Which ones have caused you trouble? Which systems need more attention? Which ones frighten you?

The Third Chimpanzee: Embracing the Primate in Us

After hearing about Charles Darwin and his theory of evolution, there is a story of one person's response that probably captures the view of many at the time and perhaps more than a few people today. On hearing one June afternoon in 1860 the suggestion that mankind was descended from the apes, the wife of the Bishop of Worcester is said to have exclaimed, "My dear, descended from the apes! Let us hope it is not true, but if it is, let us pray that it will not become generally known."

Well, we are not descended from apes, though we do share a common ancestor. The idea that we are part of the animal kingdom was repugnant to those who saw humans as being made in the image of God and whose job on earth was to subjugate the plants and animals that in their view of reality were put here for the benefit of humans.

Like the bishop's wife, there are those today who have a difficult time believing in evolution and the fact that we are part of the animal kingdom. Yet, reconnecting with our roots is part of the journey to reconnect with ourselves. What modern science tells us is that we are very close in evolutionary history to the chimpanzees, and depending on how you classify different species, we could see ourselves as "the third chimpanzee."

In his book *The Third Chimpanzee: The Evolution and Future of the Human Animal*, Jared Diamond concludes, "A zoologist from outer space would immediately classify us as just a third species of chimpanzee, along with the pygmy chimp of Zaire [also known as bonobos] and the common chimp of the rest of tropical Africa."

Seeing ourselves as separate from the animal kingdom may help us feel special, but the price we pay is that we are cut off from our heritage. We become a rogue species, more like a cancer than one member in the community of life.

Different: Gender through the Eyes of a Primatologist

Not only do we need to recognize our connection to the rest of the animal kingdom, we have to appreciate that for a billion years the animal kingdom has been made up of males and females. Frans de Waal is one of the world's leading primatologists and ethologists. He is professor emeritus of primate behavior at Emory University and the former director of the Living Links Center at the Yerkes National Primate Research Center.

De Waal is the author of numerous books including *Chimpanzee Politics, Bonobo: The Forgotten Ape, Our Inner Ape,* and *Are We Smart Enough to Know How Smart Animals Are?* In his most recent book *Different: Gender Through the Eyes of a Primatologist,* de Wall says, "Sex differences in animal and human behavior raise questions that lie at the heart of almost any debate about human gender. Does behavior of men and women differ naturally or artificially? How different are they really? And are there only two genders, or are there more?"

De Waal explores these questions in great depth. He also calls on men and women alike to accept a more accurate and positive understanding of what it means to be male. "Modern society is ready for a correction of gender differences in power and privilege," says de Waal. "Women cannot accomplish this alone, though. Gender roles are so intertwined that both men and women need to change at the same time."

He believes that getting more men involved in this healing journey is the next big challenge for humankind. "The way forward is to get men on board," says de Wall. "This is why I bristle at generalizations, such as those blaming men for all that's wrong in the world. Calling certain expressions of masculinity 'toxic' is not my idea of feminism. What is the point of stigmatizing an entire gender? I agree with American actress Meryl Streep, who saw this as unnecessary: 'We hurt our boys by calling something toxic masculinity. Women can be pretty fucking toxic. ... It's toxic people.'"

Back to the Future: Embracing the Values of the Original Affluent Societies

In their book *Our Human Story*, Louise Humphrey and Chris Stringer, researchers at the Natural History Museum, say that our human ancestry goes back at least two million years to the time of *Homo habilis* (Handy man).

In 1966, I was in graduate school at UC Berkeley and heard about a symposium at the University of Chicago called "Man the Hunter" that was organized by anthropologists Richard Lee and Irven DeVore. It brought together for the first time experts who had studied our hunter-gatherer heritage, and a book was produced from the conference presentations two years later.

We generally refer to our early ancestors as hunter-gatherers, or gatherer-hunters, since it was the gathering activities of the women that brought in the majority of food. Yet, a broader, more comprehensive name might be "affluent partnership societies" since equality, cooperation, and abundant leisure are such key elements of hunter-gatherer societies.

In their recent book *Nurturing Our Humanity: How Domination and Partnership Shape Our Brains, Lives, and Future*, Riane Eisler and Douglas P. Fry devote a chapter of their book to "The Original Partnership Societies." They say, "Nomadic foragers—also called nomadic hunter-gatherers—constitute the oldest form of human social organization, predating by far the agricultural revolution of about 10,000 years ago as well as the rise of pastoralists, tribal horticulturalists, chiefdoms, kingdoms, and ancient states."

Eisler and Fry go on to say, "There are a number of theories about how and why domination systems originated. One theory, which recently seems to have received some support from DNA studies of prehistoric European populations, is based on the proposal by archaeologist Marija Gimbutas that in Europe the shift was due to incursions of Indo-European pastoralists originating in the Eurasian steppes who brought with them strongmen rule, male dominance, and warfare."

Another theory developed by James DeMeo in his book *Saharasia: The 4000 BCE Origins of Child Abuse, Sex-Repression, Warfare and Social Violence in the Deserts of the Old World* suggests that the trigger for the shift from the hunting-gatherer-partnership life to one of domination was climate change. "Human violence appeared to have a specific time and place of origins on the Earth; antisocial violence was not distributed world-wide at all times in the past. The origins of violence was precisely timed to a major historical epoch of climate change from relatively wet towards dry conditions."

Regardless of the origin of the shift, once the domination system was in play, it spread throughout the world. The psychologist and social analyst Andrew Bard Schmookler reminds us that once one element in society chooses the dominator approach, it will spread throughout the entire society. "Power is like a contaminant," he says in *The Parable of the Tribes: The Problem of Power in Social Evolution*, "a disease, which once introduced will gradually yet inexorably become universal in the system of competing societies. Civilized society in general has been like a rabid dog. Its bite infects the healthy even though it contains the germ of its own destruction."

Carl Jung, The Collective Unconscious, and the Founding of Alcoholics Anonymous

The reason I believe that saving males is my life's work is that it calls out the best of who we are as men. It forces us to heal our personal wounds as well as our societal hubris that causes us to imagine that it's our job to dominate and control nature. It will require a moonshot-like commitment to healing ourselves and healing our relationship. But I can't think of a more important or a more exciting challenge.

To be successful we have to draw on a billion years of successful life, on our human as well as our animal elders, as well as the ancient archetypes that have shaped humanity.

I had learned a little about archetypes when I took my first psychology class at UC Santa Barbara in 1961 and was mesmerized by Carl Jung's autobiography *Memories, Dreams, and Reflections*. He begins the prologue with these words:

My life is a story of the self-realization of the unconscious. Everything in the unconscious seeks outward manifestation, and the personality too desires to evolve out of its unconscious conditions and to experience itself as a whole. I cannot employ the language of science to trace this process of growth in myself, for I cannot experience myself as a scientific problem.

It wasn't until I was in graduate school and working with drug addicts as part of my student placement at UC Berkeley that I began to explore more deeply. I was drawn to working with addicts, though I didn't have a drug problem and it would take many years before I realized my drug of choice was sex and I wrote the book *Looking for Love in All the Wrong Places: Overcoming Romantic and Sexual Addictions*.

I learned that Jung had a connection with one of the founders of Alcoholics Anonymous. In 1961, Bill W., one of the founders of Alcoholics Anonymous, wrote a letter to the famous Swiss psychiatrist in which he thanked him for helping spark the fire that was to become Alcoholics Anonymous. Carl Jung had worked with a hopeless alcoholic named Rowland H. According to Jung, Rowland's only chance to recover from his alcoholism was a "spiritual or religious experience—in short, a genuine conversion."

Jung went on to say that this type of spiritual experience had been happening to alcoholics for centuries, but that he did not know how to produce such a spiritual experience through the use of psychological methods. Jung wrote back to Bill W. and said that Rowland's alcoholism was "the equivalent, on a low level, of the spiritual thirst of our being for wholeness, expressed in medieval language: the union with God." Jung's letter went on to say that " … alcohol in Latin is *spiritus*," and that the same Latin word is used for "the highest religious experience as well as the most depraving poison. The helpful formula therefore is: *spiritus contra spiritum*."

Saving Males and Exploring the Archetypes of the Mature Masculine

I met Jungian analyst Robert Moore and mythologist Douglas Gillette shortly after the publication of their book *King, Warrior, Magician, Lover: Rediscovering the Archetypes of the Mature Masculine* in 1990. In the introduction to the book, they say, "During Bill

Moyers's recent interview with the poet Robert Bly, 'A Gathering of Men,' a young man asked the question, 'Where are the initiated men of power today?' We have written this book in order to answer this question, which is on the minds of both men and women."

They recognize that part of the problem involves families. "More and more families display the sorry fact of the disappearing father," they say, "which disappearance, through either emotional or physical abandonment, or both, wreaks psychological devastation on the children of both sexes."

But they see problems that are equally important to address. "First, we need to take very seriously the disappearance of *ritual processes* for initiating boys into manhood. A second factor seems to be contributing to the dissolution of mature masculine identity. This factor, shown to us by one strain of feminist critique, is called patriarchy. ... Feminists have seen how male dominance in patriarchy has been oppressive and abusive of the feminine—of both the so-called feminine characteristics and virtues and actual women themselves."

Moore and Gillette address the tendency of some feminists to go on to see masculinity itself as the problem. "In their radical critique of patriarchy, some feminists conclude that masculinity in its roots is essentially abusive, and that connection with 'eros'—with love, relatedness, and gentleness—comes only from the feminine side of the human equation."

Moore and Gillette offer a very strong, yet supportive, challenge to this kind of feminist critique. "As useful as some of these insights have been to the cause of both feminine and masculine liberation from patriarchal stereotypes, we believe there are serious problems with this perspective. In our view, patriarchy is *not* the expression of deep and rooted masculinity, for truly deep and rooted masculinity is *not* abusive. Patriarchy is the expression of the *immature* masculine. It is the expression of Boy psychology, and, in part, the shadow—or crazy—side of masculinity. It expresses the stunted masculine, fixated at immature levels."

That's why I don't personally use the term "patriarchy," but rather draw on the contrast Riane Eisler makes and describe this kind of masculinity as an immature and unhealthy expression of "domination" as opposed to one of "partnership."

Moore and Gillette go on to contrast Boy and Man psychology and describe the following four male archetypes:

- King—The energy of just and creative ordering.
- Warrior—The energy of aggressive but nonviolent action.
- Magician—The energy of initiation and transformation.
- Lover—The energy that connects one to others and the world.

In reviewing Moore and Gillette's work, Brett McKay, who founded the Art of Manliness website in 2008, offers an excellent review of the archetypes and the work of Moore and Gillette. "Psychologist Robert Moore took the concept of Jung's archetypes and used it to create a framework that explained the development of mature and integral masculinity in men," says McKay. "Moore argued that the problems we see with men today—violence, shiftlessness, aloofness—are a result of modern men not adequately exploring or being in touch with the primal, masculine archetypes that reside within them. Like Jung, Moore believed that men and women possess both feminine and masculine archetypal patterns— this is the anima (feminine) and animus (masculine)."

McKay goes on to say that Moore believes "the problem with modern men is that Western society suppresses the animus or masculine archetype within them and instead encourages men to get in touch with their 'softer side' or their anima. Moore would argue that there's nothing wrong with men developing those softer, more nurturing and feminine behaviors. In fact, he would encourage it. A problem only arises when the development of the feminine comes at the expense of the masculine."

The King Archetype

"The King energy," says Moore, "is primal in all men. It comes first in importance, and it underlies and includes the rest of the archetypes in perfect balance. In many ways the King energy is Father energy, but it is our experience, however, that although the King underlies the Father archetype, it is more extensive and more basic than the Father."

Moore goes on to describe the archetypal energies of the King from the actual humans who may occupy that role. "Historically, kings have always been sacred. As mortal men, however, they have been relatively unimportant. We all know the famous cry when a king dies and another is waiting to ascent the throne. 'The king is dead: long live the king!' The mortal man who incarnates the King energy or bears it for a while in the service of his fellow human beings, in the service of the realm (of whatever dimensions), in the service of the cosmos, is almost an interchangeable part, as human vehicle for bringing this ordering and generative archetype into the world and into the lives of human beings."

Brett McKay offers the following summary of Moore's qualities of the King in his fullness:

- He is centered.
- He is decisive.
- He lives with integrity.
- He protects the realm.
- He provides order.
- He creates and inspires creativity in others.
- He blesses the lives of others.
- He leaves a legacy.

The Lover Archetype

"Jungians often use the name of the Greek god Eros to talk about the Lover energy," says Moore. "They also use the Latin term *libido*. By these terms they mean not just sexual appetites but a general appetite for life. We believe that the Lover, by whatever name, is the primal energy pattern of what we could call vividness, aliveness, and passion."

Moore goes on to say, "The Lover lives through the great primal hungers of our species for sex, food, wellbeing, reproduction, creative adaptation to life's hardships, and ultimately a sense of meaning, without which human beings cannot go on with their lives."

Brett McKay offers these summary views on the Lover Archetype.

- The Lover is the archetype of emotion, feeling, idealism, and sensuality.
- Being sensual means opening up and using all of your senses in all areas of your life—touching, tasting, smelling, hearing, and seeing—or in other words—experiencing as many dimensions of life as possible, as often as possible.
- The Lover is attuned to the mysterious forces underlying our everyday existence; this is the archetype that fuels a man's spirituality, and the one in which the Muses reside.
- A man who takes time to develop this archetype will experience those hunches, insights, and premonitions more frequently than men who don't.
- A man who has fully developed the Lover archetype in his life is also often adept at reading people and social cues. He's empathetic with others and understands how to get along and connect with a wide variety of people.

The Magician Archetype

"The energies of the Magician archetype, wherever and whenever we counter them are twofold," says Moore. "The Magician is the knower and he is the master of technology. Further, the man who is guided by the power of the Magician is able to fulfill these Magician functions in part by his use of ritual initiatory process. He is the 'ritual elder' who guides the processes of transformation, both within and without."

Moore continues, saying, "One aspect of the magician's knowing, of his seeing into the depths not only of nature but of human beings, was his capacity to deflate the arrogance, especially of kings, but also of any important public official. The Magician archetype in a man is his 'bullshit detector'; it sees through denial and exercises discernment."

McKay summarizes Moore's qualities of the Magician archetype as follows:

- Intellectually curious/the holder of hidden knowledge.
- A master of technology.
- Reflective.
- Reticent.
- Alchemist of life.
- Spiritual mediator.

The Warrior Archetype

"We live in a time," says Moore, "when people are generally uncomfortable with the Warrior form of masculine energy—and for some good reasons. Women especially are uncomfortable with it because they have often been the most direct victims of it in its shadow form. Around the planet, warfare in our century has reached such monstrous and pervasive proportions that aggressive energy itself is looked upon with deep suspicion and fear."

Moore goes on to say, "The Warrior is often a destroyer. But the positive Warrior energy destroys only what needs to be destroyed in order for something new and fresh, more alive and more virtuous to appear. Many things in our world need destroying—corruption, tyranny, oppression, injustice, obsolete and despotic systems of government, corporate hierarchies that get in the way of the company's performance, unfulfilling life-styles and job situations, bad marriages. And in the very act of destroying, often the Warrior energy is building new civilizations, new commercial, artistic, and spiritual ventures for humankind, new relationships."

Here are a few summary qualities of the Warrior from McKay:

- Forceful.
- Purposeful.

- Mindful.
- Adaptable.
- Decisive.
- Skillful.
- Loyal.
- Disciplined.

Reflection: Think about how these four archetypes resonate in your own life. Which ones are most alive for you? Which ones do you feel you've engaged the most? Which ones have you engaged the least? Do you feel you could use more work integrating the archetypes?

The Warrior's Journey Home: Healing Men, Healing the Planet

I've always been interested in the warrior archetype. Like many boys growing up after World War II, I was inundated with war movies that showed males as heroes saving our country from aggression. Programs like *Victory at Sea* showed battles but never people dying. I remember seeing newsreel footage of the bombing of Japan and had nightmares for months.

My parents were peace activists and didn't believe wars solved problems, though as Jews they were ambivalent about how to protect people from aggression without going to war. I longed for a way where I could protect and serve. By the time of Vietnam, I was draft age, and I learned everything I could about why we were there, what we were fighting to achieve, and whether going to war was the right thing to do.

In college, all males were required to be enrolled in The Reserve Officers' Training Corps (ROTC). I loved marching, learning to shoot, and the comradery of being part of team. But the more I learned about Vietnam and about war in general, the more I knew I couldn't go. Wars always seemed to lead to more wars. I was hungry to find an alternative.

I found what I was looking for in an unlikely place. Shortly after I moved to Mill Valley, a friend told me about a martial arts practice called Aikido. After going to the dojo and watching the movements that seemed both powerful and fluid, I joined and became a student. One of the instructors, Richard Strozzi Heckler, told us about the founder of Aikido, Morihei Ueshiba:

> Master Ueshiba developed a martial form that empowered human beings from the inside out, without categories and contests to determine who is best. He said that the "opponent is within" and that we must first work with our own minds and bodies instead of trying to correct others. He established dignity and integrity as a priority to greed and the acquisition of fame and power. Through the techniques developed in Aikido he brought to the world an alternative to our current form of heavy-handed militarism and turn-the-other-cheek pacifism.

Over the years of Aikido practice and my own studies about a new kind of warrior spirit, I wrote a book titled *The Warrior's Journey Home: Healing Men, Healing the Planet*. In the book I shared the experiences of some of the other men who were embracing this spirit.

"Is now the time," asks Matthew Fox, author of *Creation Spirituality: Liberating Gifts for the Peoples of the Earth*, "when the Earth yearns and humankind yearns for the end of war—to take back the archetype of the spiritual warrior from the Pentagon and bastions of militarism?"

He asks, who is a warrior today? "A warrior is one who is alert, who concentrates, who contemplates, who centers oneself fully. If the warrior is not well grounded he or she may die. The warrior is one who faces death. The warrior is also one who is committed to a goal that is larger than the individual ego."

George Leonard, another one of my Aikido instructors and author of many books including *The Ultimate Athlete* and *Mastery*, has spent many years developing an understanding of what humans are like when they live fully with passion and commitment. "The Modern Warrior," says Leonard, "is not one who goes to war but rather one who exhibits integrity in every aspect of living, one who seeks to attain control then act with abandon. For the Modern Warrior, life is vivid, immediate, and joyful. He or she lives each day to the full, and is fulfilled in serving others. To achieve peace in the world and harmony in daily life, it might well be necessary for men and women to re-own the warrior ideal."

Warriors Are Needed Now More Than Ever

A Cree Indian legend says that when the earth is sick and the animals disappear, there will come a tribe of people from all creeds, colors, and cultures who believe in deeds, not words, and who will restore the earth to its former beauty. This tribe will be called the Warriors of the Rainbow.

We clearly are at a time when our relation to the earth is out of balance and the survival of the human race is at risk. We are also living at a time when males are out of balance with ourselves, with women, and the community of life. Male violence is an expression, both of the wounding that males have experienced as well as the fear and rage that this wounding engenders.

The following story told to me by Richard Heckler and recounted in his book *In Search of the Warrior Spirit* can help us begin to understand the roots of our violence:

> I'm in line at the post office waiting to mail a package to the East Coast. A young mother steps up to the long counter with her two-year-old boy. He's cranky and fidgety, she tells him to quiet down as she rummages through her purse. He puts his hand into her purse and she tells him to stop. He looks curiously into the purse reaching for something inside. Turning abruptly she slaps him hard across the face. "I told you to stop!" she shrieks. The two people in front of me drop their heads, the clerk at the desk acts as if nothing had happened. Anger surges through me. The child grows red in the face. He begins to howl. The mother turns towards him raising her hand, threatening to strike. "Don't

pull that on me," she hisses. The boy trembles and holds his sounds back in sucking gasps. I was outraged.

I wanted to pull her teeth out with my bare hands. I walked around the block twice until I was collected enough to drive my truck.

Reading an article about a bar in Dearborn, Michigan, now transforms the episode in my mind. In this establishment men are given black plastic miniature Uzi submachine guns. The miniature Uzis are built to shoot hard streams of water, not bullets. The evenings they hand out the water Uzis are called Rambo Wet-Panty Nights. On these particular nights women go on stage dressed in skimpy T-shirts and G-strings. Rock music blares out, men begin to shoot at the women's crotches. There's a lot of yelling and stamping. The bar's night manager exhorts the men on, "Shoot those guns! If you guys were like this in Vietnam, we would have won the war!" The woman who does the best job getting shot at wins one hundred dollars.

The comments of shooters are certainly explicit: "I got her. She's hot; I know she likes it. She likes it, and she knows that I know she likes it," says a computer marketing specialist.

"You work hard all day, and this is a release. I worked twelve hours today, and this is a way to get some aggression out," says a worker at a plastics manufacturing company.

"You don't get to do something like this every day. ... How many times do you get to shoot a girl in the pussy? This is great," says an auto worker.

"This gives you a feeling of power and authority. The ultimate machoism. I'm aiming at her clitoris. She knows I'm shooting at her crotch and she knows it's me and she gets stimulation from it," says a batch processor in a chemical plant.

"Maybe they don't like it at first, but when they get all wet they've got to like it. They've got to like it," the auto worker says.

It's as though the boy in the post office will someday grow up and go to a bar like this and shoot Uzis at women's crotches and not know why. His wife will be angry at him for being out without her and she'll take her anger out on their son. This son will grow up and take it out on other women.... Where does the cycle of violence end?

I've read this passage a number of times. Each time I do, I get tears in my eyes. It touches home on so many levels.

It shows us that the roots of male violence go back to the abuse we experienced as children. The often covert abuse that parents visit on their sons in the name of child-rearing leaves a deep reservoir of rage. As boys grow up the rage gets expressed toward other women and is often tied in with sexual violence disguised as "men just out having fun."

There is a suggestion that the men shooting at the women are Vietnam vets who were not good enough to win and must now redeem their honor by becoming better at violence and domination. What isn't said explicitly is that many of the men will drink a few too many and get into fights in the bar, passing on the violence to other males. The young boy in the post office, now grown to shoot Uzis, will go home after the evening's "fun" and with anger and shame will likely fight with his wife and probably with his son as well.

The connection between male violence and our child-rearing practices is borne out by a great deal of recent research.

Children reared in violent homes grow up to become violent adults. Violence begets violence. According to psychologists B. F. Steele and C. B. Pollock, "Without exception in our study group of abusing parents, there is a history of having been raised in the same style which they have recreated in the pattern of rearing their own children."

Alice Miller shows us that boys who are raised violently and come to power in a society are more likely to take their country to war. Those who look into the origins of Hitler's and Stalin's destructiveness, for instance, will find that both came from extremely abusive childhoods. It isn't just the historical murderers of the past who were brutalized as children. Saddam Hussein's father died before Hussein was born. He was raised by a stepfather who brutalized him.

We also see a similar kind of wounding in former President Donald Trump. On May 7, 2016, six months before the election in which Donald Trump defeated Hillary Clinton, I wrote an article titled "The Real Reason Donald Trump Will Be Our Next President." In the article, I noted Donald Trump's low approval ratings of 67 percent in an April 14 poll and asked, "How do we account for millions of people voting for candidates who are seen so negatively? Why do I think Donald Trump may be our next president?"

The article went on to say, "As our world becomes more complex and problems become more difficult to solve, we turn to simple solutions that give our psyches comfort. How do we deal with poverty, over-population, global climate change, endless wars? It's difficult to figure out what to do. We are all drawn to someone who seems to know the answer. 'ISIS? Trust me, I'll eliminate them in short order,' says Mr. Trump. Too many people in the world and an economic system that keeps people in poverty? 'Don't worry, I'll build a wall to keep illegal immigrants out,' says Mr. Trump, 'and I'll get Mexico to pay for it.'

"People having difficulty with the rise of female power and prestige? White men becoming uncomfortable with the non-white world? He's got an app for that, too. 'We'll ban Muslims from America and ridicule and shame women until they get back in their proper place.'

"If you think this is all ridiculous and the American people would never elect someone like this, you don't fully appreciate the way our subconscious mind works to simplify the world and protect our psyche from being overwhelmed."

I went on to say in the article, "Mr. Trump seems to have suffered abuse, neglect, and abandonment as a child. Many of us resonate with his rage."

The article continued:

"We know from Mr. Trump's own writing that he was an aggressive and violent child growing up, that he was sent to military school at a young age, and had difficulty controlling his temper. It's not surprising that we have gotten statements like these from Mr. Trump:

- 'Ariana Huffington is unattractive, both inside and out. I fully understand why her former husband left her for a man—he made a good decision.'
- 'You know, it really doesn't matter what the media write as long as you've got a young, and beautiful, piece of a**.'
- 'I would bomb the sh** out of them. I would just bomb those suckers, and that's right, I'd blow up the pipes, I'd blow up the refineries, I'd blow up every single inch, there would be nothing left.'
- 'I've said if Ivanka weren't my daughter, perhaps I'd be dating her.'

"These kinds of statements repulse many. As a trauma-informed therapist they are red flags of a person who has suffered serious abuse, neglect, and abandonment."

I wrote this six months before the 2016 election when most people felt Donald Trump was unlikely to become the next president. We know he won that election, and in the run-up to the next election with Joe Biden, he made it known *before* the election that if he lost, "the election must have been stolen." As I write this in August 2022, Donald Trump is leading a Republican Party, most of whom maintain the lie that he never lost the 2020 election.

When wounded and unhealed males come to power, they can be very dangerous, and it takes a strong populace to defend against them without becoming infected by their leader's delusion that only he can save the world, even if he has to dominate and harm others in order to do so.

Clearly a new kind of warrior is being called upon to help save the wounded males from harming themselves, each other, the women and children of the world, and the earth itself. In the next chapter, we'll address the kinds of rites of passage that will be necessary to truly protect and serve the people of our world in these perilous times.

CHAPTER 6
RENEWING RITES OF PASSAGE AND MEN'S HEALING AND SUPPORT GROUPS

If you don't initiate the young, they will burn down the village to feel the heat.

—African proverb

Throughout our human history, being part of a men's group and engaging in rites of passage were intimately connected. In indigenous cultures around the world, the young boys of the village would grow up in similar-age groups playing together, being boys, and learning skills that would be important as they got older. Later these same groups would undergo a ritual event where they would be removed from their mothers and go through a trial of some sort guided by the men of the tribe. They would return to their community as young men. For the most part we've lost both these related events in our modern lives, much to the detriment of males, females, the community at large.

Oddly enough, my introduction to my first men's group came at a weekend workshop in 1970 called "Women in Transition." I had gone with my wife, ostensibly to better understand women's liberation and the process of change she was going through. On a deeper level, I was looking for the same kind of support and understanding she was finding in the women's movement.

My wife and I had met at UC Santa Barbara in 1965 when I was a senior and she was a freshman. We'd fallen in love, gotten engaged, and were married the following year after I graduated. The women's movement was just beginning, and we both had read *The Feminine Mystique* by Betty Friedan. I still have my copy, a paperback version with a cover price of seventy-five cents and a headline above the title, "The Year's Most Controversial Bestseller." There is also a quote by the British American anthropologist Ashley Montagu. "The book we have been waiting for . . . the wisest, sanest, soundest, most understanding of contemporary American woman's greatest problem . . . a triumph."

For me, I didn't see any controversy. I grew up in a family with a mother who saw herself as a liberated woman long before there was a modern women's movement and a father who appreciated her independence and liberation and wanted the same thing for himself. I also recognized the constricting demands of a society that believed that it was a man's world and a women's place was in the home.

In the first chapter of Friedan's book called "The Problem That Has No Name," she says:

> The problem lay buried, unspoken, for many years in the minds of American women. It was a strange stirring, a sense of dissatisfaction, a yearning that women suffered in the middle of the twentieth century in the United States. Each suburban wife struggling with it alone. As she made the beds, shopped for groceries, matched slipcover material, ate peanut butter sandwiches with her children, chauffeured Cub Scouts and Brownies, lay beside her husband at night—she was afraid to ask even of herself the silent question—"Is this all?"

It didn't take much for me to imagine myself as the husband lying beside his wife and asking himself the same silent question.

Now I was attending a gathering at Asilomar, the beautiful conference center on the ocean near Monterey, California, with five hundred women in transition and a tiny contingent of men, perhaps fourteen of us. I assumed that, like me, they were drawn by the small print on the brochure describing the conference that encouraged men to attend. I also assumed that they were there as men in transition looking for ways to get support from other men so that women and men could become liberated together.

I was more than a bit frightened to be in a room with so many women regardless of small-print-encouragement of male attendance. I remembered my experience the previous year going into a feminist bookstore in San Francisco with a woman friend of mine and being greeted by cold, icy stares from the women there, even though I was as interested in the literature as the women who were browsing through aisles looking at books by Gloria Steinem, Alice Rossi, Sylvia Plath, Andrea Dworkin, Robin Morgan, Kate Millett, and bell hooks.

Engrossed in my reading, at first I didn't notice the little boy, about eight years old, obviously the child of the woman who owned the bookstore, who also looked at me suspiciously. I was only vaguely aware of him as he brushed by me while I was picking up another book, until he so obviously tripped on my foot. I had to look up and notice his angry reaction to my presence. I smiled distractedly, apologized for being in his way, and went back to my reading.

Later he finally brushed up to me and pushed a crumpled piece of paper in my hand. I almost cried when I opened it and read in his child's handwriting, "We don't like men here." I felt hurt and angry, mostly for the message that he was getting as a boy who would grow up to be a man. I thought of our own son, Jemal, who was born on November 21, 1969.

I knew that part of the reason I was with my wife at Asilomar was to be a different kind of father than my father was able to be with me when I was growing up. For the most part, the women at the conference seemed warm and supportive. The first evening we were asked to break into small groups and I found myself with four women, not surprising given the sex ratio at the conference.

The woman leading the exercise quickly amended her request and asked the men to be in a small group with each other. I was at first disappointed since I thought it would be interesting to hear from some of the women about why they were there and how they felt about having men in attendance. But I quickly shifted my thinking and thought, great, this will be a chance to connect more deeply with guys who want to talk about our own challenges.

Surely, I thought, a group of guys who had the courage to attend a conference with five hundred women would be my kind of guys. When the five us began talking, I couldn't believe what I was haring. The conversation began with sports and moved quickly to the foxy women that were around and finally to dirty joke that evolved from one man being placed in a room with two women before they realized the mistake.

I finally cut in and said I was more interested in why we were here and how each of us felt. I began talking about my nervousness and fear, but my words seemed to be dead on arrival and the conversation shifted to other guys in the group and returned the original level of banter, though at a more subdued level. I wanted to scream, what's really going on with you? How are you feeling? Why are you here? But I just tuned out their words and waited for the exercise to end.

I felt the despair I had known so much in my past. I felt like some kind of a freak and very much alone. I so wanted to talk with other men about what we were feeling, our concerns about fatherhood, and the stresses of trying to do our jobs in the world, be a good husband and father at home, and figure out what it meant to be a man.

What got me out of my despair began with a woman who smiled and told me she was glad I was there and asked me how I felt being there with so many women. I was glad to feel welcomed by a person, not just small print on a brochure. I told her about my experiences with the men in my small group the previous day. "Don't give up," she told me. "I'm sure there are some men who are wanting what you want. I know it isn't easy, and it may take time."

She was right. I soon started up conversation with a man who seemed like a kindred spirit. He said he was starting a men's group, and I almost fell over with excitement. I was ready to join until he told me he was from New York and he and his wife were visiting friends in California and had heard of the conference in Asilomar. He was encouraging, and by the end of the conference, I began looking for my own group.

I found a group shortly after I returned from the conference. My friend Brad, a social worker, whom I had met in school, asked me to join a group he was starting. We talked mostly about career issues, which were on everyone's mind, but also about our families and our challenges with fatherhood, work, and marriage. I stayed in the group for five years until I moved out of the area, but I found another group that I've been with for forty-three years now.

The End of a Marriage and the Support of My Men's Group

Like many marriages, mine didn't last "until death do us part." I had a rebound love affair that turned into an ill-conceived second marriage. I was becoming increasingly depressed with my work and my relationship and was looking for support. One day I saw a flyer tacked up on a bulletin board.

"Men, come and share a day with other men and hear psychologist Herb Goldberg, author of *The Hazards of Being Male*. We will explore the complexities of men's roles today." It was sponsored by the Men's Growth Collective, a group of guys who had been meeting as a support group for some time.

We gathered for the event on April 21, 1979, in Mill Valley. There were twelve of us, plus organizers. What stood out to me at that first gathering was a recognition that men had many challenges that needed to be addressed. In the last years of my marriage, it felt like my wife got a great deal of support from women, but it seemed that many in the women's movement either viewed men as the cause of women's problems or felt the system favored men at the expense of women.

Although I believed that many aspects of the system were harmful to women, I also saw that many aspects of the system favored women. When we were dealing with issues of child custody and support, it became evident to me that the system favored my ex-wife in many ways. It was assumed that the mother would be the best parent for minor children. When I attempted to get custody of both my children or share custody, the system thwarted my efforts. Further, though some men benefited from the system, many suffered severely from the demands of the system.

The day with Goldberg wasn't about gender politics or trying to figure out who was more harmed by the social system. It was about taking responsibility for our own wounds and supporting each other in healing. One of the exercises we did was to have each man reflect on the times we had felt dropped or betrayed by other males in our lives.

I talked about my father's anger and his leaving the family when I was five years old, something I had rarely discussed with anyone, and certainly not in front of a group of strangers. As other men talked about their own experiences, I realized I wasn't alone. Many men had experienced a father wound. But there were other hurts and betrayals.

One man talked about being the youngest in his family and having two older brothers who tormented him. Another talked about his hunger to have a child. He was willing to give up a relationship that was good in all other ways, except she didn't want children. I'd never heard a man talk so fervently about wanting to be a dad.

After the day had ended, we all had opened ourselves up to vulnerabilities and wounds we had never shared before. We felt like we had found soul brothers and wanted to continue the experience. Tom, one of the organizers, invited anyone interested to meet the following Thursday at his home in Mill Valley. Twelve of us showed up, and we discussed the idea of meeting weekly for a men's group. After a few weeks, the group was reduced to eight, and we began on a journey that continues now almost forty-three years later.

I remember feeling anxious initially. Even though we had all experienced the engagement and openness on the Herb Goldberg day, now we were in a small group, up close, without a designated leader, although Tom acted as the host to guide the initial meetings. We each "checked in" and told the other guys what was going on with each of us lately.

I was going through a major transition period in my life. My first marriage had ended. I was a part-time dad trying to navigate the conflicted feelings with my first wife and how best to work out child support and visitation. My second marriage was now more stressful than sexy, yet I was hanging in there. My reason for staying had more to do with my addiction to pain and suffering, along with depression and guilt over the ending of my first marriage and estrangement from my children, than it did with pleasure and joy.

I had gotten a temporary job at Howard Johnson's restaurant. I hadn't gone looking for a job that was more fitting. I couldn't see myself going back and working as a counselor when my own life was so out of balance. I felt I was dying emotionally, and the men's group was my place of refuge, a safe harbor from the chaos of my life.

The other guys in the group had varied backgrounds. We were all white, middle-class guys. All of us were in transition with our lives, and all of us to one degree or another were dealing with our own life wounds and our challenges with sex, love, and relationships. The format of the group was simple.

Eight of us met every Wednesday for about two hours. The first part of the evening involved a check-in. After we each had a chance to share our feelings and be heard, anyone who had an issue they wanted to get into in more depth would have a chance to delve more deeply.

The after-group time together in Tom's hot tub became an integral part of the group. We weren't working anymore. We were enacting an ancient ritual of men sitting in a circle, telling our stories, looking at the stars, and being together.

Later when we all went to hear Robert Bly tell stories and recite poetry, we heard him talk about the importance of guys being together. "Men must come together," said Bly, "in order to hear the sound that male cells sing." What a wonderful recognition that our very cells vibrate together to create a symphony of beautiful male music. The longer we've been meeting, the richer and more joyful our time together has become. Looking back over our forty-three years together, I realize there were a number of stages the group went through, which I'd like to share with you.

The Seven Stages of Our Men's Group
Stage 1: Learning to Trust and Open Up

Most of us have grown up with an ethic that says, "Real men are successful. They don't have problems. If they do have a problem, they work them out themselves. Other men are potential competitors. Anything you let slip about your life will be used against you." I expressed some of these beliefs in my first book *Inside Out: Becoming My Own Man*. I called them "The Commandments that Move Me."

1. Thou shalt not be weak.
2. Thou shalt not fail thyself, nor fail as thy father before thee.
3. Thou shalt not keep holy any day that denies thy work.
4. Thou shalt not express strong emotions, neither high nor low.
5. Thou shalt not cry, complain, or ask for help.
6. Thou shalt not be hostile or angry, especially toward loved ones.
7. Thou shalt not be uncertain or ambivalent.
8. Thou shalt not be dependent.
9. Thou shalt not acknowledge thy death or thy limitations.
10. Thou shalt do unto other men before they do unto you.

Take a moment to reflect on the commandments above. Which ones do you particularly resonate with? Which ones are the most challenging for you? Which ones do you want to let go of or change?

During the first few years of the group, we spent time testing the waters of this new world of guys to see if we could trust each other. We would share relatively safe things about ourselves and see how they were received. We spent a lot of time talking about our love lives and about the challenges we were having. We also talked a good deal about our work lives. After the group as we sat together in the hot tub, we just basked in the joy of being together.

In the summers, my two children, Jemal and Angela, came to visit and I would often bring them to the group. Tom's little house was small, and he had a bunk bed in the living room. I'd put the kids to bed, and they'd fall asleep listening to the sounds of guys talking about life, love, and work.

Years later, they both recalled the experience very positively. If, as Robert Bly suggested, children need to grow up hearing "the sound that male cells sing," Jemal and Angela got a lot of that as they listened to our voices and felt the deep vibrations of men being men.

We would also get together to watch football games on TV. It was during the time that the San Francisco 49ers were at the top of their game, and we loved rooting for our local champions. At Super Bowl time, we had a regular ritual where we'd get all our families together—men, women, and children—and we'd play a game of touch football. We all got wet and muddy and had a wonderful time. After we cleaned up, we'd watch the Super Bowl together and cheer for our team.

Stage 2: Revealing Our True Selves, Fears, and Insecurities

It took time to develop trust before we were ready to go deeper and share more sensitive aspects of our lives. One of the guys opened up about past criminal activity. He talked about being arrested for bringing drugs into the country, spending time in jail, and how it had impacted his later life. Another guy talked about his sexuality, his past marriage, and his present interest in exploring a "gay lifestyle."

Each person's openness led to another person having the courage to reveal a previously hidden part of his life. We were pleased to see that the group was safe enough for us to share. We could trust that what we said would be held in confidence and not shared outside the group. We also learned that we would be accepted no matter what we had done in our lives. It was a wonderful feeling to know that we were safe. It was something I never felt, even in my own family.

We talked about the families we grew up in and the positive things we had learned as well as the wounding that occurred. I talked about my father's "nervous breakdown," his overdose of pills, and being committed to the mental hospital. I shared my mother's fear that she would die before I grew up and that the world was dangerous and that I might die without warning. There were a number of fears that seemed to be core features of my life:

- My feelings will destroy me if I let them.
- I'll go crazy like my father.
- I'll be a failure at work and lose my family's respect.
- There's something dangerous and violent in me waiting to destroy the people I love the most.
- Women will love me, but underneath the surface, they will feel pity and contempt.

Do you resonate with any of these fears? How have they impacted your life? How have you dealt with them?

During this period, we learned that the group could deal with serious conflict. One of the guys had been studying to become a marriage and family counselor and needed to demonstrate that he had spent a number of hours learning various skills. He needed to show that he had skills leading a group. Since there was no designated leader in the group, we each contributed leadership skills.

When it was time for him to submit his hours for his license, I agreed to sign off on his application and say that he had spent a certain number of hours as the group leader. One of the other guys in the group, Norman, who like me was a licensed therapist, said that what I was doing was unethical and threatened to turn me in to my own licensing board if I went ahead and signed off on the hours of our fellow group member.

This conflict became a central focus of the group for nearly six months. There were heated discussions and angry feelings. I remained willing to sign off on the hours. Norman remained steadfast in is determination to turn me in if I did so. Most of the group sided with me, but I worked to find a solution so that we could resolve things within the group so that Norman wasn't seen as "the bad guy." We finally were able to work things out and the group was stronger as a result.

Stage 3: Baring Our Bodies and Souls

I learned in the men's group, as in life, often an emotional conflict and confrontation between men can deepen the trust level. There's often a sense that now that I've felt your emotions and know what's going on inside you, I can know you better and trust you more. Once we were able to deal with conflict in the group and learn that no one was driven out and the group was stronger as a result, we were able to continue connecting on deeper levels.

In one the groups, Tom suggested we try something different. We had gotten pretty comfortable with each other talking. We had taken our clothes off and jumped in the hot tub together, though it was in the dark and we were exposed for only a brief moment. Tom suggested we take our clothes off one at a time and let ourselves be seen in all our naked glory.

"I think it would be empowering to have us tell each man what we liked and appreciated about his body," Tom said. There was some uncomfortable discussion about why he was suggesting such a thing and what we might learn. But the consensus was "what the hell, let's give it a try."

The only time most have us had been completely naked was when we were alone in the shower or in bed with our wives or sexual partners. On a few occasions a woman had told me what she liked about my body, but I'd never experienced hearing anything from a man. We had talked about our fears of being seen as "gay" and the kind of ridicule most of us had grown up with if we were suspected of doing anything "girly." But this was different.

Taking our clothes off in front of other guys brought up hidden fears. Growing up, I was ridiculed for being short. I was teased a lot and got in fights when I couldn't talk my way out of them. There were always gay jokes that often had violent overtones. I still remember being taunted in junior high school by a group of older boys. One of them pushed me. "Hey, punk, you look like you would like a blow job."

When I backed away, the boys pushed forward. "I'll give you a blow up," the biggest boy taunted. "I'll stick my dick in your mouth and blow out your brains." I turned and ran, amid laughter and name-calling.

Now I was waiting my turn to take my clothes off in front of guys I knew I could trust. But how do you ever know for sure if you can trust someone? I realized I was sweating profusely as I took off my jeans, shirt, and undershorts and stood before these group of guys. I took a deep breath and waited. "Well, I like the pattern of chest hair you have," one guy said. There were some nods of agreement. Another guy said, "You really have strong legs." Another liked the shape of my shoulders.

I was amazed. The comments were all positive and I felt like I was awash in validation that I never knew I needed. What guys noticed and liked was very different from things that women noticed. Women seemed to like my blue eyes, long eyelashes, curly hair, and one woman said she absolutely loved my "popcorn butt." I never asked her what a popcorn butt was but was glad she liked mine. What I got from the guys felt like being seen by a whole line of fathers, brothers, uncles—all appreciating the essence of who I was. It was a magical experience that I've never forgotten.

Stage 4: Having Fun Together

Our Super Bowl football game was the first of the events we did that included families. We later had picnics, hikes, going to plays, fun dinners, and parties. We also did more things together as a men's group. We went Greek dancing a number of times and learned to do Contact Improvisation.

In the group, we often went out to dinner together. I was introduced to good food that was a new experience for me. I grew up with a mother who worked long hours and dinner was often a thawed steak with canned peas and applesauce. Now I learned about Italian food, good wine, barbequed ribs, oysters, and sea food.

Leading up to our tenth anniversary, we decided we would have dinner at "the best restaurant in San Francisco." Of course, for the guys who actually knew something about fine dining, deciding on the best restaurant was a task to be taken seriously. It was debated for six months leading up to the event in April 1999.

We decided on Masa's restaurant, and even with what I had learned about good food, I couldn't add much to the debate. I did conduct some online research and learned the following:

Masa's was opened in July 1983 by chef Masataka Kobayashi. The restaurant uses Masataka's nickname, Masa, for its name. Upon its opening, the restaurant had a six-month wait list. Masa was murdered in 1984, and sous chef Bill Galloway ran the kitchen following Masa's death.

Since this was our tenth anniversary, we decided to wear tuxedos, rent a limo, and have us delivered in style. We had the limo driver take pictures of us at sunset in front of the Golden Gate Bridge. When the seven of us walked into Masa's, heads turned. I was wearing my red hat with a long pheasant feather. We were all seated at our table, and since Masa's was a small, exclusive restaurant, we were the center of attention.

We laughed and made up a story, which we whispered to our waiter, that we were a group of retired CIA agents who had come together for one last meal before we would all be forced to go into hiding because our last covert operation went sour.

The meal was memorable, the food superb, the wine and after-dinner drinks fit for kings. The desserts so good, we ended up having seconds. The bill for us all was also grand, but it was worth it. Ten years was an accomplishment that was worth celebrating.

Stage 5: Revitalizing the Group

Our regular meetings became times of joy and appreciation. We were comfortable with each other. We laughed, played, and went deeper. These guys had become family. But like all families, we reached a point where we got too comfortable. "I feel like we've become an old married couple," one of the guys said. "Everything is nice and easy, but it's getting a bit boring. We need to find something new we can do."

I suggested we do the New Warrior weekend developed by the ManKind Project. My friend, Bill Kauth, was one of the founders. At the time, I didn't know too much about their "New Warrior Training Adventure," but I felt, intuitively, that it was what we needed. We learned that the next weekend would take place in San Diego in June 1991, and we signed up, flew down to San Diego, rented a van to drive to the site, and joined fifty other guys in connecting with a large group of guys to get to the core of what it meant to be a man in today's world, what was keeping us from our greatness, and how to find and embrace our life's purpose.

I'll describe our experiences later as I explore rites of passage. Here's how the organization describes the experience: The New Warrior Training Adventure is a singular type of life-affirming event, honoring the best in what men have to offer the planet. We are only able to recognize the powerful brilliance of men because we are willing to look at, and take full responsibility for, the pain we are also capable of creating and suffering. This is the paradox of modern masculinity, a lesson we are dedicated to learning and teaching.

We returned from the experience transformed. We felt a deeper connection with our personal paths in life and saw our group in a larger context of being part of a worldwide movement of men and women who were committed to healing our wounds and changing the social institutions that kept men locked in the Man Box.

Another adventure began for us when one of our members, our elder John Robinson, suggested we meet with another men's group. "I just attended a gathering of numerous men's groups and an all-Asian men's group said they might like to meet with an Anglo men's group to explore issues of racism and the different ways men relate in a world that is multiracial and multicultural."

We liked the idea, and though it took many months of discussions before we had our first meeting, we began to explore a host of issues. For the first time, we got to experience what minority men face in a culture that often restricts men in ways that we, as white guys, never experience.

Our group took on whole new levels of meaning and engagement, and we no longer felt like an "old married couple" but young adventurers again addressing new aspects of what it means to be a man.

Stage 6: Making a Lifetime Commitment

Although we had been meeting for a long time and developing skills that helped us improve our relationships with our partners, made us more effective at work, and made us better men, we still felt the group was a training ground for our lives. I finally voiced a need that had been rumbling around inside me for a long time but finally surfaced.

"You guys mean a lot to me," I began. I was nervous and not sure I could express what I was feeling. "You helped me get through the lowest time in my life when I was caught in a destructive marriage that was pulling me under. You've been real brothers to me, and I don't want to lose you." I had to pause. My emotions were beginning to overwhelm me. "I don't want this group to end. I want us to make a commitment to stay together forever, until death do we part."

I was prepared for laughter or disbelief. I wasn't prepared for the silence that followed. We began to discuss what it would mean to make such a commitment. It would mean that we couldn't allow ourselves to get bored to the point where someone would want to leave the group. It meant that we had to continue being honest, but to deal with each other in a respectful and caring way so that we didn't allow anger to pull us apart. It also meant that we would have to change how we did the group in response to life changes of our members.

When we began, we all lived in Marin County, across the bay from San Francisco, and met weekly. But over the years, we moved farther apart and met every other week. When Tony and his family moved to Washington state, he dropped out of the group. But since we had made a lifetime commitment to the group and each other, we changed the format again and began meeting for four days three or four times a year.

When our elder John Robinson died suddenly, we had to confront the reality of death and dying and how we would work through those issues together.

Stage 7: Dealing with Disabilities, Death, and Dying

When the group began, we were a group of guys who were mostly in our thirties and forties. Now we're a group of guys who are in our seventies and eighties. Death and disability have gradually become a real presence in our lives and therefore important issues to be shared in the group.

As we got older, we discussed the two *p*'s, the prostate and the penis. The former seemed to be enlarging in ways that were troubling, and the latter seemed to often fail to enlarge when we wanted it too. At various times we tried Viagra and other related medications that were supposed to address erectile dysfunction. Generally, the consensus was that they were helpful.

In our group, guys have dealt with joint replacement to various legs, arms, and hips. We've dealt with depression, cognitive decline, urinary tract infections, cancer, and kidney disease. One guy was in an auto accident with a driver who had run a red light. Dick's leg was badly injured, and he required surgery and spent time in a rehabilitation hospital.

He shared a room with a man who was both physically debilitated and in serious cognitive decline. When our men's group guy returned, he talked more about at what point might you decide to end your life if there was no real hope for recovery and your quality of life was compromised. As we've gotten older, we have spent more time dealing with life and death.

We continue to have discussions about these issues. At the last meeting, I brought a book that my wife was reading. She has been trained as a hospice volunteer and has worked with many individuals and families as they face end-of-life issues. The book is titled *Advice for Future Corpses: A Practical Perspective on Death and Dying* and is written by Sallie Tisdale, a fine author and an experienced nurse who has spent ten years with people going through this final stage of life.

The book is authoritative yet witty. She says at the outset, "I never died, so this entire book is a fool's advice. Birth and death are the only human acts we cannot practice." She addresses issues that we've all found to be scary but are important to discuss including:

- What does it mean to die "a good death?"
- Can there be more than one kind of good death?
- What can I do to make my death, or the deaths of my loved ones, good?
- What to say and not to say, what to ask, and when—from the dying, loved ones, and doctors.

Since we also decided not to add any new members, we are aware that there will come a time when the group itself will die. For me, writing this book helps me share the gift of the group with others who may want to join a men's group in the future. It's a way to celebrate the joy of being male.

Rites of Passage to Engage, Mark, and Celebrate Important Stages of the Male Journey

A rite of passage is a ceremony and marks the transition from one phase of life to another. Although it is often used to describe the transition from adolescence to adulthood, it applies to any of life's transitions such as marriage, birth, beginnings, endings, and eventually death.

French anthropologist and folklorist Arnold van Gennep first coined the phrase rites of passage in 1909. Interestingly, van Gennep grew up without a father in the home. All of us hunger for the guidance that comes from going through meaningful rituals as we move through important stages of our lives.

Filmmaker Frederick Marx has spent his professional career exploring and documenting rites of passage. His most well-known film, *Hoop Dreams*, documents the story of two African American high school students in Chicago and their dream of becoming professional basketball players. His new film, *Rites of Passage*, tells an inspirational story showing people exactly why ritually guided rites of passage and mentorship are necessary for all young people.

Marx says, "We have a worldwide teen crisis on our hands. It is estimated that the costs to society for teen dysfunctions—both behavioral and medical—is close to $500 billion per year in the U.S. alone." He goes on to question why there are such problems with unwanted pregnancy, STDs, school dropouts, drug and alcohol abuse, violence against self and others, depression, and a host of other problems.

He says, "It's because teens unconsciously push against the confines of their own bodies, the rules of parents and society, and the capacity of their own minds and willpower to discover the true limits of their potential." Yet, there is more to the problem than this. "They also have 'shadows,' the unconscious stories they tell themselves about who they are that fuel the coping mechanisms they adopt in order to survive a dysfunctional culture. They must become acquainted with those shadows. If they don't, they will act out and become a danger to themselves and others. They need to be initiated into adulthood."

Marx has also written a wonderful book, *Rites to a Good Life: Everyday Rituals of Healing and Transformation*. He introduces the book with a quote by ritual elder and storyteller Michael Meade. "When a culture doesn't provide formal Rites of Passage or initiations, people find their own. Or they don't find them and never really find the traction of their life. And when a society or culture doesn't attempt to create circumstances in which that can be worked on creatively, then you usually get destructive versions of them."

"I think the greatest crime of the last two centuries," says Marx, "has been the countless millions of children who have been brought into this world but never taught to discover their unique purpose in this life."

Robert Bly wrote about the need for male initiation and mentoring in his book *Iron John: A Book About Men.* "There is male initiation, female initiation, and human initiation. I'm talking here about male initiation," says Bly. "The grief in men has been increasing steadily since the start of the Industrial Revolution and the grief has reached a depth now that cannot be ignored."

Traditionally, rites of passage that helped young males transition from boyhood to manhood were initiated by the fathers and other male elders. Yet increasingly we are living in a society with absent fathers. A number of organizations have come forward recently to provide ritual initiations for males.

The ManKind Project: A Modern-Day Male Initiation and Support Network

I first met Bill Kauth in 1980 at a conference that had emerged from the consciousness of the women's movement. I immediately felt I was with a kindred spirit. We were both impressed with the positive energy of women coming together to break out of the old restrictions that society had placed on them. It felt good to support women, but we also recognized that men needed to find their own support and break free from their own restrictions.

As we talked, we realized we had a lot in common. We both had been trained as psychotherapists. We were both born the same year (1943) and both had complex relationships with our fathers. In similar ways, our "father issues" set us on a path to follow our own calling, which drew us to working with men. I talked about what I was learning in my men's group that had started in 1979, and he talked about his desire to create a way for men to come together to support each other by combining spirit and soul work and finding their own paths to authentic manhood.

In 1985, Kauth and two colleagues, Rich Tosi and Ron Hering, created the first New Warrior Training Adventure. "A premise of the New Warrior Training Adventure," says ManKind historian Hal Klegman, "was an introductory, experiential, weekend-long men's gathering and initiation focusing on deep self-examination. This initiatory training was modeled—unconsciously, at first, and later intentionally—largely on Joseph Campbell's cross-cultural research, and uses his stages of initiation: separation, descent, ordeal and welcoming back into the community of initiated men."

I still remember my own introduction to the New Warrior weekend. It was 1991, twelve years after my men's group began. We joked that we felt like "an old married couple." We knew each other well, felt safe and comfortable, enjoyed ourselves immensely, but were growing a bit bored with our time together. We decided to attend the New Warrior Weekend. Although it's impossible to describe any kind of ritual initiation because the real value is in the experience, here are some of the things I learned:

1. Being with other men in this well-crafted weekend experience was transformative. I felt a host of feelings: anxiety, confusion, exhilaration, joy, and true brotherly love. By the end, I felt more myself, more deeply connected to others, and equipped with tools that I could use to be more successful in life.

2. I broke through my Mr. Nice Guy image to share a lot of my woundedness and anger. I found that my anger didn't destroy people. In fact, it was appreciated and there was a container of supportive men to help me guide my anger and teach me ways of expressing it that would help, rather than harm, myself and others.

3. Most of my life I felt like the "lone ranger" figuring things out on my own, doing what needed to be done by myself, solving my own problems. I thought being stoic, independent, and

self-sufficient was what it meant to be a man. In the weekend, I learned to be part of a team, to work together in support of shared goals, and found that success was sweeter and more lasting when achieved together.

4. I got in touch with one of the primal emotional wounds I experienced in childhood that had never been dealt with, talked about, or healed. When I was seven or eight years old, I had a best friend named Woodrow. Everyone called him Woody, and he lived a few houses down from mine. There was a stream three blocks away where we played in the summer. In the winter it became a raging river. Woody and three friends wanted me to come play by the river one day when it was still at its peak of wildness. I couldn't go and they went without me. Later that day I learned that Woody had fallen in and drowned. I was heartbroken and felt guilty that I hadn't been there. Maybe I could have saved him, I thought. It colored my whole life. I forever felt guilty, afraid to let myself get close to others for fear they would die.

    During the weekend, I confronted my loss for the first time and was helped to let go of my guilt and let down the barriers I had erected to protect myself from the pain of his loss.

5. Although I had been doing men's work for some time, had counseled thousands of men and their families, and had been in a men's group, I had never before gotten in touch with my life's purpose. During the weekend, I was able to do so, and I still have the handwritten affirmation I had written. "My life purpose is to awaken the masculine soul to help men and the women who love them to live fully, love deeply, and make a positive difference in the world."

6. A weekend experience, no matter how powerful, is never enough to lay the foundation for real change once we are back in the real world—back to the stresses of life, the commitments we have to family and friends, the bills that must be paid, the anxieties, fears, and worries we must handle, the decisions that must be made. After the weekend ended,

we all joined a six-week "integration group" where we could learn specific techniques and practices to keep what we'd learned alive.

The Good Men Project: The Conversation No One Else Is Having

I was first introduced to The Good Men Project in 2009 by a men's health colleague, Stephen B. Siegel, MD. He had recently read the book *The Good Men Project: Real Stories from the Front Lines of Modern Manhood* by Tom Matlack. In a review, he offered the following comments:

> As a urologist, I thought that I knew all there was to know about men. Thanks to the authors of this book, I have learned so much more. It's rare that men get together and talk about these types of issues. Most of us run out of things to say after we talk about our favorite sports team and the car we want to buy. It is so important as individuals and, especially at times like these, that we define for ourselves and for our children, what it really takes to be a good man. This book breaks down our roles as Fathers, Husbands, Workers, etc. and tells amazing stories of people that either are good men or figured out how to become good men. We need these examples. We need to see that it is possible to fail initially, but succeed in the end. We need to show ourselves and our children that we get it.

To help promote the book, Matlack brought on an advertising executive and social media expert, Lisa Hickey. Following the book launch, an online program, Good Men Media, was born with Lisa Hickey as CEO. She describes online program as "a multi-media, cross-platform content site and conversation asking the question, 'What does it mean to be a good man in the twenty-first century?'"

I was impressed with the idea of the program and the potential dialogue that could occur around the simple, yet profound, question, "What does it mean to be a good man in the twenty-first century?"

As someone who has been doing "men's work" for fifty years now, I can attest to the fact that The Good Men Project (GMP) is having the conversation that no one else is having, and the conversations are just the beginning.

- GMP is changing the conversation about men with a deeply engaged, passionate, articulate, and vibrant community.
- GMP has built a vast library of original, evergreen content written by more than 6,500 contributors—with new authors joining the conversation every day.
- GMP looks at the way men's roles are evolving in society.

The thing that is absolutely unique about GMP is that they are a "participatory media company." I've written literally thousands of articles for large web-based programs. GMP is the only media company where the CEO meets every Friday with writers and readers. Everyone is invited to hear the latest updates from Lisa Hickey and discuss ideas about important issues going on in the world.

"You already know GMP has been engaged in the conversation no one else is having," she told us at one of the Friday discussions. "Well, that conversation has been getting better and deeper and even more connected to actual social change. We have been rolling out 'Social Interest Groups'—groups of people who are coming together to discuss specific areas of interest. Each group has a weekly phone call, and then participants can stay in touch during the week in the Premium Member Facebook community and our Facebook Groups."

The other unique thing about GMP is that although the focus is on what it means to be a good man, they recognize that you can never separate men's issues from women's issues or discuss issues of sex and gender without looking at the broader challenges we all face in today's world.

One of the most important things I learned from being in a men's group and going through ritual rites of passage was that there were new, more expansive, options for being a man. In chapter 7, I will explore how we need to break free from the Man Box.

CHAPTER 7

BREAKING FREE FROM THE MAN BOX AND OVERCOMING OUR FEAR OF WOMEN

So, we "man up," hold it all in,
climb the ranks, compete
for more, take the brunt,
grunt, hide in the box where
we at least know the rules
and the roles, and rationalize
living in the cave of it because
our fathers and grandfathers
did the same.

—Cameron Conaway, from *The Man Box*

As I've described earlier, the dance of male and female has been going on for a billion years in our evolutionary history. There is a simple biological truth that can help us understand the mystery of the sexes. Here's a little mind game. We all know that every one of us had a mother and a father. Whether we grew up with both our biological parents or were separated from one or both, we all were conceived by a male and a female who came together. A sperm from the male was allowed in by the egg from the female, and we were born approximately nine months later.

Now let's extend our imagining. Our father also was conceived by a man and a woman. The same was true for our mothers. This biological reality goes all the way back through time. None of our direct ancestors died childless. Think what an absolute miracle that is. We all know people who have never had children, and one of you reading this book may go through life and never have a child. But that was not true for any of our direct ancestors.

If we know bit about our recent family tree, there may have been some excellent members and there may have been some disastrous members. Some may have been wise and caring. Others may have been wounding and abusive. But all of them did at least one thing well. They managed to find a mate, have sex, and have a baby.

So we know that there had to be some degree of cooperation involved (at least for most of our ancestors). Males and females needed each other not only to survive the challenges of life in a dangerous environment, but also to have a child together and keep the child alive to continue the process into future generations.

Yet, males and females faced different challenges. Remember the biological reality that males are the ones with lots of small sex cells (sperm) and females are the ones with a small number of larger sex cells (eggs). Since it takes more nutrients and energy to create an egg, biologically, eggs are more valuable than sperm. So, sperm must compete with each other to have access to the precious egg. Likewise, males must compete with each other for access to the female.

In the case of us mammals where conception occurs inside a woman's body and she must carry the growing embryo inside and face the dangers of childbirth, she is going to be much choosier about who she mates with. Males, who face fewer risks in getting a sperm to meet the egg, are biologically more capable of impregnating women, then look for another and therefore increase their chances of passing on more genes.

So the bottom-line truth is this: men and women are equally adept at finding a partner and also face different challenges that cause them to have conflict. We talk about the age-old "battle of the sexes." I think of it more like a dance where the goal is the same, but the steps each must take to be successful are different.

Understanding the Male Matrix

I have found that a lot of the conflict that men and women have with each other is due to misunderstanding the issues that the other is facing. Our misperceptions often lead to negative judgments. Here's an example from the world-famous primatologist Frans de Waal, who we met in chapter 5.

In his book *Different: Gender Through the Eyes of a Primatologist,* he shares this personal story:

> When hard workers—always men—arrive at our house to mow the lawn or do some landscaping, they address me instead of my wife, Catherine, even though both of us are standing side by side right in front of them. They feel more comfortable talking to me. They expect me to tell them what to do, not realizing that the garden is my wife's baby. She knows every little corner, while I am about as ornamental as an azalea bush. It doesn't take them long to figure out who's boss. Catherine will make an eyeroll.

I've had similar experiences when workmen come to my house. They assume I'm in charge, and often my wife, Carlin, and I will get into conflict when she feels disrespected and wants me to confront the workmen. I'm never sure what she wants me to do or how I should handle things. De Waal offers some interesting insights.

"Men ignore women in politics, at car dealerships, in hardware stores, and many other places. There are several explanations, including, of course, plain old misogyny and disrespect. Many men just can't imagine that women know anything about what they consider male jobs."

De Waal wall goes on to say, "But the problem goes deeper. Not all men are misogynous, and not all of them automatically dismiss women's experience. Men's selective attention often has less to do with women than with the presence of other men. We need to go to a more fundamental level of understand this response."

This whole book is my attempt to help us all go to a more fundamental level, to recognize our evolutionary history, so that men and women can understand ourselves and each other so we can all have better relationships with ourselves and each other.

"Like all animals," says de Waal, "we have different social and sexual agendas with our own sex than with the other one. We also have different fears. Thus a woman walking alone at night needs to quickly determine if a group of strangers in her path is all-male or mixed gender. The latter is much less worrisome."

De Waal continues and reminds us that "our gender radar is always turned on. It's an illusion to think that we adapt to modern society without his evolutionary baggage. Our social software was written millions of years ago. For men, this means keeping an eye on their fellows. Since male-to-male combat has always been part of primate history, including ours, we can't expect men to turn off their selective attention."

I know that is true for me. I realize I'm always sizing up other men, often subconsciously. Are they a threat or a potential ally? Can he hurt me or help me? Do I have to worry about him trying to take my woman away from me? Or do I imagine I have a lot more to offer his woman than he does and could take his woman away from him?

"To prepare for physical combat is an unconscious survival mechanism," says de Waal. "It absorbs male attention not just for negative reasons, having to do with risk, but also for positive ones, because the best way to avoid conflict is to get along and make friends. I'll call it the *male matrix*: males are part of an exclusive network that makes them automatically tune in to members of their own sex. I here use the term *matrix* the way we do in biology, to refer to connective tissue within which items (such as cells) are embedded."

Understanding the *male matrix* can help us understand why guys want to hang out with their buddies, why they often get into fights but make up quickly, why we seem to be ignoring our women or not taking their side in conflicts with our friends, and much more.

Breaking Free of the Man Box

A concept related to the male matrix is the Man Box. I think of the Man Box as the set of beliefs—partly biologically based, partly culturally based—that tell men who they are supposed to be. A colleague, psychologist Ann Neitlich, was the first person to recognize that the demands placed on men were the mirror image of the demands placed on women and vice versa. In her book *Building Bridges: Women's & Men's Liberation*, she says, "It has long been clear that women are oppressed by society with men carrying out that oppression. What has not been as clear is the societal oppression of men, with devastating effects on the lives of men (and women)."

She goes on to say, "The societal oppression of men leaves most men feeling less than fully male, never quite able to live up to the standard of a 'real man'; emotionally and physically numb; unable to deeply give and deeply receive love, to nurture, to be tender, and to pay good attention to others.... Women's and men's conditioning, while different, are opposite sides of the same coin."

Neitlich says that the qualities men are taught they *must be* are the exact qualities women are taught they *must not be* and vice versa. Men *Must Be* and Women *Must Not Be*:

- Economically powerful
- Physically strong
- Courageous
- Cool and stoic
- Protective
- Responsible
- Logical

- Active
- Aggressive
- Hairy
- Muscular
- Outspoken
- Rugged
- Tough

Men *Must Not Be* and Women *Must Be*:

- Gentle
- Nurturing
- Tender
- Feeling
- Domestic
- Beautiful
- Soft

- Passive
- Receptive
- Sweet
- Hairless
- Quiet
- Giving
- Apologetic

She concludes that "one must fulfill these societally determined requirements or pay the price of not being considered a 'real' man or woman."

Tony Porter is an author, educator, and activist working to advance social justice issues and chief executive officer of A Call to Men, which educates men all over the world on healthy, respectful manhood. His inspiring TED Talk describes the Man Box and how it harms women and men. Tony is the one who originated the simple term Man Box. His book *Breaking Out of the Man Box: The Next Generation of Manhood* guides men to free themselves and become the great men they were meant to be.

Man Box culture often demands that men be aggressive and violent. Ann Silvers is one of the few women I've met who recognize that women can be abusive as well. In her book *Abuse of Men by Women: It Happens, It Hurts, and It's Time to Get Real About It*, she says, "Abuse of men by women is an everyday occurrence. The examples are all around us. If we aren't seeing them, we aren't looking for them."

In reaction to the violence inherent in the Man Box culture, many men feel ashamed of being abused by a woman and often remain silent. "Until I witnessed a male friend being abused by his wife," says Silvers, "I was among the hordes that don't appreciate the amount of abuse men are experiencing from their female partners or the devastation that it creates."

Mark Greene, author of *The Little #MeToo Book for Men*, says, "Although the Man Box defines and enforces what is considered to be 'real manhood' women are as culpable as men in the policing and the enforcing of its harsh rules. When American men attempt to express masculinity in more diverse ways, it can often be the women in their lives who force them back into the Box. This can be due to fears of economic and social isolation or out of a refusal by those women to engage in the kind of self-reflective emotional discourses that exiting the Man Box can trigger."

Gary Barker, president and CEO of Promundo-US, led a study on the Man Box culture in the US, UK, and Mexico. The study says, "The Man Box refers to a set of beliefs, communicated by parents, families, the media, peers, and other members of society, that place pressure on men to be a certain way."

The study describes seven qualities that men must follow when they are trapped inside the Man Box, along with a number of messages that embody each quality.

1. **Self-Sufficiency**

   A man who talks a lot about his worries, fears, and problems shouldn't really get respect. Men should figure out their personal problems on their own without asking others for help.

2. **Acting Tough**

   A guy who doesn't fight back when others push him around is weak. Guys should act strong even if they feel scared or nervous inside.

3. **Physical Attractiveness**

   It is very hard for a man to be successful if he doesn't look good. However, women don't go for guys who fuss too much about their clothes, hair, and skin. A guy who spends a lot of time on his looks isn't very manly.

4. **Rigid Masculine Gender Roles**

   It is not good for a boy to be taught how to cook, sew, clean the house, and take care of younger children. A husband shouldn't have to do household chores. Men should really be the ones to bring money home to provide for their families, not women.

5. Heterosexuality and Homophobia

A gay guy is not a "real man." Straight guys who are friends with gay guys are suspected of being gay themselves.

6. Hypersexuality

A "real man" should have as many sexual partners as he can. A "real man" would never say no to sex.

7. Aggression and Control

Men should use violence to get respect, if necessary. A man should always have the final say about decisions in his relationship or marriage. If a guy has a girlfriend or wife, he deserves to know where she is all the time.

The study points out that fitting in with the prescribed roles can help a man feel good about himself, but being locked in the Man Box can also be destructive, particularly to a man's mental health. Those who subscribe to the Man Box beliefs:

- are three to six times more likely to make unwanted sexual comments to women.
- are three to seven times more likely to use physical violence.
- are twice as likely to have had suicidal thoughts in the last two weeks.
- are two to four times more likely to have refrained from doing something for fear of appearing "gay."

A follow-up study looked at the costs of the Man Box for society and found "the cost of the Man Box estimates a minimum cost of $20.9 billion that could be saved by the US, UK, and Mexican economies if there were no Man Box."

How do we break free from the Man Box? The first step is knowing that there is a Man Box. We also have to realize that men who can't fit themselves into the Man Box, like my father, suffer significant physical and emotional pain. Further, we have to recognize that even those who are adept at following the rules of the Man Box suffer as well. It's time for men to expand our understanding of what it means to be a man and what the benefits are of breaking free from the rigid requirements of the Man Box.

Taking an Honest Look at Misogyny: The Male Malady

My professional background is in biology and psychology. I've learned that most of the issues we face as humans are multidimensional and cross the lines of many professional disciplines. I've long believed that if we are going to understand and solve the problems we face, we need to seek out experts in many fields. That's how I came to meet David Gilmore.

I was attending an international men's conference, and David was one of the speakers. I liked his topic "Manhood in the Making: Cultural Concepts of Masculinity" and bought his book of the same title. He had studied cultures all over the world, and though he looked like a traditional academic with a tweed jacket and short hair, he had exciting new things to say about why men are the way they are.

I reconnected with him when his book, *Misogyny: The Male Malady*, was published. I thought if anyone could give me insights into male anger toward women, David was the one. The dictionary defines misogyny as "the dislike of, contempt for, or ingrained prejudice against women." Gilmore offers a broader definition in his book:

He describes misogyny as "an unreasonable fear or hatred of women." He goes on to say that "this feeling finds social expression in the concrete behavior—in cultural institutions, in writings, in rituals, or in other observable activity."

His research is impeccable and his discoveries challenging. Gilmore explored cultures from Western Europe to the Middle East, from the jungles of South America to the remote uplands of New Guinea, from preliterate tribal peoples to modern Americans. He looks at ancient and modern cultures and all those in between. He finds that in all places around the world, there has been a tendency for men to fear and hate women.

I'm always interested in the personal perspective when looking at issues. We rarely get them in books written by professional scientists, and I was glad David shared some of his personal story about his interest in the topic.

He says, "Since I am a man writing a book about man's inhumanity toward woman, I feel I should explain my motives, if only by way of exculpation. Like most baby-boom males, I consider myself a tolerant and enlightened man, and I harbor sincere fondness for women as friends, lovers, colleagues, workmates, and of course, paragons of physical beauty."

That sounds like me and most men I know. He goes on to say, "However, I do recognize occasional negative stirrings in myself, feelings that certainly exist in most of my male friends whether they will admit it or not: these include impatience, peevishness, a tendency to scapegoat females, ancient, uncontrolled impulses (usually erotic), frustrations in trying to communicate, and anger over inherent differences."

These, too, resonated with my own experiences. But I was surprised and dismayed at the near universal findings of misogyny in men from cultures throughout the world and through time. Even the males in surviving hunter-gatherer cultures seem to exhibit this disturbing trait of misogyny. A quick summary of his findings, reported in his well-documented book, include the following:

- One of the last-surviving hunter-gatherer tribes live in the highlands of New Guinea in the South Pacific. "These men believe not only that women are inferior to men, but that women are also polluting to men, sexually dangerous to men's health. The men declare that women's monthly menstrual flow in particular is the most powerful and deadly poison on earth; one drop is absolutely lethal to men, boys, and male animals."
- The ancient Greeks often displayed a fierce misogyny, putting woman in the category of the God-given ills. Poets charged that women were the original source of kakon, or evil, in the world, which was created by the gods to torture men. The ancients populated their cosmos with she-demons

and sorceresses such as Pandora, who brought all trouble into the world, and the sinister island-dwelling Circe, a witch who turned men into pigs.

- Gentle Yurok Indians of northwestern California, like the Greeks, speak of "a woman's inside," the vagina and uterus, as the doorway through which sin and social disorder entered the world.

- The Christian Bible, the Muslim Qur'an, the Hebrew Torah, and Buddhist and Hindu scriptures condemn woman, not only for her spiritual defects, but also for her body, which they deride in the crudest terms. All these great religions blame woman for the lust, licentiousness, and depravity that men are prone to, and for committing the original sin or its theological equivalent. Weak and gullible, it is Eve, like Pandora, who introduces sin and sorrow into the world.

Lest we think that misogyny is merely an unfortunate part of our past, we need only listen to the women who have come forward under the banner of the #MeToo movement to recognize that sexual violence continues to pervade the US as well as countries throughout the world.

As I report these findings, I realize I have resistance to believing them, even though the research is solidly based and the facts are clear. I want to believe men are better than this. Humans are better than this. I am better than this. Clearly not all men engage in these practices, just as all men growing up in the slaveholding South were not racist. But the facts do show that there is a part of the male experience throughout the world that is both fearful and angry toward women.

The Other Side of the Coin: Gynophilia and Men's Worship of Women

No men I know want to feel that they "hate women." And most of us don't. When I wrote my book, *Mr. Mean: Saving Your Relationship from the Irritable Male Syndrome*, a number of my colleagues in the men's movement wrote me off. "You're demeaning men," they told me. "It's unfair, reverse sexism." But I felt that getting at the truth is not demeaning. It can be difficult, but in the long run it helps us all.

I've learned that denying the truth just causes additional pain and suffering. Whether you are male or female reading these words, notice how you are feeling inside. What do the examples of misogyny bring up in you? Do you want to dismiss them or embrace them? Do you want to run away or go deeper?

Jamie Buckingham said, "The truth will set you free, but first it will make you miserable." Gloria Steinem voiced a similar thought when she said, "The truth will set you free, but first it will piss you off." I've often said, "The truth will set you free, but first it will kick your ass."

There's another truth that I think we need to understand and recognize. Just as there are societies, and men within societies, who both fear and denigrate women, there are also groups and individuals who view women in a very positive light. They almost worship women, feeling they are goddesses and can do no wrong. I've seen that tendency in many male clients I've seen over the years.

I was surprised to learn that David Gilmore's research was clear. The same societies that denigrate and put women down also worship and elevate them. Gilmore has a whole chapter in his book describing the opposite of misogyny which he calls gynophilia. He says, "Like so much having to do with men and women, misogyny is only one piece of the puzzle. To be sure, many men hate and fear women, but just as many love and revere them. It is obvious that two edges of this mental sword are related in some labile fashion and share origins in the ancient touchstone of the primitive male cerebellum."

He suggests that both ends of the spectrum, hate and fear/ love and reverence, drive us up and down, back and forth. They frustrate and confuse us. I would add that they can drive us crazy. Gilmore describes our human dilemma this way:

Woman has the uncanny power to frustrate man's noble (but unrealistic) ideals, to subvert his lofty (hollow) ends, and to sully his (deluded) quest for spiritual perfection; but she also, and not coincidentally, provides him with the greatest pleasures of his earthly life. These pleasures are not just sexual release, but also other life-sustaining comforts that only a woman can provide (based on the organization of most societies): food, tenderness, nurturing, and heirs. It is not surprising that the men who most deplore and distrust women are the same ones who most admire, want, and need them; the most histrionic and poignant rituals of woman-adulation occur in the same societies responsible for the most egregious and sordid examples of woman-bashing.

He concludes by saying, "Like misogyny, gynophilia is kind of male neurosis, for it stems from the same unresolved conflicts and it has both a carnal and spiritual manifestation with the usual repetitive rituals and inventive folklore."

Male Ambivalence and Our Love/ Hate Obsession with Woman

One of the things I've learned over the last seventy-five years is that life is tough, and a primary reason is that relationships are tough. As I've said, I was married twice and divorced twice before I met my present wife, Carlin. We've been married, now, for nearly forty years. It hasn't always been easy, even with all I have learned about how to have a great relationship.

There was a time when I wasn't sure we were going to make it. I sought out a psychotherapist and did sessions individually and together as a couple. After one of the early sessions, in a letter to the doctor, she described the roller coaster of ups and downs that were undermining our marriage:

Dear Dr. Lacy,

The thing that is most difficult for me is Jed's rapid mood changes. He gets angry, accusing, argumentative and blaming one moment, and the next he is buying me flowers, cards and sends me loving notes with smiles and enthusiasm. He gets irritable, angry, and red in the face, demands that we talk; then he cuts me off when he judges I have said something offensive to him.

I feel like I'm living with Dr. Jekyll and Mr. Hyde. Everything seems nice and he shows me how much he loves me. Then it can change in an instant and it's like I'm living with a monster. I get frozen, feeling that no matter what I do or say, it will be "wrong" for him. At this point, he becomes competitive and I feel that he needs to win something. His intensity and the coldness in his eyes scare me at these times. I usually shut down and try to protect myself and it takes a lot of time for me to return to being loving and open with him.

When we began counseling, I acknowledged my anger, but I felt justified. In my mind she was going out of her way to provoke me. "Who wouldn't get angry when someone hits you in the head with a two-by-four," I would scream. Carlin would look at me in surprise. "I've been nothing but loving towards you until your anger blows up on me and then I withdraw to protect myself."

But even after our successful therapy and getting our relationship back on track, I observed a strange phenomenon going on inside me. At times I felt Carlin was wonderful, everything I could ever want in a partner. But then it was like a dark cloud would come over me and she seemed to change. One minute I was in bed with my friend and lover. But then, in a blink of an eye, I found myself in bed with a stranger who wanted to harm me.

It was crazy making. I knew nothing had changed. We hadn't had a fight. She hadn't withdrawn, but it was as though a switch was thrown in my brain and instead of a goddess, I was in bed with a wicked witch. I couldn't understand what was happening. It was like those perceptual illusions I learned about in my college psychology class.

From one perspective, we see a pretty woman with a red neckband looking away from us. Then the picture "flips" and we see an old hag with red lips and a big nose. That's how it felt when my mind would flip from seeing my wife change from Ms. Wonderful to the Wicked Witch of the West.

Males Feel Engulfed by WOMAN

Sam Keen is a philosopher and author of numerous books including *Fire in the Belly: On Being a Man.* I've known Sam for many years and believe he offers insights into why men are the way they are that can help us better understand men's hunger for women, along with our anger and fear.

"It was slow in dawning on me that WOMAN had an overwhelming influence on my life and on the lives of all the men I knew," Keen says. "I'm not talking about women, the actual flesh-and-blood creatures, but about WOMEN, those larger-than-life shadowy female figures who inhabit our imaginations, inform our emotions, and indirectly give shape to many of our actions."

If you knew Sam, who is tall, good-looking, and successful, you might be as surprised as I was when he shared the deeper truth about his life. "From all outward appearances, I was a successfully individuated man. I had set my career course early, doggedly stuck to the discipline of graduate school through many years and degrees, and by my mid-thirties was vigorously pursuing the life of a professor and writer. Like most men, I was devoting most of my energy and attention to work and profession."

I could definitely identify with Keen's early experience. My own life trajectory was similar as was "the rest of the story." Keen continues saying, "But if the text of my life was 'successful independent man,' the subtext was 'engulfed by WOMAN.' All the while I was advancing in my profession, I was engaged in an endless struggle to find the 'right' woman, to make my relationship 'work,' to create a good marriage. I agonized over sex—was I good enough? Did she 'come'? Why wasn't I always potent? What should I do about my desires for other women? The more troubled my marriage became, the harder I tried to get it right. I worked at communication, sex, and everything else until I became self-obsessed. Divorce finally broke the symbiotic mother-son, father-daughter pattern of my first marriage."

Sam's story is like my own and that of millions of men. When we are engulfed by WOMAN, we are out of touch with our true selves. We project all our hopes for a life of passion, joy, and meaning on to this or that woman, but it never works out because we are really longing for the mythical WOMAN of our dreams. Yet, we continually deny the reality and the power that this mythical female figure exerts in our lives.

"I would guess," says Keen, "that a majority of men never break free, never define manhood by weighing and testing their own experience. And the single largest reason is that we never acknowledge the primal power WOMAN wields over us. The average man spends a lifetime denying, defending against, trying to control, and reacting to the power of WOMAN. He is committed to remaining unconscious and out of touch with his own deepest feelings and experience."

It took a long time for me to understand my anger and fear of women and to begin the journey of becoming my own man. Sam's experiences and his words have helped me. "We begin to learn the mysteries unique to maleness only when we separate from WOMAN's world," says Keen. "But before we can take our leave, we must first become conscious of the ways in which we are enmeshed, incorporated, inwombed, and defined by WOMAN. Otherwise we will be controlled by what we haven't remembered."

As long as we are controlled by what we haven't remembered, we will continue to hate and love women, to hunger for them and also be afraid of them, to touch them tenderly and also want to hurt them.

I took my first step in remembering in a workshop for men and women. In one of the exercises, all the women sat on the floor in a big circle and the women sat in a large circle around the outside of the women's circle. The men listened while the women talked about their lives, their desire for love, and also their fears. I was amazed at the depth of the women's sharing when they were just talking to other women.

When the women had finished, they were instructed to move out and let the men create the inner circle. As the women moved to the outside the woman in front of me patted the spot on the rug where she had been sitting. It was a caring gesture, a nonverbal invitation: welcome, come have a seat here and share your story. I smiled at sat where she had invited me. Immediately I moved aside. It was as though I had sat on a hotplate, and I quickly jumped away. She looked surprised and patted the spot again, again with no word, but the intent was clear: it's OK, have a seat. You're safe here. Once again, I sat where she had offered and again felt like I couldn't sit there, moved to another spot, and burst into tears.

All this happened during the thirty seconds it took for the women to move to the outer circle and the men to move to the inner circle. "Nothing" had happened. Yet, here was a guy sitting in a circle with thirty other men weeping. The leader finally noticed that "something" had happened. "So, what's going on for you?" he asked.

It took me awhile to gather my thoughts. I described the woman's kind gesture of offering me the seat she had vacated, then continued, "by sitting on the spot where she had offered, I realized that I was doing something I had done all my life. I felt I was always trying to plug into the energy of a woman. I always acted strong and independent, but deep inside, I felt I didn't have any independent energy of my own. But in this instance, I knew I couldn't sit there, and I moved. It was terrifying to be in a new spot, to be unplugged from the force field of the woman. I was afraid I would die. When she offered the spot again, I immediately sat there, but just couldn't do it.

"The final move to my own spot was a recognition that I have to separate myself from the force field of the woman, even if it kills me. I'm not sure if I have what it takes to be my own man, but I've got to find out. My tears are about the fear and terror I feel being all alone with myself and also tears of joy for finally making the break." I soon realized I was not alone and that telling my truth in the company of other men was the first step toward manhood.

When I looked up and saw that many of the women had tears running down their cheeks, I knew that this journey to becoming my own man was one that women were coming to understand, love, and support.

Throughout Human History, Most Males Lost Out in the Competition to Be Chosen

In chapter 4, we learned about Baumeister's "most unappreciated fact about men," that throughout human history, perhaps 80 percent of women, but only 40 percent of men, reproduced. Before there was birth control, that meant that there were some males who dominated the field and had sex with many women and some men who never had sex.

"Most men who ever lived have been genetically erased from the human population," says Dr. Baumeister. "The men who didn't care about outdoing other men, who were content to take it easy and go along easily and let others push ahead (the way many women are content)—those guys did not reproduce. The men who pushed ahead were more likely to reproduce, and today's men are descended from them. To leave offspring, you had to outdo other men."

You might conclude that since we were all descended from the winners in the genetic lottery, we would all feel confident and not worried about finding a woman who would want us. But that isn't the case. Even the alpha males who got more than their share of women always had to worry that they would be replaced by younger, stronger, more aggressive, and more attractive males and that they would be cast aside.

Whether we are aware of it or not, men have a subconscious resentment toward women. *Why do women get to choose whom they accept? Why do we have to be the ones who are always competing for their attention and can never rest?* There is another subconscious resentment we feel. Since conception occurs inside a woman's body, she is 100 percent certain that any child she bears carries her genetic heritage. Males, no matter how certain his woman is faithful and any child born is his own, can never be as sure as the female. Hence the summary phrase: *mother's baby, father's maybe!*

Sneaky Fuckers, Crazy Bastards, and Incels: The Fear Extreme of Men's Universal Fear

We know that humans aren't the only species in which some males get more than 50 percent of the available females and many don't reproduce at all. Think of elephant seals, gorillas, and wild stallions—a few males dominate the other males and have sexual access to many females. If you're not the alpha male, you run the risk of having no sex at all. What's a male to do?

The term "sneaky fuckers" was coined by evolutionary biologist John Maynard Smith to describe subordinate males who take advantage of the opportunity to mate with females while dominant males are otherwise occupied. Recently, a team of anthropologists at UCLA led by Dan Fessler coined the term "Crazy Bastards" to describe males who engage in risky, daredevil behavior that may even put their lives at risk.

Until recently, I had never heard the term incel. Incel stands for "involuntary celibate," a man who cannot have sex with anyone because nobody will have sex with him. The world of Incels has come out of the shadows recently. Dr. Tim Squirrell is a researcher studying social interaction in online communities. "Incels have been on my radar for a while," he says. "Misogyny is easy to find on the internet, and there's no shortage of men willing to tell women that they have it worse. But while misogyny is inherently violent, the ideology Incels subscribe to is almost unique in the way it makes violence seem like the only solution."

The rise of the incel culture is a good example of how certain aspects of human nature can either be modified or enhanced. In recent years, we have become more aware of the large number of men, often white men in power, who feel entitled to sexually harass or abuse women. The #MeToo movement has brought these aspects of misogyny out of the closet, and more and more people are saying,

"No! No more rape, no more sexual harassment, no more domination and abuse."

Squirrell says Incels believe that "women are hard-wired to seek out men who happen to be genetically blessed and they will never consider men who do not conform to societal standards of masculinity." Because they believe this will never change, that the birth lottery has condemned them to never be loved, many of them are extremely depressed and resigned to a life of solitude and self-loathing.

They are also extremely angry at women and voice their rage in online groups. "In their more explicit posts," says Squirrell, "some Incels dream of enslaving women and forcing them to have sex with them, and murdering the other males who have been on top for far too long. There have been a number of mass murders by men who identify with Incel. Elliot Rodger, a 22-year old from California who carried out the 2014 Isla Vista massacre, was supposedly part of the Incel movement. In April, 2018, Alek Minassian was charged with ten counts of murder and fourteen counts of attempted murder after driving a van into pedestrians in Toronto. According to police the dead and wounded were predominantly women. Minassian's Facebook post praised Elliott Rodger."

Males who are involuntarily celibate have been around forever. Whether you are a low-ranking stallion, elephant seal, gorilla, or man, you run the risk of not being able to find a female who will want you. Females ultimately choose the males they want. For many males, the pain and suffering that results from feeling like a loser in the mating game can cause them to become self-loathing and hateful toward women.

Fortunately, modern humans are more monogamous than our ancestors. Most males today can find a female who will want to have sex with him. But Incels remind us that there are still men who feel left out, who don't feel there are any females who will want them, who feel ashamed, immobilized, depressed, and angry. It's unlikely that there will be a movement of females who are angry because they are involuntarily celibate. Though there certainly are females who can't find a sexual partner, most females who want sex can find a willing partner.

Warriors and Worriers, Learning to Duel and Duet

Joyce Benenson is a professor of psychology at Emmanuel College in Boston and an associate member of the Human Evolutionary Biology department at Harvard University.

In her groundbreaking book *Warriors and Worriers: The Survival of the Sexes*, she offers new insights about men and women and offers important information based on evolutionary science. She says, "For thousands of years, human females and males have faced different sorts of major problems and found different types of solutions. Women have taken primary responsibility for the long-term survival of vulnerable children. In contrast, around the world, men have taken primary responsibility for fighting wars."

As a result of these different evolutionary challenges, she concludes the following:

At essence men are *warriors* and at essence women are *worriers*.

I'm aware that a few lines of summary can trigger a negative reaction in some people. Yet, I find Benenson's research findings compelling. This does not mean that *all* men are violent or that *all* women worry about the survival of themselves and their children. It does help us better understand our gender-specific tendencies that have evolved through our evolutionary history.

Although many modern men, including myself, would like to see ourselves as "peaceful warriors," the truth is that males have evolved to fight other males. "What makes men unique compared with other species," says Benenson, "is that they like to fight and compete as a group. No example demonstrates this better than war. Unlike most other species, men band together in solidarity to risk their lives to defeat another group. For many thousands of years, human males have engaged in intergroup warfare."

These male behaviors make sense if we think about them in evolutionary terms. "Engaging in physical battle against another group would endanger the lives of everyone in the community," says Benenson. "No one's genes would survive this. The problem can best be solved by delegating fighting the enemy to one specific group: young men. Women can then protect themselves and their children. Older men can supervise from a distance. Young men should fight the enemy in a location as far away as possible from everyone else."

So, for the maximum benefit of all, women and men assume different roles. Women's first job is to take care of themselves. If they die, their children likely die. Then they must take care of the kids. Hence, it's good if they think of all possible dangers. In other words, they worry about everything. Males fight other males in order to protect the women and children. From an early age, males practice being warriors.

Benenson concludes, "We are not conscious of being warriors or worriers. Rather, being a warrior or a worrier is like having a special program continually running in the background of your mind." We are not prisoners of our evolutionary past. War is not inevitable, and societies can learn more peaceful ways to solve problems. We can do everything we can to create a society in which peaceful warriors can flourish, and at the same time we can recognize that there are still times when men will be called to battle.

Not only does our evolutionary history create warriors and worriers, it also creates communication patterns where *males duel* and *females duet.*

The different ways men and women have evolved show themselves in the ways we communicate. We all notice that men talk differently from women. Male talk and female talk aren't always obvious since when men talk to women and women talk to men, we have to accommodate each other's natural mode of talking. When I'm with my male friends, I notice that communication is shorter and has an element of friendly put downs, like when I talk to my friend Lanny about playing racquetball:

Lanny: Hey, want to play today?

Me: Sure, what time?

Lanny: Let's do one o'clock.

Me: Be there. Be prepared to have your butt whupped.

Lanny: In your dreams, little man.

Me: You've been warned.

Lanny: Bye.

Me: Bye.

If I were to write out the dialogue when my wife talks to her women friends about setting a time to meet, it would take three pages. They would talk about feelings. How other friends were doing. The recipe for the lasagna dinner they were planning to make, and so on. When I overhear a conversation like that, I think to myself, *Jesus, when is she going to get to the point?*

John L. Locke is a professor of linguistics at City University of New York. In his book *Duels and Duets: Why Men and Women Talk So Differently,* he clearly describes the way our evolution-based communication patterns have evolved into the ways men and women talk. He says, "The more dramatic differences that occur when men talk with men, and women with women, are not the 'gendered' effects of modern culture but the 'sexed' expression of ancient biological dispositions. These dispositions are as different as they are because ancestral men and women competed for the things they need in two fundamentally different ways."

Drawing on animal studies, Locke notes that "in birds and mammals, including the other primates, sexually mature males are prone to contend with each other in highly public vocal displays that are aggressive or 'agonistic' in nature. We may think of these engagements as 'duels.' In many primate species, sexually mature females have an equally strong disposition to affiliate with other females, in more private and intimate circumstances, by engaging them in subdued vocal interactions. I refer to these interactions as 'duets.'"

Locke summarizes the research on male communication. Males are more likely than females to:

1. Interrupt each other.
2. Issue commands, threats, and boasts.
3. Resist each other's demands.
4. Give information.
5. Heckle.
6. Tell jokes or suspenseful stories.
7. Try to top another's story.
8. Insult or denigrate each other.

By contrast, research indicates that females in same-sex groups are more likely than males to:

1. Agree with other speakers.
2. Yield to other speakers.
3. Acknowledge points made by other speakers.
4. Be polite.
5. Cooperate and collaborate.

Locke concludes by saying, "There is also a rule that applies to female groups: **Do what it takes to preserve group harmony.** This rule underlies the female tendencies enumerated above. In the case of males, the corresponding rule would be: **Do what is necessary to be seen as the most wonderful anything**—from strong and knowledgeable to brave and resourceful—whether that means building yourself up or tearing everyone else down." (Emphasis added)

Our language reflects our survival and reproductive needs that were different for males and females throughout our evolutionary history. Why do guys interrupt each other, issue commands, threats, boasts? Why do we tell long, elaborate stories and try and top each other's stories? Why do we playfully insult each other?

I would suggest that we are playing out our Warrior spirits. On the one hand, we are trying to outshine our male competitors so that females who are watching us will choose us, not the other guys. We are also showing the other men present that we are fighters. Given our evolutionary need to protect our tribe, we look for other guys who we can count on to stand with us if we were being attacked by other men.

In men's groups, I've had guys tell me that I can't really trust you until we've had a few fights and know where you stand. Guys can be fighting one minute, but when there is external danger, they come together as a fighting force. We are always taking the measure of other men, and so ritual conflict, including verbal duels, are ways in which we attract women and also serve to help us check out other men to see who we can trust.

The main reason men and women have such difficulty communicating is that we assume we are speaking the same language. Yet, men and women speak two very different languages that are built into our biology. We can learn to communicate in ways that are used by the other sex, but before we can do that, we have to understand why our different languages evolved in the first place.

Behavior and language continually evolve to fit our life circumstances. Yet, it's likely that male and female differences will persist, and rather than seeing these differences as fueling the battle of the sexes, accepting our differences can bring us together. "I have come to believe," says Locke, "that biologically supported sex differences in verbal behavior increase the benefits of collaboration in modern life, much as they once conspired, in antiquity, to broaden the foundation for human language."

CHAPTER 8

LEARNING THE SECRETS OF REAL LASTING LOVE

Why will the work on your marriage be challenging? Not only is the person you're married to like your parents, but the two of you are also incompatible. It's as if there is a universal design and, mysteriously, our incompatibility seems to be a key piece of the plan. Incompatibility plays a crucial role in preparing you and your partner to meet each other's needs.

—Harville Hendrix, PhD

Healing men and mankind must involve healing our relationships. For a good deal of my life, I thought of love as something that was really women's business. My part of the love story was to find the right woman, fall in love, and try to convince her I was loveable despite being short, large-eared, and big-nosed and feeling awkward and inept around women. I thought nature would just take its course. Once I found the right partner, my one and only, my dream lover, my soul partner, I looked forward to living happily ever after.

But things didn't work out that way. After two failed marriages, I was confused and depressed and had questions that I hoped could be answered:

- How can things start out good in a marriage and then turn bad?

- If our first models for love are inadequate, is it really possible to have a good relationship as an adult?
- If we're meant to find our one true love, what happens when we think we've found them and it doesn't work out?
- How do you find the courage to try again when you've failed before?
- What if all this "love and marriage" stuff just doesn't work in today's world? Should I just settle for finding a "friend with benefits"?
- Is there really such thing as real lasting love?
- What's getting in the way of finding my soul partner?

It's more than embarrassing to be a successful marriage and family counselor who can help others but seems to be making a mess of his own love life. After much resistance, I finally went into therapy myself, and being a reader, I went through every book I could find that might help me find some answers. It took some time, but I finally found what I was looking for, and Carlin and I have been together now for forty-three years.

Here are some of the important steps we took on our journey that may help you:

1. Get clear about what you really want and what you won't tolerate.

    I assumed that when the right person came along, I'd know it and I just had to wait for Ms. Right to appear in my life. Like in the old songs I grew up with, I'd find her—on some enchanted evening you may see a stranger across a crowded room and somehow you know that she is the one.

    I had to let go of my romantic-movie approach to love and get real. I sat down and wrote out all the things I wanted in a partner and all the things I knew I could tolerate. The list was many pages long and I won't bore you with the details, but getting clear was the first step to finding my perfect partner.

2. Make relationship a priority.

I had a good job and loved to work. It fulfilled me and gave me my purpose in life. But I realized I had to make relationship a priority if I was going to have one. I had to make "finding my dream partner" as important as "finding my dream job." In our stressed-out, hustle-bustle world, we often long for a relationship but never put the time and effort into finding one or keeping it alive and well once we've found one.

3. Surface your negativity.

Before meeting Carlin, I would have said, "I want to have a partner to share my life with," but I realized I had a lot of negative baggage that got in the way of having the relationship I truly wanted. I spent time looking deeply and surfacing the negative messages I was telling myself:

- I don't want to get burned again.
- I don't have time for all this dating crap.
- The woman I want doesn't exist.
- Even if I found her, she wouldn't want me.
- I can't imagine committing to having sex with only one woman for the rest of my life.
- Marriage just doesn't work for me.
- And three more pages I won't bore you with here.

But it's important to get the negativity out where you can see it. Otherwise it stays hidden and undermines everything you do.

4. Recognize that there are many perfect partners waiting for you.

Most of us grew up with the romantic notion that there is a "one and only" just for us. It's nice to think there is a perfect soul partner just waiting for you. However, the notion has unforeseen drawbacks. It creates an underlying fear that we'll never find the right person, that needle in the haystack, who is waiting for us, but like the mythical unicorn, doesn't really exist.

It also creates a tendency to move on to someone else rather than getting to know someone well. Even when we find someone, we second guess ourselves. Maybe this isn't the one. I'd better keep looking.

The truth is there are many potential soul mates. Don't get hung up thinking there is only one. That thinking works in romantic movies but is deadly for finding your soul mate in real life.

5. Become aware of your distorted love filter.

Although I had a list of the qualities I wanted in a partner, I realized I also had a subconscious filter that drew me toward certain kinds of women who weren't right for me and away from others who were. I realized I was drawn to fiery women who were risk takers but were disasters to live with. My ex-wife was like that. Shortly after we met, I found that she slept with a loaded gun under her pillow. I should have run like hell. Instead, we had a passionate, crazy year together and got married even though we nearly killed each other with our fights. I also excluded women who were nice and loving but seemed a bit boring when I first met them.

Cleaning up our filter so that we aren't subconsciously excluding partners who might be right for us and getting hooked on those who are disasters can keep you on the right track.

6. Reflect on and heal your past relationships.

We all have issues from the past that keep us from finding and holding on to our soul mate. Many of us have been married before or had serious relationships that didn't last. We all grew up in families, most of which were less than good models for soul mate love. All our previous relationships can cause distortions that keep us from finding and keeping our

soul mates. Yet, understanding and healing our past relationships helps us find the person we're destined to be with
now.

In fact, one of the hidden reasons we pick the partner we
pick is to heal wounds from the past. However, if we don't
recognize the issues from our previous relationships, including how we were influenced by our mother's and father's
relationships with us and with each other, we will find ourselves looking for love in all the wrong places.

7. Recognize the evolutionary magnets that draw you to some
and away from others.

Even though Carlin had all the qualities I wanted, the
"chemistry" just didn't feel right. When we met, she seemed
nice, but there wasn't the pizzazz I was used to having. Well,
it turns out pizzazz is another name for the evolutionary-
based magnets that are built into our brains to perpetuate
the species, not help us find our soul mates.

First, she was five years older than me. *No big deal,* my
conscious mind thought, but evolution pulls us toward youth
and beauty. Second, she was slightly taller than me. Again,
she scored twenty out of twenty on my list of wants and zero
for ten on the can't tolerate list. But something just didn't
feel right when we were together.

Often the evolutionary pulls toward that certain evolutionarily valuable mate can blind us to someone who is just
right for us. It's good to remember that the evolutionary
drives are not to make us happy but to bring about the success of our genes. Too many women will exclude a man who
isn't "tall, dark, and handsome." Too many men will exclude
a woman who isn't "short, sexy, and slim."

Yet, we hung in there with each other, talked about our
discomforts, and soon sparks were flying, and we both knew
we were with the right one, evolution be damned. Both of
us nearly walked away from a relationship that continues to

get better through time. Don't miss out on the perfect mate because the chemistry isn't there at first.

8. Committing to *us* is more important than committing to *you* or *me*.

As our relationship deepened and our love drew us to each other, we talked about getting married. Since we'd both been married twice before, we were hopeful that the "third time is the charm." But we were realistic adults and we had understandable anxiety about commitment. We both had made vows in our previous marriages about loving, honoring, and so on until death do us part. But that hadn't happened.

We were both still very much alive, and we had both gotten divorced twice. In one of our intimate conversations, I asked Carlin, "Can you really commit to me?" I felt sure that the answer was yes, but I felt I had to ask. To my surprise she said, "I can't commit to you, but I can commit to us."

I was startled and taken aback. At first, I felt hurt and afraid. All I heard is that I can't commit to *you*. But as we talked more and I sat with what we said, I realized the wisdom of what she was telling me. There are three entities in a relationship. There's *me*, *you*, and *us*. *Us* holds the best of who we are, both as individuals and as a partnership.

We had both experienced what happens when our individual selves feel hurt or wounded and how that can lead to conflict and eventually to distancing and, in our case, divorce. But a commitment to us brings in a higher power, a willingness to think beyond our separate needs to the needs of us as a couple. That larger commitment has served us well over the years.

I believe family therapist Terrence Real has a similar perspective. In his book *US: Getting Past You & Me to Build a More Loving Relationship*, he says, "*Us* consciousness says, 'We're in this together.' *You and me* consciousness says, 'Every man for himself.'"

Reflection: Think about the eight steps listed above. Which ones do you resonate with? Which ones are you doing? Which ones would you like to engage more fully?

Going Slow and Taking Your Time to Enjoy All the Steps for a Great Relationship

We all live in a world where everything is moving fast. People make quick decisions about whether someone is right for them. One of my clients, forty-six-year-old Josh, told me, "I met Cynthia at a party. We really hit it off and things went really fast. We went on a few dates, and it seemed we were meant to be together. We got married a month later. But, once we began living together, things started to go downhill. There were things about her that I didn't know. She had been abused as a child but had never dealt with the trauma and it totally messed up our sex life. She wouldn't go to therapy, and we eventually broke up."

If Josh had gone slower and followed my "take your time" approach, he would have likely found out more about Cynthia before getting married. He could have helped her get the help she needed or recognized that she wasn't the one.

These seven practices also can help a couple who are already together. I suggested them to Robert and Sue after they had been together for eighteen years and wanted to revitalize their relationship. "It really worked," Robert told me. "At first, I thought your suggestion of going back to earlier stages and imagining that we were meeting for the first time was crazy. But you were right, it actually helped us get back in touch with the romance that we had lost touch with over the years."

I've found these seven practices helpful for those just starting out with a new relationship as well as those who have been together and want to revitalize a long-term marriage.

Practice 1: Acquaintanceship

The practice of acquaintanceship allows us to recognize that each person we meet is a gift from the universe. We see each person as a jewel to be appreciated without thought of whether they would be useful to us, or if they are marriage material, or if they might be good in bed. Instead of screening out everyone except those few we think have "potential," we enjoy each person we meet simply because they are a fellow human being.

I had a friend in college named Jeannie. She had the capacity to see everyone she met as a wonder. When you were in Jeannie's presence, you felt like you were special, and Jeannie was overjoyed to be with you. Everyone she encountered felt bathed in the light of her attention. I still have memories of that gift of true acquaintanceship and try to practice it in my life.

Practice 2: Companionship

Companionship is about doing what you love to do in the presence of another person. Clients often tell me they go to places to meet people. Yet when I ask them if they enjoy the places they go and things they do, they acknowledge that they don't. "I hate going to bars," one woman told me, "but that's where I have to go to meet people." I suggest people do things they love and meet people there. It might be a book club, bird watching, or motorcycle racing. As long as you really enjoy it and there are other people there, you can begin practicing companionship.

If you want to see someone who truly understands companionship, watch a three-year-old playing in the sandbox with other children. The child is ecstatic to be alive, to play in the sand, and to be with other children having fun together. Take one child out and replace him with another, and that's fine.

When we fully engage companionship, we are fully present in the moment, enjoying doing what we love surrounded by others who are doing the same. Companionship allows us the joy of playful connection.

Companionship, like the other steps in the process, offers a double benefit. We get to enjoy each step for itself. If things don't progress further, we still have the joy of having had fun with other people doing something we love to do. Second, we get to know people before we open bodies, hearts, and souls.

Enjoying each practice before jumping ahead gives us time to reflect and see if it's a person we want to go to the next stage with. Some people just enjoy having a companion without having to go further in the relationship. Those in a long-term relationship can get back to the simple joy of finding fun things to do together.

Men often benefit from practicing companionship. We're often so busy *doing* that we don't just enjoy the present moment of being together.

Practice 3: Friendship

The practice of friendship combines being and doing. It is an interaction between two people who want to practice being themselves by doing things together with a partner. Where companionship can be done with a number of partners, the stage of friendship comes in pairs. It taps into the "power of two."

Friendship develops as we learn more about the other person and find out what we have in common. We get to know them. We learn what they like, what books they have read, what's important in their lives, and who are the people important to them.

We often think of friendship as a process of doing for the other person or having them do for us. It is really a process of getting to know another person and caring about what they are feeling. In friendship, we draw each other out. We care about who they are and how they are feeling and share more and more about who we are and what emotions are present in us.

Practice 4: Intimate Friendship

The practice of intimate friendship involves exploring the underworld. We begin to recognize in the other person things about ourselves we don't see or don't like. We may be drawn to another's warmth and ease, thinking we are more stiff and awkward. In truth, we often see in the other person qualities that are there in us but haven't been developed. We also begin to see things about the other person we don't like, which are often qualities that we don't like in ourselves.

The practice of intimate friendship allows us to reclaim lost parts of ourselves—to re-own our rage, terror, guilt, and shame and also to reclaim our ability to appreciate, accept, nurture, and love ourselves. Intimate friendship is about learning to love, heal, and accept the parts of ourselves we have rejected.

This can be a time of deep connection. It can also feel very uncomfortable. Many people bail out at this stage. I encourage people to hang in there and go deeper. The stage of intimate friendship holds up a mirror to each other showing us what has been hidden and forbidden.

Practice 5: Sensual Friendship

The practice of sensual friendship involves touching. Most of us are touch deprived. We never got enough touching as infants, children, adolescents, and adults. Many of us rush into sex looking for the skin contact we never got.

Sensual friendship does not have to become a prelude to sex. It can be its own dance. In it we relearn to hold hands and rekindle the heat of touching someone we have gotten to know. We return to the innocence of young love, where a touch of fingers or caress on the cheek could send us into paroxysms of pleasure.

To learn sensual friendship, we have to practice touching ourselves. Most of us rarely touch ourselves except when we are being sexual or when we are checking out our flaws.

In the stage of sensual friendship, we touch ourselves and our partner simply for the pleasure that we receive and give. Like all the practices, sensual friendship can lead to the next stage, but don't be in a hurry. Like a wonderful meal, savor the delights of each course.

Practice 6: Sexual-Creative Lovers

The practice of sexual-creative love recognizes that the purpose of sex is pleasure, creation, and bonding. As we have done with so much else in modern society, we have reduced the process of sexuality down to the momentary pleasure we experience in the orgasm.

For two million years of human history, we sought out sexual partners not just for pleasure, but also to create children and develop the bond necessary to nurture and raise the children. Or before birth control, nature made sex pleasurable so we'd be sure to make babies whether we wanted them or not.

Those needs have not changed. Though we may not wish to create children each time we make love, the practice of becoming sexual-creative lovers recognizes that creation is always involved in lovemaking. Each act of love creates a bond with our partner and has the potential to create new life—whether the life is a child, a poem, a dance, or an affirmation of the rebirth of the spirit.

Practice 7: Spiritual Life Partners

The practice of spiritual life partners recognizes that we cannot truly commit to be with a partner for the rest of our lives until we have gone through the other stages. It knows that the goal of spiritual life partnership is not only pleasure and happiness, but the spiritual development of both partners in the relationship and the growth of the partnership itself.

In this practice, we develop the security of knowing that the partnership is being held in the embrace of a spiritual essence. There may be many people with whom we could be joyfully partnered, but once we commit to this person, we are committed to being partners in bringing out the best in our mate, helping them heal and grow.

We also accept that the idea of making a lifelong commitment to someone is not always realistic. The world is changing rapidly, and so are we. The person we were when we first married is a different person from who we become ten or fifteen years later.

Carlin and I recognized early on that we would change through time, and that vows we had made when we first married wouldn't necessarily be appropriate for the people we would become. As a result, we review our marriage every fifteen years. We decide anew whether we want to continue. So, far, we've been married three times (to each other). We're due for our next remarriage in 2025. We'll keep you posted.

Understanding the Reality of the Male-Female Dynamic in Creating Real Lasting Love

In our first remarriage ceremony, Carlin and I were in a workshop with the anthropologist Angeles Arrien and Native American elder Brooke Medicine Eagle. They created a wonderful ceremony which included a celebration of the male and female principles. Arrien described two universal organizing principles: the Dynamic and the Magnetic.

The Dynamic, she said, has to do with the capacity to initiate, expand, and move out. In Jungian psychology, it is associated with the Animus, in Asian philosophy with yang, in shamanic cultures with the energy of the sun. It expresses the "seeker" part of ourselves.

Magnetic energy has to do with drawing in, receiving, opening, and deepening. In Jungian psychology it is associated with the Anima, in Asian philosophy with yin, and in shamanic cultures, magnetism is associated with the energy of the moon.

Like the ocean waves that alternately crash on the shore and are drawn back out to sea, the Dynamic and Magnetic are two forces that continually interplay in our lives.

There are four universal Dynamic functions and four universal Magnetic functions that both men and women must develop. According to Arrien, 95 percent of cultures around the world agree on the following functions.

The four Dynamic functions are:

1. Words, language, and logic.
2. Systems, deeds, productivity, and bringing into form.
3. Leadership and power.
4. Exploring the meaning of life.

The four Magnetic functions are:

1. Vision, intuition, and perception.
2. Beauty, nurture, care, and healing.
3. Honoring the sacred through ritual and ceremony.
4. Incubating, reflecting, and exploring the meaning of relationships.

As Angeles Arrien reminded us, we all have a mixture of Dynamic and Magnetic functions, and we can develop those aspects we may lack. Still, there are limits to how much we can change. Men and women are different, but not always in the simplistic ways a sexist society would have us believe.

Ninety percent of men express more Dynamic than Magnetic qualities, and most women express predominantly Magnetic qualities. For most men, the Dynamic is Core. For most women, the Magnetic is Core. Here's how it works. If you have a male-type brain, the foundation of your manhood must rest on the Dynamic—you feel at home in the world of structure and logic. You are drawn toward systems, understanding them and leading them. Developing your Dynamic functions is soul work for you.

Once you feel solid in owning and appreciating your Dynamic functions, you can develop the Magnetic. You will be drawn to expressing your intuition more, expressing beauty in the world, honoring the sacred, and so on. This shift often happens at midlife as our testosterone drops.

I think of my friend John, who was the elder in our men's group, before he died. Through most of his life, he had been highly effective in developing his Dynamic functions. As a young man, he served as a Navy officer on a submarine. After the war, he went back to school in Chicago and was involved in local politics. He later moved to California and served for twelve years at CORO Foundation teaching leadership skills.

At the height of his career, he became director of community relations at The Rossmoor Retirement Community in Walnut Creek for nineteen years. I remember visiting at Rossmoor where he was so well known by the ten thousand residents—it was like walking with the mayor of the city.

But when John retired, he actively developed his Magnetic side. He became very interested in art and bought beautiful paintings, but he also created his own original collage art. He became a mentor to younger men and would often meet them at local coffee houses and listen to their troubles and hear the stories of their lives. As he got older in the group, he would spend more time reflecting, meditating, and enjoying the comradery and relationships in the group.

Men and women have a mixture of Dynamic and Magnetic brain functions. "The male and female brains occur on a gender continuum," says Michael Gurian, author of *Saving Our Sons: A New Path for Raising Healthy and Resilient Boys*. "Some males and females are more 'extreme male' or 'extreme female' and some male/female brains, when scanned, look somewhat more like the other gender's brain—I call these 'bridge brains' because they bridge the genders."

I have a bridge brain. Guys like us have brains that are more similar to what is typical for females. We empathize easily. We are intuitive, receptive, and nurturing. Many of us go into the healing arts. Until I reached a point in my own personal development where I could accept the Magnetic side of my life, I always felt unmanly. As a young man, I tried to become strong, powerful, dynamic, and driving, but I never seemed to be able to pull it off.

It was only when I accepted the Magnetic qualities as part of my soul work that I began to thrive. But as I approached midlife, I realized I needed to embrace more of the Dynamic side. I began traveling more and speaking at conferences all over the world. I developed new theories and practice in gender medicine and men's health. I went back to school and got a PhD in international health. I spent more time with guys and played football with my children and grandchildren.

I found my relationship with my wife improved greatly when we each balanced our Dynamic and Magnetic sides, the yang and the yin, the sun and the moon. The sacred marriage of Dynamic and

Magnetic must occur within each person. Our soul work comes first as we embrace either the Dynamic or Magnetic side of our personality. For 90 percent of men, the Dynamic is our soul work. For the 10 percent who are like me, the Magnetic becomes our soul work.

We need both the Dynamic and Magnetic functions to be fully ourselves. We often seek the qualities of the other in a partner. Whether we are gay or hetero, we tend to look for the other quality in our partner. I'm very yin, my wife is very yang. I know many gay and lesbian couples. It's usually pretty clear who of the pair is predominantly Dynamic or predominantly Magnetic.

Reflection: Think about the Dynamic and Magnetic dimensions of your own life. How balanced are you? Which functions would you like to develop more fully in your life?

The Five Stages of Love and Why Too Many Relationships End at Stage Three

Joseph Campbell said this about the hero's journey: "You enter the forest at the darkest point, where there is no path. Where there is a way or path, it is someone else's path. You are not on your own path. If you follow someone else's way, you are not going to realize your potential." The journey toward real, lasting love is unique to each person. We can be guided, but ultimately the path is ours alone.

Currently our culture focuses a great deal of attention on finding the right partner. There are hundreds of websites that will help you find Mr. or Ms. Right. But there's much less focus on our internal love map. If our map is wrong, we're not likely to find a partner. Further, as difficult as it is to find a good mate, that turns out to be the easy part. Much more difficult is to make a good marriage that lasts and enhances the well-being of the couple.

Sharing the Five Stages of Love and marriage and some of what I have learned will help you find your own unique path to joy. Here are the stages:

Stage 1: Falling in Love
Stage 2: Becoming a Couple
Stage 3: Disillusionment

Stage 4: Creating Real, Lasting Love
Stage 5: Finding Your Calling as a Couple

Stage 1: Falling in Love Is Nature's Trick to Get Us Paired Up

We all remember falling in love, that topsy-turvy feeling of total focus on another. We think about them all the time. We are bereft when they are out of our sight. We are happy for no reason when we are together. We want them body and soul. But what causes us to fall in love?

Here's a thought experiment that can teach us a lot. Imagine the implication of this simple truth: none of your direct ancestors died childless. We know your parents had at least one child. We also know your grandparents had at least one child. You can trace your ancestry back and back and back. You may or may not have children, and you certainly know people who will never have children. But all your ancestors did.

How did they do that? Well, they fell in love, or at least they fell in lust, which often accompanies falling in love. It feels so good because all those hormones are triggered: testosterone, estrogen, dopamine, and many others.

Falling in love also feels so great because we project all our hopes and dreams on our lover. We imagine that they will fulfill our desires, give us all the things we didn't get as children, deliver on all the promises our earlier relationships failed to fulfill. We are sure we will remain in love forever. And because we are besotted with "love hormones," we're not aware of any of this.

Helen Fisher, PhD is a world-renowned scientist who has researched the reasons we fall in love and why we fall in love with that special person. She is a biological anthropologist, a senior research fellow at The Kinsey Institute, and chief scientific adviser to the internet dating site Match.com. She says that falling in love is much more than a feeling. "Romantic love," she says, "is a mammalian brain system for mate choice." Its nature's trick to get us paired up. It involves two brain/hormonal systems: lust and attraction.

Lust is a strong desire to have sexual intercourse and is driven, in both men and women, by the hormones testosterone and estrogen. When we are attracted, we lock into that special person and are truly love struck and can think of little else. Scientists think that three main neurotransmitters are involved in this stage: adrenaline, dopamine, and serotonin.

Falling in love activates our stress response, increasing our blood levels of adrenaline and cortisol. This causes our hearts to race, our mouths to go dry, and we sweat when we are in the presence of our loved one. When Fisher scanned the brains of the love struck couples, she found high levels of the neurotransmitter dopamine. This chemical stimulates desire and reward by triggering intense rushes of pleasure. It has an effect similar to taking cocaine. Serotonin is responsive for the lovely preoccupation and focus we have on our partner.

But here's something few people know. Although that wonderful feeling of falling in love doesn't go on continually forever, it does not fade away never to return. Dr. Fisher told me, "Romantic love is like a sleeping cat. It can be reawakened at any time." It may get lost, but it can return again in Stage 4. That's certainly what Carlin and I found.

It's understandable that we all have strongly positive memories of this stage of our relationship. But too many of us want to stay in this phase and feel we've lost something when the hormonally driven feelings of lust and attraction begin to wane. Further, as we hit Stage 3, Disillusionment, many couples break apart and feel there is something wrong with their marriage. "I love you, but I'm not in love with you anymore," becomes a constant refrain. As a result, too many men and women leave the relationship before reaching Stages 4 and 5.

Stage 2: Becoming a Couple and Building a Life Together

This is the stage where the power of two becomes apparent. This is a time when we may have children and raise them. If don't have children, it's the time when our couple bond deepens and develops. It's a time of togetherness and joy. We learn what the other person likes, and we expand our individual lives to begin developing a life of "the two of us."

Once again, our hormonal and brain function work together to enable us to connect more deeply with each other. Oxytocin, also known as "the cuddle hormone" and "the moral molecule," deepens the feeling of attachment and contributes to that loving feeling that we desire so strongly. Oxytocin is released by men and women during orgasm and also when they snuggle, touch, and look deeply into each other's eyes. The original purpose of oxytocin was likely to bond the mother to the baby, but like all hormones, it has multiple effects in the body. The same loving feeling that bonds a mother and father to their infant baby girl or boy is present when we bond to our mate.

Another hormone, vasopressin, also contributes to the attachment and bonding process. The power of this important hormone was recognized by biologists studying a small rodent called a vole. Prairie voles engage in far more sex than is strictly necessary for reproductive purposes. Like humans, they also form fairly stable pair-bonds. However, when male prairie voles were given a drug that blocks the effect of vasopressin, the bond with their partner deteriorated, and they lost their devotion to their partner.

During this phase, we experience less of the falling head-over-heels "in love" feelings. There is more of the feeling of deep affection for our partner. We feel warm and cuddly. The sex may not be as wild, but it's deeply bonding. We feel safe, cared for, cherished, and appreciated. We feel close and protected. We often think this is the ultimate level of love and we expect it to go on forever. We are often blindsided by the turnaround that happens at Stage 3.

Stage 3: Disillusionment: The Stage We Never Saw Coming

No one told us about Stage 3 in understanding love and marriage. Stage 3 is where my first two marriages collapsed. For too many relationships, this is the beginning of the end. We all recognize Stage 1 when we first fall in love, and most of us are familiar with Stage 2 when we start a family or settle into a warm, loving, committed relationship. We think that this is all there is to a good marriage.

I knew marriage had its ups and downs, but I thought that once I had found the right partner, it would be pretty easy to solve problems. I pictured us working together to figure out how to decorate our home, decide on a diaper service, split up parental duties as the children got older. I imagined that all the problems would be "out there" in the world.

It never dawned on me until we were deeply embroiled in conflict with each other that the most difficult problems seemed to be with my spouse, not with the outside world. Little by little, things changed at home. Our once happy household gradually filled with tension. We made love less often but justified it because we were stressed trying to make a living while taking care of small children. We became more irritable with each other.

Most of us accept the reality that a marriage will have its ups and down, but few of us understand that there is an actual stage in marriage during which we will feel disconnected and estranged from each other; we will feel as if we're living with a stranger and wonder who stole the loving partner we thought we had married. Since we're not aware of this stage or the stage beyond it, we believe that these bad times must mean that the marriage is not working. Too many people give up at this stage. They either leave the marriage or come to believe that this is the best they can hope for and accept a marriage of convenience rather than one of passion, joy, and continual growth.

The Deeper Purpose of Stage 3

I finally took stock of my life and decided I had to figure out this love thing. By the time I met my present wife, Carlin, we both had been married twice before and we both had done a lot of work figuring out the true nature of love.

Carlin and I went through the wonderful times of falling in love, merging our families, and building a life together. But when we started to have problems and became disillusioned, we were more prepared to deal with it. We hit Stage 3 after we were together for ten years. We hung in there and went deeper.

The first purpose of Stage 3, Disillusionment, is to recognize and let go of our illusions of who the other person is and how they are supposed to act. Most of us have a fairy-tale view of love and marriage. Stage 3's job is to strip away the veil of illusion so we can see ourselves and our partner as human beings, not cut out projections. It forces us to recognize the expectations that we have of ourselves and our partner and forces us to come home to the messy reality of living with a real person who has their own needs, hopes, hang-ups, and hurts.

Here are some of our illusions that we became aware of and released:

- If you are with the right person, marriage should be easy.
- If there are unresolved conflicts, something must be wrong with the marriage.
- If there is conflict in the marriage, someone must be to blame.
- A good marriage means that our love is constant and unwavering.
- If you really loved me, you should _____. We each had our own set of fill-in-the-blank shoulds.
- You should never have fantasies of being with another.
- You should always know what I need.
- You should always be kind and gentle.
- You should never be involved with other things that may conflict with the time I believe should be for me.

The second purpose of Stage 3 is to help us uncover and heal our childhood wounds. Most of the conflict we experience during this stage that we attribute to our partner is actually linked to childhood wounding. We often have forgotten the trauma from childhood and don't recognize the connection with our adult conflicts. Stage 3 forces us to address our early family history.

Much of healing practitioners avoid, or are not trained, in recognizing and exploring Adverse Childhood Experiences (ACEs) and the changes in brain function that often accompanies trauma. Many of us grow up in families where our fathers were absent physically or emotionally. It has become so common place that many of us don't recognize that absent fathers leave a would that not only causes us personal pain and suffering, but can undermine our relationships.

Often these traumas get pushed into our unconscious, so we're not even aware they are there. We just experience the results in relationship stress and too often break up. The opportunity in Stage 3 is to explore our ACEs, heal the trauma, and get our minds, bodies, and emotions more fully healed.

Marriage experts Harville Hendrix and his wife Helen LaKelly Hunt say, "Since partnership is designed to resurface feelings from childhood, it means that most of the upset that gets triggered in us during our relationship is from our past." After working with couples for more than forty years, Hendrix and Hunt have concluded, "About 90% of the frustrations your partner has with you are really about their issues from childhood. That means only 10% or so is about each of you right now."

Understanding that our present conflict will help us recognize what we need to heal from the past and our past traumas will help us know what we have to deal with in our present relationship. Even so, going through Stage 3 is always difficult. Sometimes it feels like we are going through hell. It helps to remember this bit of wisdom attributed to Winston Churchill: "If you're going through hell, keep going."

Of course, part of the hell is feeling we've been cheated. It isn't supposed to be like this. This is one of the illusions we need to release. It is supposed to be like this. To have a real relationship, we have to deal with the realities of the other person and come to peace with who they really are. It took a long time to realize that the feelings of stress, conflict, and disappointment did not mean we had chosen the wrong partner, but in fact meant that we had chosen just the right person with whom we could deepen our experience of love.

I remember meeting the legendary psychologist and therapist Carl Rogers when he gave a talk about love and marriage. He was in his eighties then, and he and his wife had been married for more than sixty years. My first wife and I had been together for less than a year and were anxious to hear the great man's wisdom about love and life.

At one point in his talk, he turned to his wife, Helen. "Remember that stretch when things were so bad in our relationship?" She smiled and nodded her head. I was amazed to hear that my idol had problems in his relationship. But I was dumbfounded to hear what came next. "There was that bad patch of nine or ten years when things were awful." Helen smiled and shook her head as she too remembered. "But we hung in there and worked things out."

You must be kidding, I thought. Nine or ten years of things being awful? I couldn't imagine things ever being awful for me and my wife, and if they ever were, I sure couldn't imagine staying in a state of awful for nine or ten years.

Now, having been married to Carlin for forty-three years, I understand that there can be some pretty difficult times that can last a lot longer than we ever imagined. But getting through those times together is how we learn about real, lasting love. The key to getting through to the other side is to understand the twin purposes of Stage 3.

Once we recognize that the conflicts of Stage 3 don't mean we've chosen the wrong person or that we've grown apart but that we're ready to go deeper, our attitude changes. We understand that Stage 3 helps us begin to accept ourselves and our partner as real beings, not projections of all our childhood hopes and dreams. We also learn that we must heal our childhood wounds in order to come to peace with our parents and other members of our family as well as to move on to the next stage of love and marriage.

Stage 4: Real, Lasting Love

The gift of Stage 4 is that we can quit trying so hard to live up to the expectations of society and of our partner. We can begin to relax and be ourselves. We all want to be loved for who we are, but until we recognize that we have been trying to please others rather than accepting ourselves fully, we remain uneasy. The longer we're in relationship, the more we have to lose and the more we feel we have to keep up the facade.

Until we hit Stage 3, we're often not even aware we are wearing a mask. We become so invested in trying to be what we think our partner wants us to be, we lose ourselves. Stage 3 gives us the opportunity to come home to ourselves.

When Carlin and I got through Stage 3 and moved into Stage 4, everything changed. She accepted that she had been depressed for many years and got help. After gentle pressure from her, I went to see a doctor and got evaluated. My anger and mood swings were diagnosed as bipolar disorder, and I took medications and worked with a psychiatrist to heal the wounds from my childhood.

We began to laugh and have more fun. We did something I thought was impossible. We fell in love again. I had thought that the "falling in love" phase only happened at the beginning and couldn't last. I learned I was wrong. Well, in a way I was right. Falling in love occurs at the beginning of a new relationship. Entering Stage 4, for us, was a new beginning. Many other couples learn the same thing.

Stage 5: Finding Your Calling As a Couple

I always thought that finding my calling was personal pursuit. It never occurred to me that couples could have their own calling in life. This came to me when my wife challenged me to write this book and offered direct support for the process. She recognized that my life's calling has to do with helping men but that I was reluctant to fully engage that calling because I didn't want to displease women.

I worried that if I focused on helping men, women would feel left out. Carlin helped me see that the best thing I can do to help women is to help the men in their lives. She was on board for helping me do that.

I believe that couples are stronger when they have a shared passion outside of their personal careers and raising their families. It doesn't have to be a passion that they both share equally. Carlin recognizes that my work has been with men. Supporting me to help others has become our joint calling. I also have helped support her in her calling to reach out in our community. She organized community events and townhall meetings to address the myriad issues a community faces. I helped in a supportive role.

We're at a time in human history where conflict is tearing us apart. Countries fight other countries; political parties fight their counterparts. The left and the right do battle for the hearts and minds of the citizens. Men and women fight each other and end up frightened and frustrated. Going through all five stages and learning to heal our love relationships can be a model of how we can heal and address all our major problems, from global climate change and depletion of resources to drug addiction and violence.

I call the Five Stages of Love a graduate program in the most important subject we will ever learn—how to love. The full journey is a rite of passage. We all need rites of passage to help us make important transitions in our lives.

Bottom Line: The Journey of Finding Real, Lasting Love Is Not for the Faint of Heart

Too often we view our past relationships as failures. Yet, they force us to ask questions that are important for us to answer in order to move ahead with our lives. They can give us a framework to guide our further journeys to finding the love we long to have. The seven practices take us from Acquaintanceship to Spiritual Life Partnership and are helpful when exploring a new relationship or revitalizing an existing one.

Balancing the Dynamic and Magnetic functions in our lives helps us to fully embrace our unique male spirit, and understanding the Five Stages of Love shows us how to understand how Stage

3, Disillusionment, is the critically important bridge between Stages 1 and 2 (Falling in Love and Becoming a Couple), and Stages 3 and 4 (Creating Real, Lasting Love and Finding Your Calling As a Couple).

Anger, anxiety, and depression are challenging emotions that can undermine relationships at every stage. They can also create fear and distance in a relationship. When we don't feel safe in a relationship, we are forever having to be on guard and protect ourselves. My most popular article of all times, "The One Thing That Men Want More Than Sex," addressed the critical issue of safety in our relationships. In the next chapter, we will give you some important tools for dealing with the difficult emotions that can undermine your peace and serenity.

CHAPTER 9

TREATING AND PREVENTING ANGER, ANXIETY, AND DEPRESSION

When women are depressed, they eat or go shopping. Men invade another country. It's a whole different way of thinking
—Comedian Elayne Boosler

I have lived with anxiety, irritability, anger, and depression literally my whole life. Often, our origin stories tell us a lot about the challenges we will face in our adult lives. I grew up with stories my mother told me about the anxiety and fear that accompanied my conception. She and my father had tried, unsuccessfully, for nine years to have a child. They finally consulted a specialist who encouraged them to try an experimental procedure at the time (1943) to inject my father's sperm into my mother's womb.

She did conceive but was terrified of losing this new life they had tried so hard to create. "I would walk down Fifth Avenue in New York," she told me, "taking small, anxious steps forever worried I would lose my child. Once you were born, I was overjoyed but afraid something would happen to you. I wouldn't let your father hold you thinking he might inadvertently drop you."

They had little money at the time, but my mother insisted on getting life insurance policies. Not only did she get a policy on herself and my father in case either of them died, but she bought an insurance policy on me. "So when you grow up and have children, your children will be taken care of in case."

In doing research for one of my weekly articles on MenAlive, I learned about the English philosopher Thomas Hobbes. He's the guy who viewed our "primitive" ancestors in such a negative light. "No arts; no letters; no society; and which is worst of all, continual fear, and danger of violent death: and the life of man, solitary, poor, nasty, brutish and short."

Then, I learned *the rest of the story* as the commentator Paul Harvey used to give us. Having been born prematurely when his mother heard of the coming invasion of the Spanish Armada, Hobbes later reported that "my mother gave birth to twins: myself and fear." When I read that, a whole lot of my early and later life experiences fell into place.

I've already told you about my father's increasing anxiety, irritability, anger, and depression that drove his adult life. I definitely am my father and mother's son, and it won't surprise you to know that my two most popular books are *The Irritable Male Syndrome: Understanding and Managing the 4 Key Causes of Depression and Aggression* and *Mr. Mean: Saving Your Relationship from the Irritable Male Syndrome*.

Reflections: Think about your own origin story. What was going on in your parents' lives when you were conceived? What was your birth like? What early experiences may have been challenging, and how might they have impacted your life and relationships?

The Roots of American Rage

Irritability and anger seem to be dominating our personal, professional, and political lives these days. A cover story in a recent issue of *The Atlantic Magazine* was titled, "The Real Roots of American Rage." Written by Pulitzer Prize-winning writer Charles Duhigg, the article gives us "the untold story of how anger became the dominant emotion in our politics and personal lives—and what we can do about it."

Duhigg notes that anger can be positive. It energizes people to solve problems and can bring about positive political change by uniting people to address social ills such as sexism and racism. But anger can also be divisive and destructive. What the article doesn't address, though it is clear from the examples given, is that irritability and anger are problems that are much more common in men than in women.

We've all known a grumpy old man or two. Maybe he was the guy down the street who chased you off his lawn when you were a kid. Hollywood turned grumpy old men into comic icons in movies starring Jack Lemmon and Walter Matthau. While we sometimes laugh off the chronic crabbiness of a friend, we're just as likely to dismiss it as an unfortunate, but inevitable, part of being a man. But as we will see, there is more to this kind of behavior than what we see on the surface, and it is no joking matter for those who are experiencing it or those who must live with a chronically irritable man.

For some, this kind of irritability has come on slowly over a period of months and years. For others, it seems like someone has flipped a switch, and Mr. Nice has turned into Mr. Mean. "God, it's like he's hormonal," one woman told me. When I told her she wasn't too far from the truth, she snapped back, "I knew it."

When I was conducting research for my book *The Irritable Male Syndrome*, I conducted a survey in partnership with *Men's Health* magazine. The response was overwhelming. Nearly six thousand men filled out the Irritable Male Syndrome Questionnaire, and nearly 3,500 filled out the Male Depression Questionnaire. The respondents ranged in age from ten to seventy-five. The results were surprising and gave an initial look into the world of men:

- **Stress is a significant issue for men.**
  Only 8% said they are almost never stressed.
  46% said they are often or almost always stressed.
- **Sex is a major concern.**
  46% of the men said they are almost never sexually satisfied.
- **Depression and irritability are related.**
  21% of men said they are depressed often or almost always.

Only 9% said they are almost never irritable; 40% are irritable often or almost always.

- **Emotions related to depression are significant.**

  Only 7% said they almost never have a desire to get away from it all, but 62% said they often or almost always desire to do so.

  Only 11% said they almost never have a strong fear of failure, but 55% said they often or almost always have a strong fear of failure.

  Only 12% said they almost never feel burned out, compared to 44% who said they feel burned out often or almost always. 12% said they almost never feel empty inside, while 48% said they feel empty often or almost always.

Millions of Men Are Depressed and Don't Know It

I began my journey to understand male-type depression when I was five years old and went with my uncle to the mental hospital to visit my father. I didn't know it at the time, but I hungered to understand what happened to him and learn how I could prevent it from happening to me and other men.

When one of our adult sons began having problems with alcohol and drugs, I helped him get into a treatment program. One of the requirements was that parents attend a weekend session to learn about addictions, causes, and recovery.

My wife Carlin and I walked tentatively into the nicely restored old building to attend the "family weekend." As part of the weekend experience, all family members were given a number of questionnaires. One was a depression questionnaire. We dutifully filled it out, and my wife scored "high" while I scored "low."

Carlin talked to a counselor, who suggested that Carlin might want to be evaluated for depression when we returned home. Driving back, we talked, and it became clear that Carlin had been feeling depressed for some time. Once home, she saw a doctor, was evaluated, and subsequently put on antidepressants. Her life and mine changed for the better. It was as if she had come out of a fog. Her joy returned, and she became much more fun to be around.

A few months into her treatment, Carlin suggested that I might be depressed as well and suggested I see her doctor. I promptly refused.

"I'm not depressed," I insisted. "If I were, I'm sure I'd know it. I'm a therapist and I treat depression. I'd certainly recognize it in myself."

"OK, it was just a suggestion," she said. She gave me a gentle smile.

"Anyway," I reminded her, "I took the depression quiz at the treatment center, and I scored low."

As far as I was concerned, the case was closed. Nevertheless, disturbing thoughts would pop into my head. My father had suffered from manic-depressive illness all his life and had tried to commit suicide. I knew that the disease ran in families. Though I kept telling myself I was immune—God knows we therapists can be the most pigheaded people when our own mental health is questioned—still there were those doubts. Plus, I found I was often irritable, angry, preoccupied, and withdrawn. But that couldn't be depression, could it?

I convinced myself that my irritability and anger were justified. "Who wouldn't be upset with what I have to put up with?" I would argue. "I'm stressed out at work, the kids seem to go out of their way to get on my last remaining nerve, and my wife is going through menopause."

Carlin received the brunt of my anger, which she fought to deflect. But what did she expect? If she'd just be nicer, more loving, more interested in sex, everything would be okay. It never occurred to me that my constant anger made it nearly impossible for her to be nicer, more loving, or more interested in sex.

More and more often I found I was having fantasies of running away from it all. I'd see myself getting in my car and just driving into the sunset. Other times I saw myself with another woman, someone who was kinder and gentler and who understood me—someone like Carlin used to be. Those thoughts both excited and scared me. I knew we couldn't go on like this, but I had no idea what to do.

Finally, Carlin made the decision for me. "Look," she told me directly, "we're both miserable. If our marriage is going to survive, you've got to see someone." Reluctantly, I made an appointment with the doctor she had seen. He did a complete evaluation, and I was sure he would say I was a normal guy who had to deal with a lot of stress in his life.

Instead, he told me I was suffering from depression and would benefit from treatment. I was shocked. I thanked him and was about to leave when he said something that hit me between the eyes.

"You need to be aware that men often experience depression differently than women, and highly successful and intellectual men, in particular, often deny that they are depressed."

When I got home, Carlin was anxious to hear the results. I told her what the doctor had said, and she seemed relieved. I told her I wanted a second opinion.

She blew up. "You want a second opinion? I'll give you a second opinion. You're depressed and you need treatment just as I did. It helped me and it will help you." She turned and walked out of the room.

I didn't want to believe I was depressed. It just didn't fit with my view of myself. And it didn't fit with what I knew were the symptoms of depression. My mood wasn't depressed most of the time. I hadn't lost interest in my work or activities I loved. I slept fine and my energy was OK. I didn't feel worthless, and I didn't think of killing myself.

I did decide to see another doctor. Even though I liked this one much better than the first, she told me essentially the same thing as doctor number one. She also explained that men who are depressed are often hypersensitive, irritable, and angry. She gave me a book to read by a world-renowned psychologist, Kay Redfield Jamison. In *An Unquiet Mind: A Memoir of Moods and Madness*, Jamison describes depression in a way that cut to my core. This line nailed what I was feeling. "You're irritable and paranoid and humorless and lifeless and critical and demanding, and no reassurance is ever enough."

I could no longer deny the truth. I was dealing with depression. I agreed to begin therapy and try medications. I found that my life turned around. I wasn't so hypersensitive. Little things didn't bother me as much. I wasn't so reactive, and I felt less irritable. As Carlin described it, "You used to look at me in a way that chilled me. Your eyes were narrow and beady. Now when you look at me, I feel your love. It's wonderful."

It was partly the result of these experiences that I decided to return to graduate school in my sixties. It was an exciting and frightening prospect. I was a successful therapist, and I didn't need any other credentials to show I was competent. It was clear that there were millions of men who were depressed and didn't know it. There were millions of women living with depressed men who didn't know what to do. The women were often blamed for the emotional outbursts that were so common with irritable, angry, and depressed men.

Male versus Female Depression: Why Men Act Out and Women Act In

It took me a long time to find a graduate school where I could learn more about gender medicine and men's health. I finally found a program, but it took me much longer than I expected. The doctoral program was in international health, and we studied everything from pandemics to how to prevent them to the different health problems that are more common in men and women. The course work was interesting, and I breezed through it.

When it was time for the dissertation study that was the capstone for doctoral level study, I realized why so many dissertations examined some minuscule issue that seemed to have limited relevance to real-world issues. Designing and carrying out a study that is scientifically sound and then writing it up is very demanding. I learned why so many people who start a doctorate end up with an ABD rather than a PhD. An ABD (all but dissertation) is where too many graduate students end up.

It took me seven years and more money than I want to remember, but I finished the program, did significant research on men's depression, and published my results as a book: *Male vs. Female Depression: Why Men Act Out and Women Act In.* From my own clinical work over the years, I knew that the first step in treating or preventing a problem is to understand it clearly. Both my experience treating depression and my research studies convinced me that our traditional ways of understanding and treating male depression were inadequate.

A New Way of Assessing Depression in Men: The Diamond Male Depression Scale

Prior to my study, most of the professional literature in the field indicated that women experience depression at twice the rate of men even though men commit suicide at rates much higher than women. My hypothesis was that men were being underdiagnosed and undertreated because the depression scales that were commonly used did not include many of the symptoms, such as irritability and anger, that depressed men experience. My studies showed that to be true.

A total of 1,072 individuals (323 females and 749 males) filled out the Diamond Male Depression Scale (DMDS) questionnaire. Ages ranged from eighteen to eighty with a mean age of fifty-one. Most respondents were from the United States, but people responded from a total of forty-five countries. Previous research indicated that men, particularly depressed men, would be less likely to respond than women, so a specific effort was made to reach out to that group.

The DMDS questionnaire was administered online to a population of men and women. The questionnaire had seven sections. The first included demographic information on age, sex, marital status, relationship happiness, children, race, employment, income, education, and veteran status. Additional information was sought in this section on whether the subjects had been diagnosed with a depressive illness or other common mental illnesses and whether family members had been so diagnosed.

The second section presented fifty-one questions that included atypical symptoms thought to be associated with male-type depression. The selection of questions was based on clinical experience of the author over the past forty years as well as previous research focused on atypical symptoms thought to be more common in males than females.

The third section contained the twenty-question Center for Epidemiologic Studies Depression Screen (CES-D), which is one of the most well-known and accepted scales for measuring depression.

The fourth section focused on suicidal ideation and intent and included four questions taken from the Beck Hopelessness Scale as well as two questions that asked directly about suicidal thinking and intent.

The fifth section addressed issues surrounding the drinking of alcoholic beverages. It contained the four questions from the CAGE scale assessing alcohol abuse and one question that asked about the quantity of alcohol consumed.

The sixth section asked about possible comorbidities, including a number of physical illnesses and medications thought to be associated with depression.

The seventh section included the questions from the Gotland Male Depression Scale, which at the time was the only scale that examined symptoms thought to be present in depressed men.

Three Important Subscales Help Us Better Understand Depressed Men

Based on my analysis of the full questionnaire, I was able to determine that were three subscales within the full scale that led to three different ways males experience depression.

Sub-Scale 1: Emotional Acting-In Depression

This scale focused on feeling negative, stressed, empty, and other internal expressions of depression and included the following items from the full fifty-one-item questionnaire:

- d28: I feel I'd like to get away from it all.
- d34: I feel that things are stacked against me.
- d35: People I count on disappoint me.
- d36: I feel stressed out.
- d40: I feel emotionally numb and closed down.
- d41: I feel hopeless about the future.
- d42: I feel powerless to improve things in my life.
- d43: I feel my life has little worth or value.
- d44: I have little interest or pleasure in doing things.
- d45: I find I am complaining about things in my life.
- d46: I feel sorry for myself.
- d48: I feel burned out.
- d49: I feel empty inside.
- d50: I feel tired even when there is no reason to be so.
- d51: I have difficulty making everyday decisions.

Sub-Scale 2: Emotional Acting-Out Depression

This scale focused on such things as being difficult, irritable, angry, and other external emotional expressions of depression and included the following items from the full fifty-one-item questionnaire:

- d1: I flare up quickly.
- d2: I have trouble controlling my temper.
- d22: I am easily annoyed, become grumpy, or impatient.
- d27: Other people "drive me up the wall."
- d29: When others disagree with me, I get very upset.
- d37: It doesn't take much to set me off.
- d38: I have difficulty maintaining self-control.

Sub-Scale 3: Physical Acting-Out Depression

This scale focused on such things as violence, gambling, alcohol abuse, and other external, physical expressions of depression and included the following items from the full fifty-one-item questionnaire:

- d4: I have hit someone when I was provoked.
- d8: I work longer hours because going home is stressful.
- d10: I gamble with money I have set aside for other things.
- d11: I drive fast or recklessly as a way of letting off steam.
- d12: If I'm feeling low, I'll use sex as a pick-me-up.
- d23: I have felt I should cut down on my drinking or drug use.
- d30: I feel like picking a fight with someone.
- d31: I get so jealous or possessive I feel like I could explode.

I use these scales when I see clients. The questions help us assess what areas are problematic and give us better understanding of possible depression. I don't use it as a formal way to diagnose people but a way to collaborate with each person by finding ways to help them solve problems that are causing them to feel the way they do.

Reflection: Ask yourself which of the above symptoms might be causing problems in your own life.

Males and Females Often Experience Depression Differently

J. Douglas Bremner, MD, is a professor of psychiatry at Emory University where he conducts research on stress-related illnesses. In a very interesting experiment, he gathered a group of former depression patients. With their permission, he gave them a beverage that was spiked with an amino acid that blocks the brain's ability to absorb serotonin, the neurotransmitter that is associated with happiness. The most popular antidepressants, such as Prozac, Celexa, and Paxil, are among a class of medications called *selective serotonin reuptake inhibitors*, or SSRIs. By blocking the brain from absorbing serotonin, Bremner was creating an instant chemical depression.

What I found fascinating were the gender-specific differences in the way men and women reacted to the potion that blocked the effects of the serotonin. Typical of the males was John, a middle-aged businessman who had fully recovered from a bout of depression thanks to a combination of psychotherapy and Prozac. Within minutes of drinking the brew, however, "He wanted to escape to a bar across the street," recalls Bremner. **"He didn't express sadness… he didn't really express anything. He just wanted to go to Larry's Lounge."**

Contrast John's response with that of female subjects like Sue, a mother of two in her mid-thirties. After taking the cocktail, **"She began to cry and express her sadness over the loss of her father two years ago,"** recalls Bremner. "She was overwhelmed by her emotions."

Ron Kessler, PhD, a professor of health care policy at Harvard, describes depression in men this way. "When you study depression among children, they don't talk about being sad, they talk about being angry and irritable," he said. "Children don't have the cognitive capacity to make sense of all their feelings. There's a great similarity between children and men. Men get irritable; women get sad."

I have developed a chart to describe the main differences in the ways males and females experience depression. I want to emphasize that this is a shorthand summary of thousands of people I have seen. Most depressed people will find they identify with some things on both sides of the chart. Some men will find themselves predominantly on the female side, and some women will find themselves predominantly on the male side. But generally speaking, these differences hold true for depressed females and males.

Ron Kessler, Ph.D., a professor of health care policy at Harvard, describes depression in men this way. "When you study depression among children, they don't talk about being sad, they talk about being angry and irritable," he said. "Children don't have the cognitive capacity to make sense of all their feelings. There's a great similarity between children and men. Men get irritable; women get sad."

Depressed Females	Depressed Males
Blame themselves for problems	Blame others for problems
Feel sad and tearful	Feel irritable and unforgiving
Sleep more than usual	Have trouble sleeping or staying asleep
Are vulnerable and easily hurt	Are suspicious and guarded
Try to be nice	Are overtly or covertly hostile
Withdraw when feeling hurt	Attack when feeling hurt
Often suffer in silence	Overreact, often sorry later
Feel they were set up to fail	Feel the world is set up to fail them
Feel slowed down and nervous	Feel restless and agitated
Maintain control of anger or may have anxiety attacks	Lose control of anger or may have sudden attacks of rage
Feel overwhelmed by feelings	Feelings are blunted, often numb
Let others violate boundaries	Have rigid boundaries; push others away
Feel guilty for what they do	Feel ashamed for who they are
Are uncomfortable receiving praise	Are frustrated if not praised enough
Accept weaknesses and doubts	Deny weaknesses and doubts
Have a strong fear of success	Have a strong fear of failure
Need to "blend in" to feel safe	Need to be the "top dog" to feel safe
Use food, friends, and "love" to self-medicate	Use alcohol, TV, sports, and "sex" to self-medicate
Believe their problems could be solved if only they could be a better… (spouse, coworker, parent, friend)	Believe their problems could be solved if only their… (spouse, coworker, parent, friend) would treat them better
Wonder, "Am I loveable enough?"	Wonder, "Am I being loved enough?"

The Evolution of Treatments for Male Depression

When my father was committed to the state mental hospital in 1949, treatment involved being locked up away from the pressures of life, being fed and clothed, and given high doses of psychiatric medications. If there was a theory at all about what caused depression, it was assumed that the person had some kind of brain disease, and they hoped they had a drug that would cure it or at least control the symptoms.

If the person didn't get well, they increased the dose of the drugs and hoped for the best. It my father's case, which was true for many others who were hospitalized back then, he continued to get worse, and the doctors told my family that he may need to be "treated" long-term until he got well. My father had other ideas and finally escaped and never returned.

By the time I was in graduate school in 1965, there were more options. Psychotherapy was more readily available to treat psychological aspects of depression, and new medications were available. But really, not much had changed. Once he left the mental hospital, my father got better, mainly because he stopped being locked up and getting high doses of drugs that were making him sicker. However, he still wasn't healthy. He was still irritable, angry, and often depressed. What changed things for my father was being admitted to God's Hotel.

My Father's Stay at God's Hotel: A Slow-Medicine Approach to Healing Mental Illness

After my father had escaped from Camarillo, he stayed hidden and I didn't see him for many years. I learned later that he had walked more than a hundred miles back to Los Angeles and took up residence in Santa Monica. An uncle unexpectedly ran into him years later and told me where he was living. I went to see him and was struck by two things. He was, as the song goes, "still crazy after all these years." But he could also be kind and gentle, and he put on puppet shows for the children in the neighborhood.

He would seem normal for a while, but then would become agitated and paranoid. His anger would escalate, and he would become consumed by it. Eventually he would scream at me, tell me he never wanted to see me again, and threaten me until I would reluctantly leave. He refused to get help for his "mental illness," which I could understand, given his experiences in Camarillo. I saw him numerous times over the years, but our encounters always ended the same way. I eventually gave up having a father I could trust and moved on with my own life.

One day after work, I received an unexpected call from a man who said he knew where my father was. He had read my book *Inside Out: Becoming My Own Man* and was moved by what I had said about my dad. He told me he had been visiting a friend at a hospital in San Francisco and met a man there who was putting on puppet shows. He recognized my father based on the description I had written in my book about the puppet shows he put on in Berkeley and San Francisco.

He told me he was sure my father would like to see me, and I told him I doubted that since all my recent encounters over the years were negative. I decided to write my father a letter and see how he responded. In the letter I told him the truth about my feelings:

Dear Dad,

I heard from a man who read my book that you were in Laguna Honda Hospital. He said you would want to see me, but our last encounters were pretty hurtful for me. It seems that every time I've reached out to you over the years, you get angry, blame me or someone in the family for all your troubles. Well, I'm tired of being the brunt of your anger. You are my father and I'll always care about you, but I'm done with being dumped on. If you keep on like this you are going to die a lonely old man. If you want to see me, you have to change, if that's even possible.

Your son, Jed

I thought this might finally be the end for us, but I was wrong. I was surprised to receive the following letter.

Dear Jed,

No one has ever talked to me like that. It made me angry. But you're right. I've spent my life blaming others for my problems. It's true there are things people have done that have been hurtful and harmful to me, but I

know I've done my own share of shit. I do want to change and I feel I'm
actually getting better here. I would like to see you and I hope you'll come.
Your father, Tommy the Puppet Man

These were words I had never expected to hear. I was still apprehensive about meeting, but something had changed in him. There was an honesty that I had never heard, a willingness to accept responsibility for his own problems I had never seen. I felt real hope, not just blind desire to have my father back in my life. Something had also changed in me. I was no longer the wounded little boy. I was a forty-two-year-old man, and I had finally stood up to my father and said no more shame and blame. I'm done feeling responsible for your unhappy life.

A week later when I arrived at Laguna Honda Hospital in San Francisco, I felt a shudder of remembrance from my visits to Camarillo State Hospital so many years ago. Laguna Honda also looked like an old California mission with stucco walls and red-tiled roofs. But once inside, I knew I was in a different world. The walls were lined with beautiful murals by the artist Glenn Wessels painted in 1934 depicting the four elements—earth, air, fire, and water. People were friendly and two chickens greeted me as I asked directions to Clarendon Hall where I was told my father stayed. Yes, chickens in a hospital. This was my first clue that this was not your typical medical center.

I asked the person at the information desk about the chickens. "Yes," she told me. "That's unusual. We actually have other animals as well including rabbits, ducks, guinea pigs, and cats."

When I looked surprised at animals in a hospital, she continued. "They really raise the spirits of the patients here. Even those who are withdrawn in their own world and won't talk to staff seem to come alive when the animals visit."

I learned that the animals have a long history at Laguna Honda, which first opened in 1867 as an almshouse for the gold rush pioneers, at least the ones who didn't strike it rich. The almshouse grew its own food and had livestock on the eighty-seven-acre complex. The hospital had changed over the years, but the animals were still there.

I met my father in Clarendon Hall for the first time in seven years. I was directed to the well-lit visitor's room. Tommy got up and walked toward me. He had a smile on his face and gave me a hug. I was surprised. He had never hugged me since I was a child. His embrace was strong, yet gentle. "I'm so glad you came," he told me with a strong feeling of warmth and welcome in his voice. I felt hopeful for the first time since I was five years old, but I held back. I wanted to see more before I got my hopes too high.

He asked about my family, and I told him about Carlin, our marriage in 1980, my two children, Jemal and Angela, from my first marriage, and Carlin's three sons, Dane, Evan, and Aaron. I asked about his life at Laguna Honda. "I've been here for five years," he told me. "And I'll be happy to spend the rest of my life here."

I was surprised. "You escaped from Camarillo State Hospital and said you'd never be locked up in a hospital again. What happened?"

"This place isn't anything like Camarillo," he told me. "That place really was like a concentration camp. Whatever problems I had at the time just got worse there. Here I'm not locked up. The staff respect us, and the other people here are just people like me. I come and go as I please. I usually have breakfast in the morning, take a bus out in front of the hospital, and go into downtown San Francisco. I put on puppet shows anywhere there are people. When the kids see me coming, they cry out, 'puppet man, puppet man.' I make people happy. I come back at the end of the day feeling like a million dollars."

"Wow, that's not like any hospital I've ever seen." I told him. I was beginning to understand the changes I was seeing. Maybe there was hope for a real reunion.

"Someone called it 'God's Hotel,' and I can't disagree," he told me. "I've never been religious, but since I've been here, I feel like I've been touched with the spirit of God. It's really the result of being seen, cared for, and respected by the people here."

I visited Tommy at God's Hotel often after that and brought the family. We watched as he put on puppet shows for the residents, and when we met him in San Francisco, I marveled at how many people on the street knew him. As Carlin and our two youngest kids watched, one young woman came up to Tommy after one of his puppet shows with a little girl in hand. "Tommy, thank you for the show," she said. Her six-year-old daughter smiled at Tommy's puppet Tomaso, who looked like a miniature of my father. "Thank you, Tomaso," she said beaming. The little hand puppet rubbed the little girl's cheek and kissed her.

Her mother continued, "My mother brought me to one of your puppet shows when I was a little girl. I still remember seeing you on the campus of San Francisco State and how your puppets were angry like many of the students."

Tommy smiled. "Yes, I was there. I used to go to all the colleges and put on shows, even UC Berkeley. It was an angry time, and I was angry with the world. Things are different now."

"It's so nice to bring my daughter to see you." She gave Tommy a big hug and my own family watched with tears in our eyes. It was wonderful to see how much joy my father had brought to families, and I felt proud of his accomplishments. He had cut the marionette's strings that had controlled his life and became the master of his own future. He was the puppet man.

A number of years later, one of the doctors at the hospital, Victoria Sweet, who had known my father, wrote a book titled *God's Hotel: A Doctor, a Hospital, and a Pilgrimage to the Heart of Medicine*. It helped me better understand the unique setting that my father had found so late in life, a place that allowed him to truly heal and for a father and son to find our soul connection.

I met Dr. Sweet at a local bookstore where she was giving a talk on her book about the hospital. "San Francisco's Laguna Honda Hospital is the last almshouse in the country, a descendant of the Hôtel-Dieu (God's Hotel) that cared for the sick in the Middle Ages," Dr. Sweet told us.

Having a Dr. Sweet in your life certainly is a good thing for healing painful wounds. In the book, she describes the people who came there over the years. "Ballet dancers and rock musicians, professors and thieves—anyone who had fallen, or, often, leapt, onto hard times and needed extended medical care—ended up here."

After I read her book, I went to see her to ask her about my father and what magic enabled him to truly heal after so many years during which he was crazy, angry, blaming, and shaming. She had retired from Laguna Honda, and we met in a little café in San Francisco. "Because we dealt with the misfits of society, we were largely ignored by the medical establishment and its modern focus on efficiency and medications. We practiced a kind of slow medicine that allowed us to get to know the patients as full human beings, not just as a medical diagnosis."

"Tell me more about slow medicine," I said. Just the name was intriguing.

"There's a secret that modern medicine has missed in its attempts to treat patients most effectively and efficiently. And that secret is that what one wants as a patient and as a doctor is the right diagnosis and the right treatment. But modern medicine is focused on speed, technology, and efficiency—in other words, Fast Medicine. But that's not enough. What patient and doctor also need, in addition to wonderful technologies, is time. Time may not heal all wounds, but it heals very many of them, and having enough time, though so inefficient on paper, turns out to be the most efficient health care of all.

"Your father was an example of the kind of patient we helped there," she continued. "He was irascible and had his own ideas about what he needed. He was fiercely independent, and you couldn't get him to do anything he didn't want to do."

I smiled, thinking how exactly she had understood my father. "Instead of seeing ourselves as the experts who know everything," she continued, "we took time to listen deeply to those at the hospital and respected their own strengths and abilities."

"I've worked in health care my entire adult life," I told her. "This makes perfect sense, but it seems so foreign to the way most of the health care system operates today."

"You're right. I have always been interested in medical practices from the past. I became intrigued by the teachings of a Benedictine abbess named Hildegard von Bingen. Born in 1078, Bingen practiced medicine in premodern times. Through Bingen's methods, I began to appreciate the value of taking time, paying attention to the details about the patients' lives, and treating the practice of medicine more like the work of a gardener than a mechanic."

"Does that include chickens as healers?" I asked. "They were the first ones to welcome me when on my initial visit to the hospital." We both laughed.

"You'd be surprised how therapeutic animals can be," she went on. "Many of the patients also worked in the large gardens we had growing food that they could eat. It was really slow medicine at its best."

"But you wrote about things changing at Laguna Honda. What happened?" I wanted to know.

"The modern world found us," she told me. "Health regulations forced all the animals out and closed down the garden. Patient privacy regulations closed the open dormitories where everyone slept together, socialized, and knew if someone was having a problem. A lot was lost."

"Well, I feel blessed that my father was able to be there while the chickens still walked the hallways." We both laughed together, and I gave her a hug of thanks. "My father is doing great. He lives in San Francisco in a residence hotel in the Tenderloin, but he still talks fondly about his stay in God's Hotel."

Walking Your Blues Away: An Ancient Practice for Preventing Depression

Another thing that helped heal my father's depression was walking. As he said, he would leave the hospital every day and go into downtown San Francisco. He'd bring his bag of hand puppets with him and put on shows wherever people gathered. Over the years, he walked slowly, but I believe the exercise was healing. Studies have demonstrated that the benefits of exercise—particularly walking—are therapeutic. I know this is true in my own life. I turned seventy-eight last year and have been active my whole life. When COVID-19 came into our world, I decided to increase my exercise routine to strengthen my lungs since I often get pneumonia in the winters and I definitely didn't want to catch the virus.

I used to walk regularly around town. For the last two years, I have been walking every day and adding hills to my walking route. I haven't caught COVID-19, and I'm healthier than I have ever been in my life. I walk up and down hills easily now that I wouldn't have even attempted before.

Although I took medications for depression and bipolar disorder in the past and believe that medications can be helpful, I haven't taken them in years. I feel that walking offers benefits that no medication can ever give. A man who believes as I do is Thom Hartmann. Hartmann is a best-selling author and one of the major thought leaders in the world. He hosts the number-one progressive talk show in the country with over seven million weekly listeners.

Among Thom Hartmann's many books is a gem that is not as well known as some of his others. It's called *Walking Your Blues Away: How to Heal the Mind and Create Emotional Well-Being*. It was written in 2006 and is even more relevant today. In the introduction, he offers a compelling statement of the world in which we live:

> Trauma is nothing new to the human race. We are certainly familiar with trauma in the modern world, from acts of war and terrorism to crime, child abuse, and the pain of our dysfunctional, standards-driven schools cause so many of our children. And many of us don't handle trauma well: suicide is the third leading cause of death among Americans ages fifteen to twenty-four. In the last decade over 51 million prescriptions were written in the United States just for SSRI family of antidepressants (including Prozac, Paxil, and Zoloft), with sales topping $3.6 billion for the six most popular SSRIs, and the numbers have more than doubled since then.

He goes on to ask a compelling question. "So how has humankind historically dealt with trauma for the past two hundred thousand years, before the advent of psychotherapy? Humans experienced mental and emotional wounds in ancient times."

The answer to his question, what Hartmann discovered is both obvious, simple, and profound: it's walking. Clearly, our human ancestors walked a lot. They had to walk to find food. Hartmann combines walking with simple practices based on modern science. "I've identified a specific healing mechanism and process that nature has built into the human mind and body that enables us to process trauma in a way that is quick, functional, and permanent."

I have used this technique over the years, which is basically just walking, with the normal swing of the arms that creates a rhythmic side-to-side stimulation of the body while bringing to mind a problem or traumatic memory from the past. I was skeptical at first that something so simple and easy could actually cure the traumatic memories that underlie many depressions, but I found it does.

Hartmann concludes, "When we stimulate the nervous system in this bilateral manner while calling to mind a present emotional distress, the emotional 'change' associated with that memory quickly and permanently dissipates. This isn't a process of producing amnesia or forgetting; instead, it's a way of reframing the past, a way of re-understanding, of putting into context that which has been so 'unnerving' for us."

I highly recommend Thom Hartmann's book. It also brings to mind other ancient practices that have been shown to produce real cures for depression and for many more of our society's present ills.

Ancient Health Practices and Modern Applications: Welcome to the Blue Zones

"I've spent over a decade studying the areas in the world where people live longer and healthier lives than anywhere else on the planet," says Dan Buettner, author of *Blue Zones: 9 Lessons for Living Longer from the People Who've Lived the Longest*. "These 'Blue Zone' regions are incredible because the people there live not only longer, but better. Besides having a large percentage of people that live to 100, the aging population also remains active well into their 80s and 90s, and typically do not suffer the degenerative diseases common in most of the industrialized world."

The original region they studied was in the Barbagia region of Sardinia, Italy. When they discovered areas where people lived unusually long and healthy lives, they circled them with blue ink on their map. They later found long-lived people in other areas of the world: Ikaria, an island in Greece; Okinawa, an island in Japan; Loma Linda, a small city in California; and the Nicoya peninsula in Costa Rica.

Buettner goes on to say, "With my Blue Zones team of medical researchers, anthropologists, demographers, and epidemiologists, I found the evidence-based common denominators of all the Blue Zones regions. We call them the Power 9:

1. Move Naturally. Moving naturally throughout the day—walking, gardening, doing housework—is a core part of the Blue Zones lifestyle.

2. Purpose. The Okinawans call it *ikigai* and the Nicoyans call it *plan de vida*. Knowing why you wake up in the morning makes you healthier, happier, and adds up to seven years of extra life expectancy.

3. Down Shift. Stress is part of life, but Blue Zones centenarians have stress-relieving rituals built into their daily routines. Adventists pray, Ikarians nap, and Sardinians do happy hour.

4. 80% Rule. People in Blue Zones areas stop eating when their stomachs are 80% full and eat their smallest meal in the early evening.

5. Plant Slant. Beans are the cornerstone of most centenarian diets. Vegetables, fruit, and whole grains round out the rest of the diet and meat is eaten in small amounts.

6. Wine @ 5. Moderate but regular consumption of wine (with friends and/or food) is part of the Blue Zones lifestyle.

7. Belong. Being part of a faith-based community adds four to 14 years to life expectancy.

8. Loved Ones First. Having close and strong family connections (with spouses, parents, grandparents, and grandchildren) is common with Blue Zones centenarians.

9. Right Tribe. The world's longest lived people have close friends and strong social networks."

Bringing Blue Zones to Communities Through the US

"After spending so much time in these Blue Zone areas and traveling around the world lecturing and presenting my research, I wanted to find a way to bring these longevity lessons home," says Buettner. "In 2009, I partnered with Healthways to start the Blue Zones Project, which brings the Power 9 longevity principles to whole communities. To do this, we focus on changing built environments—we want to make the healthy choice the easy choice. Instead of just focusing on the individual, the Project creates sustainable, long-term changes that affect the entire community and future generations."

Recently, the Blue Zone Project came to my community. I'm working with a team from Healthways where I live in Mendocino County. Here, we're using the experiences that have been garnered throughout the world and adding what I have learned about gender medicine and men's health to help our communities work well for everyone.

In chapter 10, I will share our vision for the future.

Chapter 10

Join Our Moonshot Mission for Mankind and Humanity

As I began writing this chapter, an event occurred that reminded me how important this mission of healing is in my life. My wife, Carlin, received a call from her close friend, Rosamond, who was like a little sister to us. She and her husband, Doug, were the first people we met in Willits when we moved here in 1992. Rosamond was in tears as she told Carlin that Doug had just been killed. His motorcycle had been hit by a car going the wrong way.

Carlin immediately went to be with our little sister to help in the aftermath of the tragedy, and our community rallied around. I remembered numerous occasions where we held large men's gatherings on their land, and Doug was a wonderful host and support for men's health. Doug's untimely death reminds me of how fragile all our lives are and why we need a close, supportive community to support us all in these challenging times. I dedicate this book to Doug and Rosamond and to all the men whose lives are cut short and the women who must carry on without them.

By joining together, we can all help improve the lives of men, the women and children who love them, and the entire community of life on this earth we call Gaia. When I shared my vision of our moonshot mission with a colleague, she had an interesting response:

I imagine sometimes you get pushback when you first describe your project as one helping men, as the first thought might be, "Really, do we need to help men, especially white men, anymore? Don't they get enough?" But then when you describe the details of what you're doing, the lightbulb goes off and the answer is YES!! This is exactly where men need some help!

In November 2021, I invited a few of my colleagues to join me in this adventure of a lifetime. My criteria in choosing this initial group were these:

- I wanted people who I knew were doing exceptional work in the field of men's mental, emotional, and relational health.
- I wanted males and females.
- I wanted those who had been working in the field for more than twenty years and those who were newer to the work.
- I wanted those who were committed to collaborating and who were seriously committed to creating a world where men would live fully healthy lives for the benefit of themselves, women, children, and the community of life on earth.

The following people have been working together with me since January 2022. They are the first to join the moonshot mission. As Joseph Campbell reminded us, "The call to adventure signifies that destiny has summoned the hero." I've asked each of them to share the stories, what they do, why they were drawn to this mission, and their visions for the future.

Frederick Marx, WarriorFilms.Org

Somehow a good portion of my adult life has been devoted to advocating for the initiation and mentorship of young people, especially boys. That journey began when I was nine when my father died and my uncle told me I was the man of the house. When I got home from school that day, right away I knew something was different.

Two of my father's college students were holding each other on the living room couch. They seemed startled to see me. My child mind made up the story that I caught them necking and they were embarrassed. The male student told me solemnly, "Your mother wants to see you in the bedroom."

I walked into her room. She was working at the little desk in the corner by the windows. I stepped toward her. She turned and said, "Fred, your dad is dead." She might've said more. I don't remember saying anything, maybe, "Oh." Maybe she said, "He died of a heart attack." But what I remember is her turning back to the work on her desk. "I guess it's time for me to leave," I thought. I walked into the bedroom I shared with my brother Larry, who was four. He was sitting on the floor playing a game with our family friend Ruth Lorbe.

He looked up brightly. "Hey Fred, did you hear Dad is dead?"

"Yeah," I said, and walked out. It was only then I remember hearing my eleven-year-old sister crying behind the closed door of her bedroom. I looked into the living room and saw the student couple "necking." Maybe they looked forlornly at me. I don't know. They were probably consoling each other. What I suddenly did know was that there was no place for me to be alone.

I went to the only place left in our small house where I could close the door and be alone with my confusion. I went to the bathroom. I put the toilet lid down and sat. "What does this mean?" I couldn't wrap my head around it. I listened to my sister crying across the hall. My agitation bloomed. I needed someplace to be. I felt stupid sitting in the bathroom on the toilet. I didn't want to be there, but I had to be somewhere. But where? The restlessness in my body needed some place to go that could hold it. I walked out through the living room to the utility room, got my coat and hat, and went outside.

I remember a sunny day, though it was February and there was snow on the ground. Outside, I had no better idea where I could park my body, but at least I had escaped the house. I found my best friend Steve Osborn coming home from school. We exchanged pleasantries. How does one talk about these things? I felt like a liar and a fool.

When we got to his house, his mother was at the door. "How's your father, Fred?" Parents seemed to have secret modes of communication; they knew everything. I blurted out "My dad's dead!" and threw myself into her arms and sobbed. "I didn't know!" Steve called out guiltily. Fade to black.

On the way to my dad's funeral, I walked to the car with my dad's younger brother—the man who at ten was led by my fifteen-year-old father out of the rioting city of Frankfurt following Kristallnacht to the care of Dutch refugee officials, who spent those next twelve months as the war began with a Dutch farm family, only to be fetched by their half-dead father who somehow managed to escape Buchenwald to claim his boys and spirit them across the Atlantic on one of the last ocean liners to make the voyage to NYC in January, 1940. My uncle put his hand on my bony shoulder and said, "Well Freddy, you're the man of the house now."

Nowadays we laugh at the inappropriateness of such statements. Maybe in the back of his mind he was thinking about what he would have done if my father hadn't been there to save his life. But his words didn't seem inappropriate to me. I wanted to be that man, to care for my mother, older sister, and younger brother. I wanted to live up to that responsibility.

I thought my father's death and my uncle's recognition somehow combined to anoint me a man. It would be many years before I understood the conceit of that. I was no more a man than my sister or brother or mother. But that moment planted a seed in me, one that would continue germinating throughout my lifetime. How to become that man of integrity and honor I yearned to be? How to hold responsibility for the well-being of those I love?

That's why I joined this moonshot mission. Over the years I've found good answers to those questions, but I'm still reaching for pathways to bring some of this accumulated wisdom to society's main stage. That's why I made the TV miniseries *Boys to Men?* along with other films that examine the issue of men's maturation, and that's why I wrote the book *Rites to a Good Life* with a chapter titled "The Mature Masculine." Like Jed and the other members of this accomplished team, I aim to provide some of the tools to enable people everywhere to reach for their own human transformation and to lend a hand in support of men everywhere.

My simple, albeit ambitious, prayer is that male teens worldwide get initiated and mentored into adulthood. To help get us there, I envision thousands of men's organizations worldwide partnering with us to sign and promote a simple Five-Point Men's Wellness Vow:

- I will remain healthy in mind and body.
- I will nourish and grow my emotional awareness.
- I will become familiar with my internal darkness and never harm another man, woman, or child.
- I will ask for help and strive to live cooperatively, not competitively, with men.
- I will become the best man I can be, living with honor and pride in my masculinity.

Our goal? One hundred million men signatories! You can reach Frederick at WarriorFilms.org.

Shana James, Shana James Coaching. Shanajamescoaching.com/tedx

In my twenties, I was part of an intentional community. We decided to be honest and vulnerable with each other. We committed to working things out when they got tough instead of bailing when it got uncomfortable.

Two men who were part of the community felt they grew so much from the honest feedback, especially from women, that they started a workshop called the Authentic Man Program (AMP). They invited me and a few other women to participate. Our role was to give men honest and loving feedback. This supported them to strengthen their self-awareness and understand why women were reacting to them in undesirable ways. Most of the men were in heterosexual relationships, but not all.

After the first workshop, as we debriefed with participants, a man spoke up. With tears in his eyes, he shared that our team of women brought him back to life. He said our acceptance and love was a balm to his heart in a very challenging time as he went through a divorce and figured out how to be a father. Before the weekend, he hadn't been sure if he wanted to be alive.

I did not stop crying for hours. I realized that through my love, and becoming an ally to men, I could help keep men alive and support them to thrive. I realized I could be a safe woman for men to be vulnerable with. I could see a bigger vision for how this would impact not only these men, but families, communities, and the earth. I saw that men being understood and supported, especially in their most vulnerable places, would allow them to love themselves and bring more love to the world.

What made me decide to join the Moonshot Mission? When Jed was on my podcast for men—*Man Alive*—to talk about the father wound and male depression, I was impressed. He brought depth, love, and wisdom to the listeners, and it was clear to me that he was an expert in men's healing.

When he created the mission for men to live longer, happier, and healthier lives, I jumped at the chance to be involved. Even as my work focuses on supporting men to feel connected and confident in their romantic relationships, there is a deeper mission. I want men to feel more self-love, aliveness, and fulfillment. I want men to thrive, first for themselves and then to become stewards of a healthier world and communities.

Collaborating with those who support different facets of men's well-being allows us to create the cultural change necessary to help men break free from the Man Box that fosters depression, anxiety, and even suicide.

For men (and most humans), relational health is one of the determining factors of emotional health and a fulfilling and longer life. But many men were taught to "man up" and struggle alone. So, when relationship challenges arise (and they always do), men often tend toward shame and isolation. They do not get the help they need to transform their pain into deeper connection and become more self-respecting and loving.

As a relationship coach, I support men to be sovereign and connected—to know, and then communicate, their wants, fears, and vulnerabilities in a way that creates understanding and intimacy. I support men to have clarity about the impact their actions and words have on others, empowering them to collaborate to create the outcomes they desire.

There is no doubt men's work and rites of passage are powerful and important for men's growth. There is a certain kind of healing men need to do with other men. There is also healing men need to do with women. As men return from workshops or men's circles, it can be a challenge to translate their learnings into effective communication and collaboration with women in their lives. I am a practice ground for men to cultivate the awareness to consciously create their relationships. As I support men to know their own worth, they then isolate and explode less often. They generate their own safety, which allows them to open their hearts and reveal their humanity, creating the kind of intimacy that is a foundation of thriving.

What is my vision for the future of this movement?

Hurt people hurt others. The destructive power dynamics that plague our world result from the pain so many are feeling internally. Men hold a specific piece of this pain, and it is driving the suicide rate up and life satisfaction down.

In order to support men to live healthier and longer, I see the need for a cultural shift. Men need the encouragement to take care of their health and receive care. They can be released from the culturally induced shame of needing to pretend they have it all together. I see this movement bringing awareness to men's humanity and vulnerability. I see organizations around the world partnering to create a support network for men. I see us rallying people around the goal of men living longer, more fulfilling lives, and how this creates a more just and peaceful world.

You can learn more about my work here: https://shanajames-coaching.com/

Joe Conrad, Founder & CEO, Grit Digital Health.
https://www.gritdigitalhealth.com/

Man Therapy—taking care of your mental health is the manliest thing a man can do.

At some point in my life, I went from acting like a boy to behaving like a man. For me, it happened at Colorado State University sometime during my senior year. I had a job writing for the *Rocky Mountain Collegian*, which is where I found my voice. I was covering campus stories and writing articles about America's undercover, CIA-lead war in Nicaragua. I wrote a series of stories about US military veterans returning from Vietnam and their difficult transition back to civilian life. I covered issues around the growing environmental movement. And I wrote my first editorial encouraging students to vote in the upcoming election and the importance of being informed citizens. I was creating something, putting it out into the world, and it felt great.

In 1990 I started Cactus, a purpose-driven ad agency focused on working with nonprofit organizations, foundations, and brands to help bring a powerful voice to their work. Since day one, our mission has been to create sharp ideas for brands that help people thrive.

One day while leading a workshop for the Colorado Department of Public Health and Environment, I was approached by the director of the Office of Suicide Prevention, Jarrod Hindman. He said, "Joe, do you know that there is an epidemic out there and that working-age men are killing themselves at an alarming rate?" I had no idea that five out of seven suicides were men from all walks of life, demographics, and socioeconomic backgrounds. As our friendship grew, he would visit my office every month to talk about the issue, and we decided that somehow, some way, we would do something. We recruited Sally Spencer Thomas, who led a suicide prevention foundation, to join our team, and the three of us set out to find a path forward.

We looked at a number of creative approaches, but one idea stood out and was the obvious choice: Man Therapy. The centerpiece of the campaign is a website, ManTherapy.org, hosted by a fictional thera-pist named Dr. Rich Mahogany. However, Dr. Rich is not your typical therapist. He tells it like it is and uses humor to convince guys that taking care of their mental health is the manliest thing a man could do. When landing on the website, visitors are greeted with the gruff, direct, and hilarious Dr. Rich. He explains what Man Therapy is about and encourages men to take the twenty-point head inspection, an assessment that helps them examine their own mental health.

We realized early on that if we waited until men were in crisis, we would be too late. When a man decides to take his own life, they are often successful on the first attempt, usually by lethal means, and most often with a gun. Our team set three early goals for Man Therapy:

1. Break through the stigma surrounding mental health by making therapy approachable.
2. Encourage help-seeking behavior.
3. Reduce suicidal ideation.

Through research, men told us to just give them the informa-tion they needed to fix themselves, so we built a website that pro-vides a broad range of information, resources, and tools to do just that.

On July 9, 2012, Man Therapy was launched to the world, and we were fortunate to land a feature article in the *New York Times* calling the campaign a groundbreaking approach to suicide pre-vention. ManTherapy.org suddenly had hits from seventy-two dif-ferent countries and ten thousand unique visits in the first couple of days. That night, I received an email intended for Dr. Rich from a combat veteran in Baton Rouge, LA, who was referred to the site by a therapist. He wrote a two-page note about how powerful the website was and what a huge difference it made for him and the soldiers in his platoon.

Since then, Man Therapy has had visits from more than two million men, spending an average of five minutes per visit, with five hundred thousand head inspections completed. Dr. Rich Mahogany is the hardest working therapist in the world and is there for men 24/7/365. Over the past ten years, we have received hundreds of emails from men and their loved ones sharing stories about how Man Therapy has helped them. Five years ago, the CDC sponsored a $1.2 million research study to evaluate the effectiveness of the campaign and found that it improves help-seeking behavior and reduces suicidal ideation in men. It has been an honor to be involved with this campaign, and I am grateful for the many team members, partners, and suicide prevention advocates that have been a part of this effort.

Little did I know at the time, but the ripples from Man Therapy were just beginning. In 2014, I was asked by Colorado State to help them address the issue of suicide on college campuses after they suffered seventeen student suicides in a two-year academic period. We lose about 1,200 college students in the US every year to suicide, so we decided to do something about it. Building on our experience with Man Therapy, we knew college students would require a different approach. After conducting interviews with students, we had a vision to create a comprehensive mental health and well-being platform that supported every aspect of the student experience to help them thrive, succeed, and matter.

In 2015, I started a company called Grit Digital Health to harness the power of innovation, creativity, and technology to support mental health and well-being. We launched the YOU at College well-being hub at Colorado State in 2016, and today our solution is on two hundred campuses around the US. We have since created well-being hubs for veterans (OperationVeteranStrong.org), first responders (ResponderStrong.org), and community mental health centers (youatyourbest.org).

About a year ago, I received an email from Jed Diamond, who came across an old article on Man Therapy. Even though Man Therapy had been out in the world for ten years, Jed Diamond, a man who has committed his entire career to men's health, was just learning about the campaign. Crossing paths with Jed's work helped reinforce the fact that we have only scratched the surface on the potential impact this campaign could have. Jed asked me to join his Moonshot Mission for Mankind movement, and getting to know him and the other people behind this project has inspired me to keep doing the work. You never know where the ripples may lead, but I'm excited to see the kind of impact we can have on helping men live longer and healthier lives in the years ahead.

> *Never forget that you are one of a kind. Never forget that if there weren't any need for you in all your uniqueness to be on this earth, you wouldn't be here in the first place. And never forget, no matter how overwhelming life's challenges and problems seem to be, that one person can make a difference in the world. In fact, it is always because of one person that all the changes that matter in the world come about. So be that one person.*
>
> *—Buckminster Fuller*

MaLe Corona <3, Trauma-Informed & Body-Oriented Male Wholeness Coach, https://malewholeness.com/

Biologically, I was born a female; psychologically, it wasn't until I turned thirty that I could finally start to embrace my femaleness. Now, it is clear to me that having been raised immersed in the context of a *machista* Mexican culture, while also being surrounded by flashes of influence from the women's empowerment movement slowly rising to its crescendo, were all sources of mixed messages that caused me to experience profound gender identity issues as I was growing up.

During my childhood, I had the impression that being male was easier, much more fun, and way more advantageous than being a female. Unconsciously, I promised myself I'd never become a submissive woman like my mother and to never let any man dominate and devalue me as I saw my father do with my mom. At such tender age, it seemed that the only way I was going to be able to avoid such miserable fates was through slaughtering the disempowered girl in me and learning how to grow up as an almighty boy instead.

By the time I became a teenager, part of me was ready to publicly claim my identity as a trans male, while another part of me felt scared and ashamed due to experiences of bullying from peers, my own father's disparaging rage, and a group of homophobic teachers advocating for me to be expelled from the all-girl Catholic school I was attending after they all found out I had a romantic relationship with a young lady in my class.

At some point, the levels of physical and emotional pain I was enduring due to my looking like a *freak* in other people's eyes became excruciating, and the only way to endure them, at least until I finished high school, seemed to be opting for a more silent and secret life. My sense of personal worth started depending on how much I excelled intellectually and how well I disconnected from my emotional needs. A few years later, I managed to become an honor roll university student in the mornings while keeping a consistent employee-of-the-month record in my afternoon job and transforming into a party animal who used women and alcohol to numb myself down several nights a week. I seemed to have figured out how to have it all together, but little did I know that my late twenties would bring with them a physical, mental, emotional, and even spiritual collapse.

At the time, I had achieved everything I was told I needed to succeed in life—I was covering a top position at a marketing company, traveling abroad to renowned conferences; I had my own apartment, car, and cutting-edge gadgets, along with active loans and a decent amount of savings in the bank—yet I felt empty, mentally, and physically ill and extremely lonely. All of a sudden, along with my health, everything I relied on to sustain my image of the "perfect life" started to fall apart. I was extremely overweight, lost my high-end job, got ditched by my partner at the time, and even my dog died.

Eventually, I went bankrupt as well. It was obvious that I had hit rock bottom as neither my work addiction nor my superficial social life nor my substance abuse were doing the trick anymore. My constant panic attacks, the soreness in my body, and the acute depression I was experiencing forced me to look at myself again after so many years of just reaching outward for the next achievement and the next adrenaline hit only to find that behind my apparent mask of success, I was physically ill, mentally and emotionally trapped in addictive patterns that were only making me more and more depressed. And spiritually, I didn't have the slightest clue about who I really was or what life meant to me.

Until then I had been living by the book rather than by my heart. I had also been living exclusively in my mind, completely neglecting my body and soul. It was time to learn how to become healthy and whole if I wanted to make it alive to my thirties and beyond. And so, they say that when the student is ready, the teacher appears. I sincerely wanted to learn how to feel at home in my body, my mind, and my life; as a result, during the next months and years, the right workshops, books, and people started showing up, each bringing with them little hints of direction to a new way of living that could be truly sustainable in the long run. And since I didn't have anything left to lose anymore, I just surrendered to the process.

First, I was guided to start with the basics: my physical health. I learned how to listen to my body for the nourishment it needed from food, as well as for the amount of movement and rest it required. I was impressed at how easy it was to lose weight just by being mindful about the kind and amount of food my body craved for each day and by spending just a little time connecting with my breath and bodily sensations through yoga several times a week. However, the most amazing side effect of connecting with my body was that my addictive desire to consume alcohol started to vanish.

Second, I was guided to work with my mind and emotions. I learned to meditate, to seek support in other human beings. I learned to be mindful about the type of information I choose to consume and to hold space for my little inner child no matter what she's going through. I also started trying different practices to channel emotions, like keeping a journal, creating art, and my favorite one: dancing!

Third, I was guided to define my own version of spirituality and the devotional practices that would keep me connected to source on an ongoing basis. I was raised in a Catholic household, so I needed to expand my felt experience of God to find my unique spiritual path. Sometimes I'd chant at the Christian church, then I'd do community service at the Buddhist temple, sometimes I'd study Kabbalah, and other times I'd be drawn to attend a Mayan ceremony. All of those experiences together helped me discern how I want to engage with the spiritual realm while still remaining grounded in my humanness.

Having gone through such a self-discovery process is supporting me to safely explore deeper areas of my life like relationships, sexuality, and my own life's purpose. In terms of my gender identity, I've been able to find my authentic sexual expression, and to my surprise, it's an interesting mix of feminine and masculine traits. Knowing my wholeness more and more each day has inspired me to inspire others to get to know themselves deeply as the magnificent human beings they truly are deep down. In particular, I have developed a great sense of love and respect for men as I understand, even if not at a biological level, the psychological and cultural split that rigid masculine roles create between mind, body, and soul.

Something that all the steps I've taken to heal share in common is the body-mind-spirit connection. Through connecting the mind to the body, we are able to access an inner source of wisdom that can become our GPS in life—some call it our *soul*; others just call it *intuition*. Through the practice of embodiment, we can get a felt sense of who we are and what most matters to us. Additionally, by connecting with our bodies in a mindful way, we inherently learn how to connect with other bodies and the earth's larger body in respectful and cocreative ways. In my experience, it is through getting to know ourselves that we get to know our place in the cosmos.

Currently, I support male-identified BodyMinds in the restoration of their embodied self-awareness through my work as a somatic coach at malewholeness.com.

Ed Frauenheim, with Ed Frauenheim
& Friends. Edfrauenheim.com.

A hockey game lies at the root of my involvement in men's work. A championship hockey game. One I played in when I was about twelve years old. I let my team down by not playing nearly as well as my counterpart on the opposing team. I cracked under pressure. Choked.

In those days—the late 1970s—there was little as humiliating to a young man as failing to come up big in the clutch. And that was me. I not only failed to seize the moment, I shrank from it.

As I look back on the game today, I'm struck that I beat myself up so much because the other team didn't actually beat us. We tied. Neither team lost.

Still, I felt like a loser. A poor excuse for a man. And those painful feelings have followed me for much of my fifty-five years. That game haunted me. Which is to say the conventional, confined rules of manhood in American have plagued me.

Be strong? I was skinny. Dominate others? I lost my one fist fight in sixth grade and froze in key moments of hockey, basketball, and soccer games.

Woo the ladies? I was more emo than alpha male—more successful at befriending women than causing them to swoon. Climb the corporate ladder? I've managed one person for one day. I may have the smallest management career in history.

None of this is to say that my life has been a mess. Thanks largely to privileges including a middle-class upbringing and being an able-bodied, heterosexual man, I've made a decent living as a writer. And I've been fortunate to be in a twenty-year marriage with a wife I love and two healthy teenage kids.

But I'm a sensitive guy. Which means that even though I've played the game, not "measuring up" as a man has been difficult.

It also has been helpful. It's allowed me to see, I think, the water in which we men swim. The near-constant contests in which we find ourselves. Not just in sports, but in school and work. The way emotions other than anger are off limits, and the way we define vulnerability as "weak."

For the last several years, I've been exploring the way my personal story speaks to a wider one. The way our cramped definition of masculinity hurts us as men, which prompts us to hurt others.

At the same time, I noticed a converging trend in my professional life. As a journalist, researcher, and book author on workplace culture, I saw that the traditional way men showed up at work no longer works well in a world that is faster, flatter, and fairness focused. Guys who are barking bosses or calculating corporate climbers come across as rigid, cold, and isolated in a world now calling for agility, warmth, and connection.

So in 2020, I cowrote *Reinventing Masculinity: The Liberating Power of Compassion and Connection*. My coauthor, psychologist Ed Adams, and I tell the story of how we are moving from a "confined" version of manhood to a "liberating" one that frees men and all those around them to live fuller lives.

I now work to reinvent masculinity, organizations, and our broader society. My goal is a more soulful world—one that is more loving, just, peaceful, truthful, and joyful. I'm convinced that healing and transforming men is critical to creating that future.

A future where winning isn't everything. Where performance and achievement are not the foundation of our self-worth as men. And where sharing a championship is cause not for shame, but for celebration.

I joined the moonshot mission because it aligns perfectly with my personal mission to reinvent masculinity and create a more soulful world.

The moonshot goal of enabling men to live as long as women is worthy in its own right. But it also comes with brilliant side effects. Closing the lifespan gap between the sexes will require the kind of healing and transformation that I believe are critical to men and humanity overall.

Physical healing, yes. But also moving through emotional and spiritual trauma that I believe men have suffered from a cramped ideology around manhood.

We men need to embrace not only the "arrow" aspects of the masculine symbol, but also the "circle" aspects. Not just assertiveness, goal orientation, and self-reliance. But also compassion, connection, and receptivity.

We must allow ourselves to live into the sacred masculine archetypes as well as the sacred feminine ones. For centuries, boys and men have had the circle-feminine aspects beaten out of us.

That's a fundamental cause of men's hurt and lack of health today. It's a fundamental cause of the way men hurt others. It's a fundamental cause of the challenges facing the human race—war, obscene inequality, the looming climate catastrophe.

When we do the deep healing called for in the moonshot mission, men will live longer lives. They will live better lives. So will all human beings.

I contribute to men's mental, emotional, and relational health in a number of ways and through a number of partnerships. I give talks and workshops on the reinvention of masculinity underway today. I connect this change to specific challenges men are facing in organizations especially. These challenges include burnout, the need to embrace allyship, and the call for emotionally intelligent leadership.

I also focus on particular segments of men and specific professions. My colleague Jennifer Kahnweiler, a pioneer on the topic of introverts in the workplace, and I have researched the intersection of introversion and gender roles. The result is our conclusion that "now is the time for quiet men." We believe introverted men have long been marginalized in workplace cultures governed by loud, domineering men. But quiet men have superpowers fit for the emerging world, including calmness, deep listening skills, and a willingness to advocate for other less-powerful peers.

I also work with men (and women) in law enforcement through Project Compassion, an initiative to bring new questions, new perspectives, and a new set of practices to public safety. Among these new practices is "self-compassion" for police officers. Many cops are men suffering intense job-related stresses yet socialized to suppress emotions like sadness and fear. By putting compassion at the center of policing, my colleagues and I believe we can heal wounds, improve the lives of police officers, and foster safer, healthier communities—for all.

My vision for the future of this movement is a hopeful one. I believe the moonshot mission has the potential to take off. It can ignite passions and attract increasing numbers of men and women.

It has the potential to be a transformative mass movement in part because it avoids partisanship in our deeply divided society. Who can oppose men living as long as women?

As with the original moonshot of the 1960s, we are poised to stir people's souls. We are poised to launch a worldwide effort that succeeds in healing men, closing the lifespan gap, and offering hope to humanity.

If you'd like to know more about me, you can do so here: https://www.linkedin.com/in/ed-frauenheim-685294/

Lisa Hickey, Publisher and CEO of The Good Men Project & Good Men Media Inc. https://goodmenproject.com/

Sometimes there is a moment that changes your life. Something awesome or catastrophic or serendipitous happens. Maybe it is out of your control. Or maybe you make a choice. You try something new. Get an insight. An epiphany. Your life veers in a direction you never saw coming.

And everything changes.

For me, it started innocuously enough. I had been introduced to Tom Matlack; we were meeting for the first time to discuss a book he was putting together. He had asked me to lunch because he had heard I knew something about social media. As we rode down the elevator from his office, he carried the unfinished manuscript in his hands, about a hundred pages, unadorned, double-spaced on white copier paper.

As we walked the block to the restaurant from his office, he told me that the book was a collection of "essays." My heart sank. In my mind, essays were boring, academic exercises. But a few steps later he explained that they were first-person stories held together by the fact that they were all "defining moments" in men's lives. The moment—Tom explained as we were walking—when a guy woke up one morning, looked in the mirror, and everything he knew about being a man—everything he knew about being a good man—seemed to be in question.

The story of the guy who wanted to divorce his wife but didn't want to lose his son, and the only person he could talk to was a janitor in the buildings he had to inspect for demolition. The dad who had watched doctors try to jump-start his son's heart after his first son had died of a drug overdose. The guy who had been to Iraq taking photos of the war, who had come back to Brooklyn and realized he no longer knew how to function as a civilian. "You know," Tom said, "those moments."

We weren't even seated at the lunch table before I realized the brilliance of Tom's idea.

⚜ ⚜ ⚜

My life changed in a heartbeat.

I went on to help start The Good Men Project, one of the largest worldwide conversations about what it means to be a good man in the twenty-first century. The book was published. A website created at the cornerstone, an online community that attracts millions of people from around the globe every month. Tens of thousands of writers. Live storytelling events. Talking to schools, colleges, universities, organizations, and corporations. Thousands of live phone calls with our community that happen almost every day of the week so that people can call in and truly participate in the conversation.

And here's the thing about The Good Men Project. We are trying to create big, sweeping, societal changes—overturn stereotypes, eliminate racism, sexism, and homophobia, and be a positive force for good for things like education reform and the environment. We also give individuals the tools they need to make individual change—with their own relationships, with the way they parent, with their ability to be more conscious, more mindful, and more insightful.

For some people, doing all that, having goals that big, could get overwhelming. But for those of us here at The Good Men Project, it is not overwhelming. It is simply something we do—we do it with teamwork, with compassion, with an understanding of systems and how they work, and with shared insights from a diversity of viewpoints.

❖ ❖ ❖

Over lunch that day, Tom passed me the bread. I sipped ice water. I told him just how much I believed in the idea. The idea of sparking a conversation about the changing roles of men. The idea of talking about the moment that a man woke up, looked in the mirror, and said, "I thought I knew what it meant to be good. I thought I knew what it meant to be a man. I realize I didn't know either."

I looked up at Tom and said, "I don't know if I can sell a million copies of the book. But I can sell a million people on that idea."

❖ ❖ ❖

When Jed Diamond told me about his idea for the moonshot mission, I felt exactly the same way as I felt that day I decided to help launch The Good Men Project.

The moonshot mission is an extraordinary idea with a big, hairy, audacious goal. I may be dating myself by mentioning a BHAG, but that's what it is. Yet the goal of closing the gap between the life expectancy of men and women and getting men to live longer, happier, more enriched lives also feels like an attainable goal.

There are some simple things that can be done. For example, getting men to go to the doctor as often as women, especially as they age. To erase the current shame of men dealing with mental health issues. To stop the cultural pressures of "work till you drop," which seems to be such a part of the narrative told to men, both overtly and covertly. To look at rates of smoking, gun violence, and risk-taking in men versus women and ask why.

To understand how embracing the full spectrum of gender and sexuality might help men achieve some of these goals. And to help, really help men develop a wide variety of relationships that go far beyond the stereotypical relationships coveted by our culture and media. Men can have deep, long-lasting, intimate, empathetic, collaborative, and caring relationships with every kind of human in existence without it being an affront to their manhood.

Have a vision, work to create it. We put a person on the moon without knowing exactly how. We can do this too.

My personal mission statement is "I like to create things that capture the imagination of the general public and become part of the popular culture for years to come."

The goal of the moonshot mission—helping men live longer, healthier, happier lives—will make the world a better place. It's a goal to heal men, close the lifespan gap, and offer hope to humanity. It captured my imagination, and I hope it captures yours as well. Come visit me here: https://goodmenproject.com/author/lisa-hickey/

Boysen Hodgson, https://boysenh.com/, ManKind Project - https://mkpusa.org

Men's work—physical, social, emotional, spiritual, and relational work—with folks who are socialized as men in our culture, has the potential to transform and heal some of the most damaging patterns of harm on the planet. This is why I'm part of the moonshot mission and why I hope you'll engage.

I was born in Hickory, North Carolina, and spent the first couple of years of my life learning to crawl in red dirt. I grew up in the social-emotional gauntlet of the 1970s, surrounded by boys and men, and contained in the love of two wounded, beautiful, and ambitious parents. I'm one of six boys birthed over a span of twenty years from the late '60s through the late '80s. I am the second son of a charismatic country veterinarian and a powerful woman with deep southern roots who, from today's perspective, I would describe as a libertarian feminist hippie.

At the age of two, my parents moved north. We settled in Cato, New York, a tiny village far upstate at the intersection of New York State Routes 370 and 34. The village was rural, stunningly homogeneous, and deeply suspicious of anything beyond the fields and rolling hills. There are good men there—loving and hardworking men. And it was a place where going outside of the bounds of what makes a "real" man was dangerous.

The first decade of my life was a Norman Rockwell painting with overalls and a lot of facial hair. My family raised and showed Percheron horses. On our fifty acres, we had a cow, goats, chickens, pigs, rabbits, cats, dogs, and even a donkey. I rode my bike, played in the barn, built tree forts, got poison ivy, and swam in ponds, streams, and two-hundred-gallon galvanized feed troughs. I helped bale hay, shovel horse manure, and stack firewood.

I rode my bike down the old railroad bed into town to see my best friend and go to Diz's IGA for penny candy. I also ate an astounding number of vegetables my mom grew in a garden that covered close to an acre. In the winter, a wood stove heated the house, and we ate canned cherries, beans, tomatoes, beats, pickles, and even watermelon that my mom put away in the cellar.

At the age of eleven, my parent's marriage rather abruptly—it seemed to me at the time—imploded. Life turned to chaos. Both of my parents remarried in the next year and a half. My dad was divorced again inside of two years and married again inside of a year and a half. My mom divorced in six years and married again in three more. We moved. We moved again. We moved again.

I was the child of a man in a permanent midlife crisis with a slow-moving stream of stepmothers, hot rods, and Harleys. I was also the child of a sometimes-single mom raising four, then five, then six boys. At the darkest time in my adolescence, I was a born-again

Christian with an alcoholic chain-smoking stepfather. On any given day, we were poor. On Wednesday nights and every other weekend with Dad, I was middle class.

I coped by hiding and performing. I learned to not take chances. I learned to not risk friendships or connections that might expose the darkness and confusion I felt at home. I was the "good" kid, the "smart" kid, the well-behaved kid. I lived a painful and secretive double life, never allowing anyone to get close enough to know what was really happening with me.

And I grew. Being a boy, manhood was an impossible contradiction. Don't be like your dad. You're just like your dad. In many ways, I internalized this as "don't be a man." Eventually I learned that not knowing what was happening within me, numbing myself, and repressing my feelings was the safest way to be.

Being a man (like my dad) will lead to success, power, and access to fun, money, and the love of women. Being a man (like my dad) will lead to loneliness, shame, and the hatred of women.

And so it was for decades. I was a young man in constant internal conflict that caused a lot of pain—to me and others. Especially to the young women I dated. So much potential, so little expressed. So nice, so distant.

It was the beginning of my fourth decade before the pain became great enough to change direction. My pain and conflict prevented me from creating lasting success in any area of my life. Though I was a well-read seeker of self-knowledge and wisdom, it was not until I found men's groups through the ManKind Project that I found a place where I could express what had been hidden and begin to make healthier decisions. I began to reclaim my emotions and take responsibility for my impacts.

That was nearly two decades ago, in 2004. Having a place to do embodied emotional work with a group of trustworthy men has changed my life. I discover more of who I am and support other men in their pursuit of a more empowered and purpose-driven life.

This work did not change who I am. I am more of the best of me, a me who I can recognize as being present even in my earliest memories. Except now I have practices and skills to release shame, fear, and self-hatred I carry from my childhood, supported by other men on a path of emotional growth, accountability, and compassion.

This is what I've found as the potential of the ManKind Project's trainings and men's groups, and it's just one of the possible paths to take in doing men's work.

It is in this experience of sacred and healthy connection that I met Jed, and that I have been part of the moonshot mission. I believe in the moonshot, and in men's work, because I believe that only when we change the culture we socialize men into will we create opportunities to heal some of the most damaging impacts we have on one another and the planet.

Hurt men hurt others. Healed men heal others. We cannot shame or punish men into healing. The ManKind Project is one place for this healing to happen. And I hope that the moonshot will bring together more people of all genders to support all kinds of paths of healing.

Contact - boysenhodgson@gmail.com

Learn more about the ManKind Project - https://mkpusa.org

Learn more about me - https://boysenh.com

Jed Diamond, Founder/VHS (Visionary, Healer, Scholar in Residence) MenAlive—www.MenAlive.com

I began working in the field of gender healing and men's mental health on November 21, 1969. I was with my wife as she went through hours of labor preparing for the birth of our first child. When she was ready to go to the delivery room, the nurse said, "OK, Mr. Diamond, your work is done. You can go to the waiting room now. We'll let you know when the blessed event happens." I knew the hospital rules at the time. I kissed my wife as she was wheeled to the left toward the delivery room as I went to the right. But before I could exit, I couldn't make myself go through the doors. I felt a calling from my unborn child. *I don't want a waiting-room father. Your place is with us.*

I turned around and went back and pushed my way into the birthing room. There was no question of leaving for me. It wasn't long until our son, Jemal, was born. He was handed to me amid tears of joy and relief. As I held him, I made a promise that I would be a different kind of father than my father was able to be for me and to do everything I could to help bring about a world where fathers were fully involved with their families throughout their lives.

In support of that commitment, I graduated from college, got my master's degree in social welfare, and later a PhD in international health. I launched MenAlive as a central focus for my work. I began writing articles and books, including international best-sellers *Male Menopause, The Irritable Male Syndrome: Understanding and Managing the 4 Key Causes of Depression and Aggression*, and *The Enlightened Marriage: The 5 Transformative Stages of Relationships and Why the Best is Still to Come.*

When I first began working in the field in 1970, there were very few good programs focused specifically on men's mental health. Now there are many. It became increasingly clear to me that what I could do as a single program would not ever come close to solving the problems in addressing men's issues. Comedian Elayne Boosler, humorously, but insightfully, described the problem. "When women get depressed, they eat or go shopping. Men invade another country. It's a whole different way of thinking."

Male violence is worldwide problem. Although things like school shootings, terrorism, and war grab the headlines, most violence involves self-harm. According to "The World Report on Violence and Health" published by The World Health Organization (WHO):

- War-related violence accounted for 18.6% of the total.
- Homicide accounted for 31.3%.
- Suicide accounted for a whopping 49.1% of the total violence in the world.

In his book *Dying to Be Men*, social scientist Dr. Will Courtenay cites CDC statistics showing that the suicide rate for males is much higher than it is for females and increases with age while female rates are much lower and rates decrease:

Age Group	Male Suicide Rate	Female Suicide Rate	Male/Female Ratio
35–44	23.9	6.8	3.5
45–54	25.8	8.8	2.9
55–64	21.4	7.0	3.1
65–74	21.5	3.4	6.3
75–84	27.3	3.9	7.0
85 or older	38.6	2.2	17.5

At this stage of my career, spanning more than fifty years, I want to use the time I still have to make the most positive impact in the world.

My colleagues Randolph Nesse, MD, and Daniel Kruger, PhD, examined premature deaths among men in twenty countries. They found that in every country, men died sooner and lived sicker than women, and their shortened health and lifespan harmed the men and their families.

They concluded with four powerful statements:

- Being male is now the single largest demographic factor for early death.
- Over 375,000 lives would be saved in a single year in the US alone if men's risk of dying was as low as women's.
- If male mortality rates could be reduced to those for females, this would eliminate over one-third of all male deaths below age fifty and help men of all ages.
- If you could make male mortality rates the same as female rates, you would do more good than curing cancer.

For me, the finding of Drs. Nesse and Kruger constituted a call to action. In November 2021, I reached out to a number of colleagues who I knew were doing good work in this broad field of men's mental, emotional, and relational health and invited them to join me in working together to bring about positive change in the world by focusing our joint efforts. Our collective work has inspired me to continue to expand our efforts to reach out to individuals and organizations who share our belief that by healing *mankind*, we can improve the lives of millions of men, women, and children, and the community of life on planet earth.

At MenAlive, we focus on helping men and the families who love them to live fully authentic lives, to love deeply and well, and to make a positive difference in the world. We offer the following resources:

- A free weekly newsletter with updated programs and resources announcements.
- Weekly articles with information you can use to improve men's mental, emotional, and relational health.
- Online programs that address issues including the following: healing the family father wound; navigating the Five Stages of Love; stopping male anger from destroying your relationship; healing the Irritable Male Syndrome; dealing with male depression, and more.

In my vision for the future, I see millions of individual men and women committed to their own healing and helping men live fully healthy lives. I see thousands of organizations working together in support of the Moonshot Mission for Mankind and Humanity. I hope you will want to join us.

As Joseph Campbell reminded us, we are all on our own hero's journey, and our stories and myths are metaphors for the work we are called to engage in our lives. "People say that what we're all seeking is a meaning for life," says Campbell in *The Power of Myth*. "I don't think that's what we're really seeking. I think that what we're seeking is an experience of being alive, so that our life experiences on the purely physical plane will have resonances with our own innermost being and reality, so that we actually feel the rapture of being alive."

If you resonate with our mission, I hope you will join us. You can learn more here. https://moonshotformankind.com/.

Let's Connect

I hope you have found this book helpful. For me, the Moonshot Mission for Mankind is the beginning of a worldwide community of individuals and organizations who are committed to helping men live long and well for themselves, their families, communities, and the world. I look forward to connecting with you. You can reach me through my website at www.MenAlive.com and you can drop me an e-mail at Jed@MenAlive.com and put "Long Live Men" in the subject line.

INDEX

www.ingramcontent.com/pod-product-compliance
Lightning Source LLC
Chambersburg PA
CBHW031150270326
41931CB00006B/213